Lecture Notes in Computer S

Commenced Publication in 1973
Founding and Former Series Editors:
Gerhard Goos, Juris Hartmanis, and Jan van Leeuwen

Raghunath Nambiar   Meikel Poess (Eds.)

Topics in Performance Evaluation, Measurement and Characterization

Third TPC Technology Conference, TPCTC 2011
Seattle, WA, USA, August 29–September 3, 2011
Revised Selected Papers

 Springer

Volume Editors

Raghunath Nambiar
Data Center Group
Cisco Systems, Inc.
3800 Zankar Road
San Jose, CA 95134, USA
E-mail: rnambiar@cisco.com

Meikel Poess
Server Technologies
Oracle Corporation
500 Oracle Parkway
Redwood Shores, CA 94065, USA
E-mail: meikel.poess@oracle.com

ISSN 0302-9743   e-ISSN 1611-3349
ISBN 978-3-642-32626-4   e-ISBN 978-3-642-32627-1
DOI 10.1007/978-3-642-32627-1
Springer Heidelberg Dordrecht London New York

Library of Congress Control Number: 2012944423

CR Subject Classification (1998): C.4, D.2.8, J.1, H.2.7-8, K.6, H.4, K.1

LNCS Sublibrary: SL 2 – Programming and Software Engineering

Typesetting: Camera-ready by author, data conversion by Scientific Publishing Services, Chennai, India

Printed on acid-free paper

Springer is part of Springer Science+Business Media (www.springer.com)

Preface

The Transaction Processing Performance Council (TPC) is a non-profit organization established in August 1988. Over the years, the TPC has had a significant impact on the computing industry's use of industry-standard benchmarks. Vendors use TPC benchmarks to illustrate performance competitiveness for their existing products, and to improve and monitor the performance of their products under development. Many buyers use TPC benchmark results as points of comparison when purchasing new computing systems.

The information technology landscape is evolving at a rapid pace, challenging industry experts and researchers to develop innovative techniques for evaluation, measurement, and characterization of complex systems. The TPC remains committed to developing new benchmark standards to keep pace, and one vehicle for achieving this objective is the sponsorship of the Technology Conference Series on Performance Evaluation and Benchmarking (TPCTC). With this conference, the TPC encourages researchers and industry experts to present and debate novel ideas and methodologies in performance evaluation, measurement, and characterization.

The First TPC Technology Conference on Performance Evaluation and Benchmarking (TPCTC 2009) was held in conjunction with the 35th International Conference on Very Large Data Bases (VLDB 2009) in Lyon, France, during August 24–28, 2009.

The Second TPC Technology Conference on Performance Evaluation and Benchmarking (TPCTC 2010) was held in conjunction with the 36th International Conference on Very Large Data Bases (VLDB 2010) in Singapore during September 13–17, 2010.

This book contains the proceedings of the Third TPC Technology Conference on Performance Evaluation and Benchmarking (TPCTC 2011), held in conjunction with the 37th International Conference on Very Large Data Bases (VLDB 2011) in Seattle, Washington, from August 29 to September 3, 2011, including 12 selected papers and two keynote papers.

The hard work and close cooperation of a number of people have contributed to the success of this conference. We would like to thank the members of TPC and the organizers of VLDB 2011 for their sponsorship; the members of the Program Committee and Publicity Committee for their support; and the authors and the participants who are the primary reason for the success of this conference.

Raghunath Nambiar
Meikel Poess

TPCTC 2011 Organization

General Chairs

Raghunath Nambiar (Cisco)
Meikel Poess (Oracle)

Publicity Committee Chair

Nicholas Wakou (Dell)

Program Committee

Alfredo Cuzzocrea	University of Calabria, Italy
Alain Crolotte	Teradata, USA
Neoklis Polyzotis	University of California, Santa Cruz, USA
Badriddine Khessib	Microsoft, USA
Brian Cooper	Google, USA
Harumi Kuno	HP Labs, USA
Kai Sachs	SAP, Germany, USA
Marco Vieira	University of Coimbra, Portugal
Masaru Kitsuregawa	University of Tokyo, Japan
Michael Brey	Oracle, USA
Michael Molloy	Dell, USA
Patrick O'Neil	University of Massachusetts at Boston, USA
Peter Thawley	Sybase, USA
Tilmann Rabl	University of Toronto, Canada

Publicity Committee

Andrew Masland (NEC)
Matthew Lanken (Oracle)
Peter Thawley (Sybase)
Michael Majdalany (L&M Management Group)
Forrest Carman (Owen Media)

Keynote

Umeshwar Dayal (HP Labs)

Invited Talk

Karl Huppler (IBM)

About the TPC

Introduction to the TPC

The Transaction Processing Performance Council (TPC) is a non-profit organization that defines transaction processing and database benchmarks and distributes vendor-neutral performance data to the industry. Additional information is available at http://www.tpc.org/.

TPC Memberships

Full Members

Full Members of the TPC participate in all aspects of the TPC's work, including development of benchmark standards and setting strategic directions. The Full Member application can be found at http://www.tpc.org/information/about/app-member.asp.

Associate Members

Certain organizations may join the TPC as Associate Members. Associate Members may attend TPC meetings, but are not eligible to vote or hold office. Associate membership is available to non-profit organizations, educational institutions, market researchers, publishers, consultants, governments and businesses that do not create, market, or sell computer products or services. The Associate Member application can be found at http://www.tpc.org/information/about/app-assoc.asp.

Academic and Government Institutions

Academic and government institutions are invited join the TPC and a special invitation can be found at http://www.tpc.org/information/specialinvitation.asp.

Contact the TPC

TPC
Presidio of San Francisco
Building 572B(surface)
P.O. Box 29920 (mail)
San Francisco, CA 94129-0920
Voice: 415-561-6272
Fax: 415-561-6120
Email: info@tpc.org

How to Order TPC Materials

All of our materials are now posted free of charge on our website. If you have any questions, please feel free to contact our office directly or by email at info@tpc.org

Benchmark Status Report

The TPC Benchmark Status Report is a digest of the activities of the TPC and its technical subcommittees. Sign-up information can be found at the following URL: http://www.tpc.org/information/about/email.asp.

TPC 2011 Organization

Full Members

AMD
Bull
Cisco
Dell
Fujitsu
HP
Hitachi
IBM
Ingres
Intel
Microsoft
NEC
Oracle
ParAccel
Sybase
Syncsort
Teradata
Unisys
VMware

Associate Members

Ideas International
ITOM International Co
Telecommunications Technology Association
University of Coimbra, Portugal

Steering Committee

Karl Huppler (IBM), Chair
Charles Levine (Microsoft)
Mike Nikolaiev (HP)
Raghunath Nambiar (Cisco)
Wayne Smith (Intel)

Public Relations Committee

Nicholas Wakou (Dell), Chair
Andrew Masland (NEC)
Meikel Poess (Oracle)
Peter Thawley (Sybase)
Raghunath Nambiar (Cisco)

Technical Advisory Board

Jamie Reding (Microsoft), Chair
Peter Thawley (Sybase)
Dave Steinhoff (ParAccel)
Matthew Emmerton (IBM)
Mike Nikolaiev (HP)
Nicholas Wakou (Dell)
Wayne Smith (Intel)

Table of Contents

Shaping the Landscape of Industry Standard Benchmarks: Contributions of the Transaction Processing Performance Council (TPC)

Raghunath Nambiar[1], Nicholas Wakou[2], Andrew Masland[3], Peter Thawley[4], Matthew Lanken[5], Forrest Carman[6], and Michael Majdalany[7]

[1] Cisco Systems, Inc., 3800 Zanker Road, San Jose, CA 95134, USA
rnambiar@cisco.com
[2] Dell Inc., One Dell Way, Round Rock, TX 78682, USA
Nicholas_Wakou@dell.com
[3] NEC Corporation of America, 14335 NE 24th Street, Bellevue, WA 98007, USA
andy.masland@necam.com
[4] Sybase, an SAP Company, 1 Sybase Drive, Dublin, CA 94568, USA
peter.thawley@sybase.com
[5] Oracle Corporation, 500 Oracle Pkwy, Redwood Shores, CA 94065, USA
matthew.lanken@oracle.com
[6] Owen Media, 3130 E. Madison St., Suite 206, Seattle, WA 98112, USA
forrestc@owenmedia.com
[7] LoBue & Majdalany Magt Group, 572B Ruger St. San Francisco, CA 94129, USA
majdalany@lm-mgmt.com

Abstract. Established in 1988, the Transaction Processing Performance Council (TPC) has had a significant impact on the computing industry's use of industry-standard benchmarks. These benchmarks are widely adapted by systems and software vendors to illustrate performance competitiveness for their existing products, and to improve and monitor the performance of their products under development. Many buyers use TPC benchmark results as points of comparison when purchasing new computing systems and evaluating new technologies.

In this paper, the authors look at the contributions of the Transaction Processing Performance Council in shaping the landscape of industry standard benchmarks – from defining the fundamentals like performance, price for performance, and energy efficiency, to creating standards for independently auditing and reporting various aspects of the systems under test.

Keywords: Industry Standard Benchmarks.

1 Introduction

Originally formed in 1988, the Transaction Processing Performance Council (TPC) [1] is a non-profit corporation focused on defining database processing benchmarks and disseminating objective, verifiable performance data to the IT industry. The TPC

R. Nambiar and M. Poess (Eds.): TPCTC 2011, LNCS 7144, pp. 1–9, 2012.
© Springer-Verlag Berlin Heidelberg 2012

was originally founded in response to a growing trend at the time, affectionately known as "benchmarketing." Effectively, this was the not-so-uncommon practice of vendors to publish amazing claims based on their own performance data in order to increase sales. Without independent and objective oversight, a number of vendors created highly suspect workloads and test environments while often ignoring crucial operational and sometimes even "correctness" requirements in order to improve the market's perception of their product.

"Benchmarketing" effectively enabled vendors to exaggerate performance and even reliability claims in order to boost sales. The need for a vendor-neutral standards organization that focused on creating and administering fair and comprehensive benchmark specifications to objectively evaluate database systems under demanding, but consistent and comparable workloads, quickly became apparent. Several influential database academics and industry leaders began working to establish an organization charged with leading the effort to impose order and consistency to the process of benchmarking products fairly and objectively – this effort ultimately culminated in the formation of the TPC.

Over the years, both vendors and end-users have come to rely on TPC benchmarks to provide accurate and dependable performance data that is backed by a stringent and independent review process. Vendors publish TPC benchmarks to illustrate performance competitiveness for their products. In addition, many vendors use TPC workloads internally to improve and monitor release-to-release progress of their products using TPC-C and TPC-H benchmarks. End-users use TPC benchmark results as a reliable point-of-comparison when considering new technologies and purchasing new computing systems.

The key to providing end-users with the promise of reliable and comparable results across both hardware and database systems starts with a well-defined specification to ensure consistency in workload and measurement. Although some might argue these specifications are too large and detailed, it is precisely this which prevents vendors from "bending" the rules to their advantage. To ensure this, TPC benchmark publications mandate extensive documentation of the configuration and benchmark process which are carefully vetted and certified by a TPC-certified and independent Auditor before it can be released as a formally approved TPC benchmark result.

A key innovation the TPC popularized was the notion of Price/Performance. While vendors could often reach bigger and bigger performance results simply by adding more capacity or faster components, price/performance acts as a counter-balance to provide transparency to the cost of getting that level of performance. To enforce consistency in the costing aspects of these tested solutions, the TPC developed a Pricing Specification [2] designed to ensure uniformity between benchmark results. Auditors must also validate that each benchmark follows the requirements set forth in the pricing spec to ensure this. The pricing specification sets guidelines for how vendors must price the hardware, what hardware components must be included, the rules for licensing of all the software used in the benchmark, and the contract costs for three years of maintenance and support for all hardware and software.

In recent years, energy efficiency has become one of the leading factors in evaluating computer systems. To address this shift, the TPC has developed the Energy Specification [3], intended to help buyers identify the energy efficiency of computing systems in addition to the performance and price/performance requirements. Like the TPC Pricing Specification, the TPC Energy Specification is a common specification ensuring consistency across all TPC benchmark standards currently in use, including TPC-C, TPC-E and TPC-H specifications.

To better understand the TPC's contributions to the industry, let's explore the different benchmark specifications.

2   TPC Benchmark Standards

Over the years, TPC benchmarks have raised the bar for what the computing industry has come to expect in terms of benchmarks themselves. Though the original focus has been on online transaction processing (OLTP) benchmarks, to date the TPC has approved a total of nine independent benchmarks. Of these benchmarks, TPC-C, TPC-H and TPC-E are currently active, and are widely being used by the industry. TPC-ETL, TPC-V and TPC-DS are under development. The timelines are shown in Figure 1.

Benchmark Standards																								
TPC-A																								
TPC-B																								
TPC-C																								
TPC-D																								
TPC-R																								
TPC-H																								
TPC-W																								
TPC-App																								
TPC-E																								
Common Specifications																								
Pricing																								
Energy																								
Developments in Progress																								
TPC-DS																								
TPC-ETL																								
TPC-V	1988	1989	1990	1991	1992	1993	1994	1995	1996	1997	1998	1999	2000	2001	2002	2003	2004	2005	2006	2007	2008	2009	2010	2011

Current industry standard benchmarks include TPC-C, TPC-H and TPC-H, each of which addresses distinct industry requirements. TPC-C and TPC-E are standards for benchmarking transaction processing systems, while TPC-H is the standard for benchmarking decision support systems. The longevity of these benchmarks means that hundreds of results are publicly available over a wide variety of hardware and software platforms.

The top contribution of the TPC is defining the fundamental metrics that the industry uses to analyze and compare computer server technologies. All TPC results must report three primary metrics; Performance, Price/Performance and Availability Date. All three primary metrics must be reported for a valid TPC result.

Performance is a measure of the throughput of database transactions being performed on a System Under Test (SUT) in a given operating environment. Each benchmark standard has a defined performance metric; TPC-C uses tpmC (transactions per minute), TPC-H uses QphH (queries per hour) and TPC-E uses tpsE (transactions per second). TPC performance results are widely used in the industry to analyze server performance and compare the performance of various vendor offerings. The performance must be reported in, or derived from, measured values. The result has to be repeatable. The use of estimated values in describing a TPC result is strictly prohibited.

Price/Performance is a measure of the cost of delivering the stated performance. The motivation for price/performance was driven by the need for sponsors to use configurations that are commercially viable. This metric has been used widely for purchasing decisions, especially in a highly competitive market place, where the most effective use of resources is a key objective. The Pricing Specification gives guidelines on how the Total Cost of Ownership (over three years) of the SUT is calculated. The TCO is composed of the line item costs of the hardware and software components, based on the SKUs that ship with the systems plus the cost of a three year maintenance service. The TPC pricing specification defines the process that enables these costs to be verified for accuracy.

Availability Date, the third TPC primary metric, defines the vendor's commitment in delivering the product. Having the option of using a future availability date enables vendors to preannounce, and hence generate demands for, their products. The Availability Date as per TPC definition is when the all the components of the SUT are orderable and are being shipped to customers. The Availability Date must be within 185 days of the date when the result is submitted to the TPC.

Introduced in 2009, the TPC-Energy specification defines the methodology and requirements for measuring and reporting energy metrics. TPC-Energy metrics are optional and are not required to publish a TPC benchmark result. Watts per Performance was a metric that was inspired by the realization that the high performance of a SUT usually comes at a cost of high power consumption. With the ever rising energy costs for data centers, a measure of the power a configuration consumes is relevant business information for IT managers. A key objective of this metric is to encourage and spur the development of power efficient computer technologies.

TPC benchmarks have permanently raised the bar; vendors and end users rely on TPC benchmarks to provide real-world data that is backed by a stringent and independent review process. The main user and vendor benefits of TPC benchmarks are listed below:

- Cross-platform performance comparisons. TPC benchmarks enable server configurations and solution offerings to be compared. The ability to verify vendor marketing claims is a key contribution by the TPC to the industry. By providing a basis on which server platforms are compared, the TPC has encouraged and driven better performing technologies.

- An objective means of comparing cost of ownership. The TPC has been the most successful benchmarking group in developing a standard means of comparing the price and price/performance of different systems. All TPC testing requires vendors to detail their hardware and software components, along with the associated costs and three years of maintenance fees, in order to provide the industry's most accurate price and price/performance metrics.
- An objective means of comparing energy efficiency. The TPC Energy metric provides an additional dimension to computing systems' performance and price. As with the TPC's price/performance metrics, which rank computing systems according to their cost-per-performance, the TPC Energy metric ranks systems according to their energy-consumption-per-performance rates.
- Complete system evaluation vs. subsystem or processor evaluation. The TPC benchmarking model has been the most successful in modeling and benchmarking a complete end-to-end business computing environment. This has helped TPC benchmarks gain recognition as credible, realistic workloads. Most past and many current benchmarks only measure the hardware performance (including processor and memory subsystem). TPC benchmarks have led the way in developing a benchmark model that most fully incorporates robust software testing.
- Peer review and challenge. TPC results are used widely within the industry and the TPC has defined processes that ensure that these results are credible and compliant with the benchmark specification under which they are published. All results are checked by an independent TPC-authorized Auditor for accuracy and compliance with the benchmark specification before they can be published. A result's sponsor must publish an Executive Summary (ES) and Full Disclosure Report (FDR) detailing how the SUT was measured. Both these documents are available to the public. TPC member companies can review these documents and raise a challenge if they find any inconsistencies with the prevailing TPC policies or specifications. The Technical Advisory Board (TAB) considers these challenges in a timely manner and recommends a course of action to the TPC General Council. If a result is found non-compliant, it is withdrawn. The use of TPC results to make false and unverifiable marketing claims (benchmarketing) is strictly prohibited and can lead to a TPC Fair Use violation. This can subsequently lead to a reprimand and/or fine.

3   Defining a Level Playing Field

TPC benchmarks provide a credible way to comparatively evaluate the price, performance and energy requirements of complete systems, subsystems and/or processors. To make this possible, the TPC has taken considerable efforts to establish a level playing field, in which end-users and vendors can agree on an objective means of comparing disparate computing architectures.

Two key components to the TPC's success include the organization's rigorous benchmark result auditing process and the pricing component of existing TPC benchmarks. These items are described in detail below.

3.1 Auditing Process

The TPC's stringent auditing process has been integral to the organization's success as a leading publisher of industry-standard benchmarks. Independent TPC-certified Auditors verify all benchmark results as a prerequisite for publication. Organizations performing benchmark tests are required to fully document the system components, applications under test and benchmark procedures. This full disclosure makes it possible to question and challenge each result, and ensures that all published results are both credible and verifiable.

Even after a benchmark result has been published, the TPC encourages a 60-day Peer Review process. During the Peer Review, every member organization in the TPC has the right to challenge the published result.

A comparison of the TPC's auditing process to that of other industry-standards organizations is provided at the end of this section. First, however, the TPC's auditing process is outlined below in further detail for added clarity:

- Verifying the compliance of all components in a SUT, including software programs, hardware configurations, purchase and maintenance pricing, etc.
- Ensuring that the methodology used to implement the benchmark tests produces results that demonstrate compliance.
- Verifying the compliance of benchmark execution by examining the results produced.
- Encouraging comment: The establishment of an audit protocol allows Test Sponsors and Auditors to document, in detail, a required set of steps which produces the specified benchmark results. The protocol also documents test methodology and the resulting test data, which is captured and communicated to the Auditor.
- Verifying the compliance of the result, based on applicable Technical Advisory Board (TAB) and General Council (GC) rulings. Additions to the audit process may be required if there are outstanding issues that have not been previously covered.
- The Test Sponsor is responsible for attesting to the veracity of all information disclosed to the TPC Auditor and in the Full Disclosure Report (FDR).
- The Auditor may choose to examine and test disclosed information at his/her discretion. The Auditor's focus is on verifying the methodology used for reaching compliance, rather than verifying the information disclosed by the Test Sponsor.

The TPC's auditing process differs from other organizations involved in creating and publishing benchmark results. The Standard Performance Evaluation Corporation (SPEC), for example, emphasizes a Peer Review process after publication in lieu of auditing benchmark results independently. This is intended to help improve consistency in the understanding, application, and interpretation of SPEC benchmark run rules. Critically, although SPEC reviews results and accepts them for publication on its Web site, the results themselves remain the responsibility of the tester. This stands in contrast to the TPC, which makes substantial efforts to ensure benchmark results are independently certified prior to publication.

Like the TPC, the Storage Performance Council (SPC) utilizes both Peer Review and independent auditing. An SPC benchmark measurement becomes a new benchmark result upon successful submission and completion of the SPC audit process, which is required. The submitted result is then given the status "Submitted for Review" for a minimum of 60 days, during which time the Peer Review occurs. Like the TPC's Peer Review process, the SPC Peer Review allows members an opportunity to review the details of the benchmark result and raise any compliance issues. If there are no issues raised during this period, the status of the benchmark result changes to "Accepted." If, however, the SPC result is found to be non-compliant during the Peer Review, the benchmark result must either be withdrawn or revised prior to additional review.

3.2   Pricing

The TPC-Pricing specification is designed to guide both customers and vendors implementing TPC benchmarks. Additionally, the specification directs TPC Auditors on what is acceptable pricing for the purposes of publication. The pricing methodology reflects the purchase price of the benchmark SUT, software licensing used in the benchmark and the contracts for maintenance.

The TPC-Pricing specification also establishes an availability metric, which provides information on whether a specific benchmark configuration can be purchased immediately or if some of the components of the configuration are not immediately available. The availability requirement limits the length of time before a promised result must be fully available. Ideally, all systems would be available immediately upon publication, but the TPC must balance the benefits of allowing sponsors flexibility in showcasing systems where one component may not be available, and currently allows 185 days from the date of publication – although most results are available immediately or within a few weeks.

To meet the requirements of being fair, honest and comparable, while allowing for a variety of pricing and business strategies, the following requirements exist for the pricing information across all TPC benchmark publications:

- Pricing must be based upon a pricing model that the sponsoring company employs with existing customers.
- The published price must be a price that any customer would pay for the priced configuration. In a competitive environment, aggressive discounting

may occur in certain situations, such as sales or closeouts. Since these situations are unique, they do not meet the requirements of the TPC-Pricing specification. Therefore, the pricing model employed for TPC benchmark publications may not represent the best or lowest price a customer would pay.

- The methodology used must generate a similar price for a similar configuration for any customer. The pricing model must represent the pricing that could be obtained by any customer in a request for bid to a single vendor. Situations that occur when requests for bids go out to multiple vendors, and then those bids are used in negotiations to get a better price, are not represented.

Benchmark sponsors are permitted several possible pricing models to construct a price for their configuration. The pricing models used must adhere to TPC disclosure requirements. Competitors often try to confirm price accuracy by calling into sales offices anonymously and attempting to purchase an actual system.

4   A Look Ahead

The information technology landscape is evolving at a rapid pace, challenging industry experts and researchers to develop innovative techniques for evaluation, measurement and characterization of complex systems. The TPC remains committed to developing new benchmark standards to keep pace, and one vehicle for achieving this objective is the sponsorship of the Technology Conference on Performance Evaluation and Benchmarking (TPCTC). With this conference, the TPC encourages researchers and industry experts to present and debate novel ideas and methodologies in performance evaluation and benchmarking.

The first TPC Technology Conference on Performance Evaluation and Benchmarking (TPCTC2009) [4] was held in conjunction with the 35th International Conference on Very Large Data Bases (VLDB2009) in Lyon, France during August 24–28, 2009, supported by the TPC in a silver sponsor role. The paper acceptance ratio was 47%. The conference was keynoted by Mike Stonebraker, recognized as one of the top five software developers of the 20th century and an adjunct professor at the Massachusetts Institute of Technology. The formation of TPC's Virtualization working group (TPC-V) was a direct result of the papers presented at this conference. Proposals like dependability aspects are under consideration for future benchmark enhancements. The conference proceedings have been published by Springer-Verlag, and are available via the following URL: http://www.springer.com/computer/hardware/book/978-3-642-10423-7.

The second TPC Technology Conference on Performance Evaluation and Benchmarking (TPCTC2010) [5] was held in conjunction with the 36th International Conference on Very Large Data Bases (VLDB2010) in Singapore during September 13-17, supported by the TPC in a silver sponsor role. The paper acceptance ratio was 58%. The conference was keynoted by C. Mohan, IBM Fellow at IBM Almaden Research Center in San Jose, who is recognized worldwide as a leading innovator in transaction management. There are several new benchmark ideas, enhancements to existing benchmarks and lessons learnt in practice presented at this conference. The conference proceedings have been published by Springer-Verlag, and are available via the following URL: http://www.springer.com/computer/communication+ networks/book/978-3-642-18205-1.

With the third TPC Technology Conference on Performance Evaluation and Benchmarking (TPCTC2011) proposal, the TPC encourages researchers and industry experts to submit novel ideas and methodologies in performance evaluation, measurement, and characterization. Authors are invited to submit original, unpublished papers that are not currently under review for any other conference or journal. We also encourage the submission of extended abstracts, position statement papers and lessons learned in practice. The accepted papers will be published in the workshop proceedings, and selected papers will be considered for future TPC benchmark developments.

Areas of Interest:

- Appliance
- Business Intelligence
- Cloud computing
- Complex event processing
- Database performance optimizations
- Green computing
- Data compression
- Disaster tolerance and recovery
- Energy and space efficiency
- Hardware innovations
- High speed data generation
- Hybrid workloads or operational data warehousing
- Unstructured data management
- Software management and maintenance
- Virtualization
- Very large memory systems
- Lessons learnt in practice using TPC workloads
- Enhancements to TPC workloads

Acknowledgements. The authors would like to thank the past and present members of the TPC for their contribution to specifications and documents referenced in this paper.

References

1. Transaction Performance Council website (TPC), http://www.tpc.org
2. TPC Pricing Specification, http://www.tpc.org/pricing/default.asp
3. TPC Energy Specification, http://www.tpc.org/tpc_energy/
4. Nambiar, R., Poess, M. (eds.): TPCTC 2010. LNCS, vol. 6417. Springer, Heidelberg (2011) ISBN 978-3-642-18205-1
5. Nambiar, R., Poess, M. (eds.): TPCTC 2009. LNCS, vol. 5895. Springer, Heidelberg (2009) ISBN 978-3-642-10423-7

Metrics for Measuring the Performance of the Mixed Workload CH-benCHmark

Florian Funke[1], Alfons Kemper[1], Stefan Krompass[1],
Harumi Kuno[2], Raghunath Nambiar[3], Thomas Neumann[1],
Anisoara Nica[4], Meikel Poess[5], and Michael Seibold[1]

[1] Technische Universität München, 85748 Garching bei München, Germany
firstname.lastname@in.tum.de
[2] HP Labs, 1501 Page Mill Road, Palo Alto, CA 94304, USA
harumi.kuno@hp.com
[3] Cisco Systems, Inc., 3800 Zanker Road, San Jose, CA-95134, USA
rnambiar@cisco.com
[4] Sybase, An SAP Company, 445 Wes Graham Way, Waterloo ON, N2L 6R2, Canada
anica@sybase.com
[5] Oracle Corporation, 500 Oracle Parkway, Redwood Shores, CA-94065, USA
meikel.poess@oracle.com

Abstract. Advances in hardware architecture have begun to enable database vendors to process analytical queries directly on operational database systems without impeding the performance of mission-critical transaction processing too much. In order to evaluate such systems, we recently devised the mixed workload CH-benCHmark, which combines **transactional load** based on TPC-C order processing with **decision support load** based on TPC-H-like query suite run **in parallel** on the **same tables** in a **single database** system. Just as the data volume of actual enterprises tends to increase over time, an inherent characteristic of this mixed workload benchmark is that data volume increases during benchmark runs, which in turn may increase response times of analytic queries. For purely transactional loads, response times typically do not depend that much on data volume, as the queries used within business transactions are less complex and often indexes are used to answer these queries with point-wise accesses only. But for mixed workloads, the insert throughput metric of the transactional component interferes with the response-time metric of the analytic component. In order to address the problem, in this paper we analyze the characteristics of CH-benCHmark queries and propose normalized metrics which account for data volume growth.

Keywords: mixed workload, real-time business intelligence.

1 Introduction

Today, businesses typically employ operational database systems to service transaction-oriented applications that are vital to their day-to-day operations. These

R. Nambiar and M. Poess (Eds.): TPCTC 2011, LNCS 7144, pp. 10–30, 2012.

operational database systems focus on providing high availability and low latency to a large number of concurrent users. Data warehouse systems are used for analyzing large amounts of business data to support strategic decision making, e. g. computing sales revenue of a company by products across regions and time. Consequently, data warehouses are especially designed to support fast scans and complex data algorithms for a relatively small number of users. Early attempts to run analytical queries directly on the operational database systems resulted in unacceptable transaction processing performance [4]. Instead, companies deployed separate systems, one for the operational side and one for the analytical side of their business. As part of an Extraction, Transformation and Load process (ETL), the data warehouse is periodically updated with data that is extracted from the operational databases and transformed into a schema optimized for analytical processing. While allowing each system to be tuned separately according to the characteristics of their respective loads, this staging approach suffers from inherent drawbacks. On the one hand, two or more software and hardware systems must be purchased and maintained. On the other hand, analyses do not incorporate the latest data, but work on a stale snapshot in the data warehouse.

Lately, the case has been made for so called real-time Business Intelligence, to overcome the disadvantages of the data staging approach. SAP's co-founder Hasso Plattner [5] emphasizes the necessity of analytical queries to be performed on current data for strategic management and compares the expected impact of real-time analysis on management with the impact of Internet search engines on the world. This trend is supported by advances in hardware architecture, which allow keeping large amounts of data in main-memory and may help to process both loads in a single database system.

Recently, a mixed workload benchmark, called CH-benCHmark has been proposed [3], that bridges the gap between existing single-workload benchmarks and allows analyzing the suitability of database systems for real-time Business Intelligence. This hybrid benchmark is based on TPC-C and TPC-H, two standardized and widely used benchmarks addressing either transactional or analytical workloads. The CH-benCHmark produces results that are highly relevant to both hybrid and classic single-workload systems, as it is derived from these two most widely used TPC benchmarks [6]. A related benchmark is the Composite Benchmark for Transaction processing and operational Reporting (CBTR) [1,2], which includes OLTP and reporting components. As discussed in [3], the CH-benCHmark is intended as a step towards modeling complex mixed workloads and models the components: continuous data loading, batch data loading, and large numbers of standard reports.

In this paper we analyze the workload characteristics and performance metrics of the mixed workload CH-benCHmark. Based on this analysis, we propose performance metrics that account for data volume growth which is an inherent characteristic of the mixed workload benchmark.

This paper is organized as follows. Section 2 gives an overview of the mixed workload CH-benCHmark. Section 3 describes the performance metrics of CH-benCHmark and introduces the proposed normalized metrics. Section 4 presents the results of our experiments. Section 5 describes how CH-benCHmark deviates from TPC-C and TPC-H specifications. Section 6 concludes the paper by restating the reason why the proposed performance metrics are needed and mentions alternative approaches.

2   Overview of the Mixed Workload CH-benCHmark

The CH-benCHmark represents a mixed database workload comprised of transactional and analytical loads that are executed in parallel on the same tables in a single Database Management System (DBMS). The transactional load is based on the business transactions of TPC-C. Since the TPC-C tables are used unchanged, benchmark sponsors [1] can use their TPC-C benchmark kits to run the transactional load of CH-benCHmark. The analytical load consists of a read-only query suite modeled after TPC-H. The TPC-H refresh functions are omitted, as the database is continuously updated (and expanded) via the transactional load.

2.1   Schema and Inital Database Population

CH-benCHmark extends the TPC-C schema (see gray boxes in Figure 1) with three additional tables from the TPC-H schema: SUPPLIER, REGION and NATION (see white boxes in Figure 1). These additional tables are read-only, as they are not modified during a benchmark run. The combined schema allows formulating slightly modified TPC-H queries on TPC-C-like schema and data.

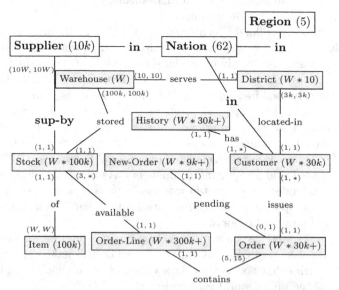

Fig. 1. Entity-Relationship-Diagram of the CH-Benchmark Database

---

[1] Benchmark sponsors are hardware and software vendors who publish TPC benchmarks.

Figure 1 denotes the cardinalities of the initial database population in brackets after the name of each entity. The + symbol is used after the cardinality of an entity to indicate that the cardinality is subject to change during a benchmark run, as rows are added or deleted. The initial database population follows the official TPC-C specification. (min,max)-notation is used to represent the cardinalities of relationships after initial database population and during benchmark runs. As in TPC-C, the WAREHOUSE table is used as the base unit. The cardinality of all other tables (except for ITEM) is a function of the number of configured warehouses (cardinality of the WAREHOUSE table). The population of the three additional read-only tables is defined as follows. The relation SUPPLIER is populated with a fixed number (10,000) of entries. Thereby, an entry in STOCK can be uniquely associated with its Supplier through the relationship STOCK.S_I_ID $\times$ STOCK.S_W_ID mod $10,000 =$ SUPPLIER.SU_SUPPKEY. A Customer's NATION is identified by the first character of the field C_STATE. TPC-C specifies that this first character can have 62 different values (upper-case letters, lower-case letters and numbers), therefore we chose 62 nations to populate Nation (TPC-H specifies 25 nations). The primary key N_NATIONKEY is an identifier according to the TPC-H specification. Its values are chosen such that their associated ASCII value is a letter or number. Therefore no additional calculations are required to skip over the gaps in the ASCII code between numbers, upper-case letters and lower-case letters. Region contains the five regions of these nations. Relationships between the new relations are modeled with simple foreign key fields: (NATION.N_REGIONKEY and SUPPLIER.SU_NATIONKEY).

2.2   Transactional Load

The original TPC-C workload consists of a mixture of read-only and update-intensive business transactions: New-Order, Payment, Order-Status, Delivery, and Stock-Level[7]. The TPC-C schema contains nine tables: WAREHOUSE, STOCK, ITEM, HISTORY, NEW-ORDER, ORDER-LINE, DISTRICT, CUSTOMER, and ORDER (see grey boxes in Figure 1). The transactional load of the CH-BenCHmark is very similar to the original TPC-C workload. Unchanged TPC-C business transactions are processed on unchanged TPC-C tables. Even the initial database population follows the official TPC-C specification. But the CH-Benchmark does not simulate terminals, as TPC-C does with keying times and think times. Instead a given number of transactional sessions issue randomly chosen business transactions in a sequential manner without think times or keying times. The distribution of the different business transaction types follows the official TPC-C specification. The home warehouses of business transactions are randomly chosen by each transactional session and are evenly distributed across warehouses.

2.3   Analytical Load

The original TPC-H workload consists of a database load, the execution of 22 read-only queries in both single (a.k.a. Power Test, see Clause 6.3.3 of [8]) and multi-user modes (a.k.a. Throughput Test, see Clause 6.3.3 of [8]) and two re-fresh functions (RF1 and RF2). The power test measures a systems ability to parallelize queries across all available resources (i.e. memory, CPU, I/O) in or-der to minimize response time. The throughput test measures a system's ability to execute multiple concurrent queries, allocate resources efficiently across all users to maximize query throughput. The queries are intended to test the most common query capabilities of a typical decision support system. In order to fa-cilitate the understanding of TPC-H queries and the mapping of the benchmark queries to real world situations, each query is described in terms of a business question. This business question is formulated in English explaining the result of the query in context of TPC-H's business model. The business questions are translated into functional query definitions that define the queries using the SQL-92 query language. TPC-H queries are chosen to perform operations that are relevant to common data warehouse applications. Accordingly, the demand a query places on the hardware (processor, IO-subsystem) and software (operating system, database management system) of the tested system varies from query to query. To assure that the benchmark remains dynamic, each TPC-H query contains substitution parameters that are randomly chosen by the benchmark driver immediately before its execution, to mimic ad-hoc workloads. The refresh functions are intended to test the periodic update of the database. RF1 inserts new rows into the ORDERS and LINEITEM tables while RF2 removes rows from the ORDERS and LINEITEM tables to emulate the removal of stale or obsolete information. The amount of data inserted and deleted scales with the scale factor SF.

The CH-benCHmark uses the 22 TPC-H queries. Since the CH-benCHmark schema is different from the TPC-H schema, the queries are rewritten to match the schema. However, their business semantics and syntactical structure are pre-served. Business queries read data from the extended schema, including data from the TPC-C tables and the three additional read-only tables. The contents of the unmodified TPC-C tables change during the benchmark run, as business transactions update and insert tuples. These changes have to be accounted for by the business queries depending on data freshness requirements. Analytical performance in the CH-benCHmark cannot be easily inferred from the perfor-mance of a similarly-sized TPC-H installation. The analytical load is generated by a given number of analytical sessions. Each analytical session submits busi-ness queries sequentially. All 22 business query types are issued in continuous iterations over the query type set, while each analytical session executes all 22 query types in a randomly chosen permutation sequence to avoid caching effects.

2.4   Benchmark Parameters

Figure 2 illustrates parameters of the CH-benCHmark and shows some exem-plary values. Database systems can be compared based on performance metrics by performing benchmark runs with the same parameter values on all systems.

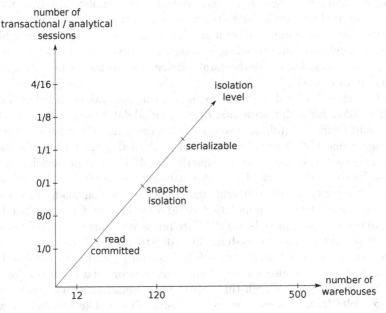

Fig. 2. Benchmark Parameters

Similar to TPC-C, the size of the initial database is specified by the number of warehouses, which determines the cardinalities of the other relations.

The composition of the workload is specified by the number of transactional sessions and analytical sessions. This parameter allows to specify purely transactional, purely analytical and mixed workload scenarios.

The isolation level which has to be provided by a system under test, is a parameter of the CH-benCHmark. Lower isolation levels, like read committed, can be used to measure raw performance with limited synchronization overhead. More demanding isolation levels can be used to account for more realistic synchronization requirements. The isolation level parameter can be specified separately for the transactional and the analytical load.

For mixed workload scenarios, the data freshness parameter allows to specify the time or number of transactions after which newly issued queries have to incorporate the most recent data.

2.5   Data Scaling

TPC-C and TPC-H employ different scaling models. A scaling model maintains the ratio between the transaction load presented to the system under test, the cardinality of the tables accessed by the transactions, the required space for storage and the number of terminals or sessions generating the system load. TPC-C employs a continuous scaling model, where the data volume has to be increased for higher transaction load. The number of warehouses determines not only the cardinality of the other tables, but also the number of terminals that generate a limited load each due to think times and keying times. For increasing transaction load, the number of terminals has to be increased, requiring a higher number of warehouses and resulting in a larger data volume. TPC-H employs a fixed scale factor model, where the database size is set by a scale factor regardless of system performance.

The CH-benCHmark deviates from the continuous scaling model of TPC-C in order to allow for high transaction rates on small database sizes that are common in main-memory database systems. On the one hand, the continuous scaling model may cause higher response times for analytical queries when transaction load is increased, because analytical queries would have to process larger data volumes. In this case it would not be meaningful to compare query response times of two systems with different maximum transaction loads, as even the size of the initial database population could vary largely. On the other hand, the continuous scaling model of TPC-C requires very large data volumes and expensive secondary storage systems in order to fully utilize modern CPUs. However, the CH-benCHmark was designed not only for traditional disk-based database systems, but also for emerging main-memory database systems. For measuring performance of high-throughput OLTP main-memory database systems like VoltDB, Stonebraker et al. propose a TPC-C-like benchmark which does not adhere to continuous scaling [9]. The CH-benCHmark determines maximum system performance for a fixed initial data volume. Similar to TPC-H, the initial database population is determined by a scale factor regardless of system performance. The scale factor is the number of warehouses which determines the initial data volume like in TPC-C. But unlike TPC-C, the number of transactional sessions is fixed and there are neither sleep nor keying times. Therefore higher system performance can be achieved without increasing the initial data volume.

During the course of a benchmark run business transactions add new orders, adding tuples to relations ORDERS, ORDERLINE, HISTORY and NEW-ORDER. Since the SUPPLIER relation is read-only, the ratio of the cardinalities of these relations changes relative to the SUPPLIER relation. The cardinality ratio relative to the SUPPLIER relation does not change for the relations WAREHOUSE, DISTRICT, STOCK, CUSTOMER, and ITEM, which are read-only or only updated in-place. Due to continuous data volume growth, refresh functions like in TPC-H are not required. The challenges posed by data volume growth during benchmark runs is discussed in the next section.

3   Performance Metrics

Currently, the mixed workload CH-benCHmark uses performance metrics similar to those of single-workload benchmarks like TPC-C and TPC-H (see Table 1). The two most important metrics are *Transactional Throughput* for transactional load and *Geometric Mean* of response times for analytical load.

It may seem obvious to combine the *Transactional Throughput* metric and the *Queries Per Hour* metric in order to obtain a single metric, but competing systems under test may prioritize transactions and analytical queries differently and this aspect would get lost if a single metric were used.

Table 1. Performance Metrics

Transactional Throughput (tpmCH)	Total number of New-Order transactions completed during the measurement interval divided by the elapsed time of the interval in minutes; New-Order transactions that rollback due to simulated user data entry errors must be included; Similar to the Maximum Qualified Throughput metric of TPC-C
Geometric Mean (ms)	For each query type the average response times of queries completed during the measurement interval is determined and the geometric mean of the average response times of all query types is reported.
Duration Per Query Set (s)	Query set consists of 22 queries, one query per query type; Sum of the average response times of all query types; Reported in seconds
Queries Per Hour (QphCH)	Completed queries per hour; This metric is based on the composite performance metric of TPC-H (QphH), but differes largely, as there are no refresh functions in CH-benCHmark; Can be deduced from *Duration Per Query Set* metric as follows: $$\frac{60\ minutes}{\frac{Duration\ Per\ Query\ Set\ (in\ seconds)}{60}} \times 22$$

But data volume growth caused by the transactional load of the mixed workload poses a challenge. The problem is that higher transactional throughput may result in larger data volume which in turn may result in longer response times for analytical queries. Therefore, currently reported performance metrics cannot be compared individually, as systems with high transactional performance may have to report inferior analytical performance numbers, although analytical queries have been performed on larger data volumes. The insert throughput metric of the transactional component interferes with the response-time metric of the analytic component of the mixed workload. Note that TPC-H does not consider a database that grows over the course of a benchmark run. To overcome this issue, we propose performance metrics that account for data volume growth which is an inherent characteristic of a mixed workload benchmark like CH-benCHmark.

3.1 Response Times and Data Volume Growth

During the course of a CH-benCHmark run, data volume grows over time due to inserts caused by transactional load of mixed workload. Figure 3 illustrates how response time of a query may increase with growing data volume.

During the course of a CH-benCHmark run, cardinality of the following tables increases: ORDER, ORDERLINE, HISTORY and NEW-ORDER. The cardinality ratio between the relations ORDERLINE and ORDER should be approximately ten and should be more or less constant during a run, because an order includes ten items on average according to the TPC-C specification and thus there should be ten orderlines per order on average. The HISTORY relation is not read by any query in the TPC-H-like query suite of CH-benCHmark. One could think that the cardinality of the NEW-ORDER relation would be more or less constant, as each delivery transaction delivers a batch of ten new (not yet delivered) orders and the TPC-C specification states: "The intent of the minimum percentage of mix ... is to execute approximately ... one Delivery transaction ... for every 10 New-Order transactions". But in practice our CH-benCHmark implementation, like any other implementation of TPC-C, tries to maximize the number of processed New-Order transactions and only processes the required minimum of the other transaction types. This strategy results in approximately 45% New-Order transactions and only 4% Delivery transactions that deliver ten new orders each. Therefore the Delivery transactions cannot keep up with orders created by New-Order transactions and therefore the cardinality of the NEW-ORDER relation increases during a benchmark run, as approximately 11% of new orders remain undelivered.

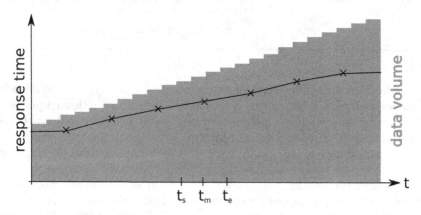

Fig. 3. Response Times and Data Volume Growth

Whether the response time of a given query is affected by growing data volume, depends on the required data access patterns, available indexes and clustering of the accessed data. Data volume growth may affect response times of 19 out of the 22 analytical queries (see Appendix for SQL code of analytic queries), as they access tables whose cardinality increases during the course of a benchmark run. Response times of queries Q2, Q11 and Q16 should not be affected by growing data volume, as they access only tables whose cardinality does not change during the course of a benchmark run. Also Q22 should not be affected, if a suitable index on the ORDER table is available.

3.2 Analytical Model and Normalization

We propose to monitor data volume growth during a benchmark run and to normalize response times based on an analytical model to compensate the "handicap" caused by larger data volumes.

The number of non-aborted New-Order and Delivery transactions can be monitored. Based on this figure, data volume growth of the ORDER, ORDERLINE and the NEW-ORDER relation can be estimated. CH-benCHmark, like any other TPC-C implementation, has to monitor the number of New-Order transactions anyway for reporting the throughput metric.

For each analytic query, the analytical model has to capture how data volume growth affects query response times, e.g. based on the accessed relations and the complexity of required basic operations (scan, join, etc.).

For a given point in time, cardinalities of accessed relations can be estimated and the analytical model can be used to determine a compensation factor. This factor can be used to normalize query response times and thereby compensate the "handicap" caused by larger data volumes.

The point in time used for estimating data volume of a given query execution depends on the configured isolation level. Depending on the chosen isolation level, a query may even account for data which is added while the query is executed. For example, in Figure 3 data volume grows even during query execution as query execution starts at t_s and ends at t_e. Response times of queries may increase over time when more data has to be processed. For snapshot isolation and higher isolation levels, the start time of query execution (t_s) can be used. For lower isolation levels, t_s would ignore cardinality changes during query execution and t_e could favor longer execution times. As a compromise, the middle of query execution (t_m) may be used.

4   Experimental Evaluation of the Query Performance

We conducted our experiments on a commodity server with two Intel X5570 Quad-Core-CPUs with 8MB cache each and 64GB RAM. The machine had 16 2.5 SAS disks with 300GB that were configured as RAID 5 with two logical devices. As operating system, we were using an Enterprise-grade Linux running a 2.6 Linux kernel.

In order to evaluate how data volume growth affects response times of analytical queries, we need the ability to evaluate analytical performance on CH-benCHmark databases of different sizes. For reproducibility, we always use the same fixed data set for a given data volume size. We generate the data sets by configuring CH-benCHmark for a purely transactional workload scenario and dump database contents to disk after a given number of New-Order transactions have been performed.

As described in Section 3.1, normalization is based on an analytical model and an estimation of data volume growth. We estimate data volume growth based on the characteristics of typical TPC-C implementations. Figure 4 shows a comparison between the estimated cardinalities and the actual cardinalities of the relations in the used data sets. The x-axis represents the factor by which data volume is increased (2x - 64x) in a given data set and the y-axis represents actual or estimated cardinality of the relations.

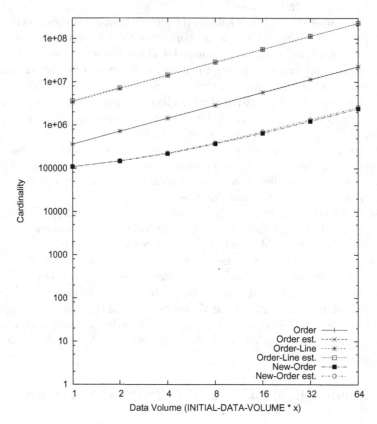

Fig. 4. Estimated and Actual Cardinalities of Relations

In order to compare purely analytical performance of different database systems, we load data sets of different sizes into two database systems which represent different kinds of database systems. Database system "P" is a general-purpose disk-based database system and adheres to a traditional row-store architecture. Database system "V" adheres to emerging column-store architecture, is highly optimized for analytical loads and represents a main-memory database system. We measure response times of analytical queries for each data set. Each query is performed N times on each data set with warm cache and the average response time is compared.

Figure 7 shows the measured average response times for each of the 22 queries on system "P" and Figure 8 shows the corresponding normalized response times. Figures 5 and 6 show the same for system "V".

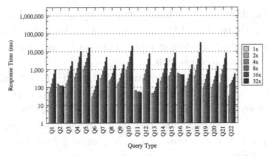

Fig. 5. Average Response Times of System "V"

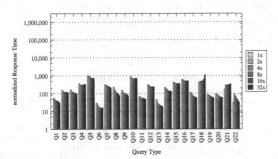

Fig. 6. Normalized Average Response Times of System "V"

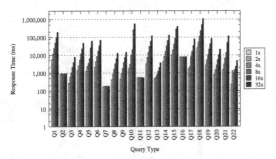

Fig. 7. Average Response Times of System "P"

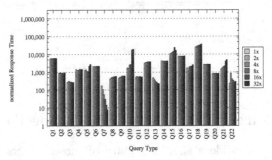

Fig. 8. Normalized Average Response Times of System "P"

The experiments show data volume growth of CH-benCHmark affects response times of analytic queries. Our analytical model can be used to normalize response times. Normalized response times can serve as a performance metric that accounts for data volume growth.

[3] defines a tabular format for reporting CH-benCHmark results. In Table 2 we show our results according to this format and have added columns and rows for the proposed normalized metrics. The normalized metrics are determined in the same way as the original ones, but with normalized response times. The presented results do not correspond to a full mixed workload, but only one query stream is performed on fixed data sets with increasing data volume. The advantage of this approach is, that the same data set of given size can be used for both systems. We decided not to compare the two system with a full mixed workload, because System "V" is highly optimized for analytical loads and is not intended for transaction processing.

Table 2. Reported CH-benCHmark Results

| | 1 Q. stream on data set with increasing data volume | | | |
| | System "V" | | System "P" | |
	average response times (ms)	average normalized response times	average response times (ms)	average normalized response times
Q#				
Q1	368	42	63632	6001
Q2	126	126	890	890
Q3	1012	121	2606	281
Q4	3368	319	15202	1403
Q5	5722	818	17104	1624
Q6	168	20	22549	2125
Q7	1782	260	177	65
Q8	729	131	4270	517
Q9	703	105	4829	551
Q10	6760	725	141634	7510
Q11	57	57	538	538
Q12	2497	254	39550	3619
Q13	120	27	1437	314
Q14	1430	163	42819	4165
Q15	2876	368	141051	14804
Q16	525	525	7767	7767
Q17	651	79	23405	1926
Q18	7828	587	332413	30598
Q19	614	70	27786	2683
Q20	517	73	6863	819
Q21	2552	280	31812	2710
Q22	245	53	1847	396
Geometric mean (ms)	146		1621	
Normalized geometric mean	859		10814	
Duration per query set (s)	41		931	
Normalized duration per query set	6		92	
Queries per hour (QphH)	1949		86	
Normalized queries per hour (QphH)	15222		868	

5 Deviations from TPC-C and TPC-H Specifications

In the following we provide a short summary of those aspects in which CH-benCHmark deviates from TPC-C and TPC-H specifications.

The transactional load of CH-benCHmark deviates from the TPC-C specification in the following aspects. First, client requests are generated directly by transactional sessions instead of simulating terminals. The number of transactional sessions is a parameter of the CH-benCHmark. Therefore, home warehouses of business transactions are randomly chosen by each transactional session and are uniformly distributed across warehouses, instead of statically assigning home warehouses to terminals. Second, a transactional session issues randomly chosen business transactions in a sequential manner without think times or keying times. But, the distribution of the different business transaction types follows the official TPC-C specification. Third, the number of warehouses is a parameter of the CH-benCHmark and does not have to be increased to achieve higher throughput rates. These changes can be easily applied to existing TPC-C implementations, only small modifications of the benchmark driver configuration and implementation may be required.

The CH-benCHmark specification has to define the additional tables which have to be added to an existing implementation of TPC-C. Furthermore, the business queries, the scaling model and the performance metrics have to be specified.

6 Conclusions

In this paper we analyzed the workload characteristics and performance metrics of the mixed workload CH-benCHmark. Based on this analysis, we proposed performance metrics that account for data volume growth to tackle the problem that higher transactional throughput may result in larger data volume which in turn may result in inferior analytical performance numbers. Put differently, the reason why we need the proposed performance metrics is not data volume growth itself, but the fact that data volume growth varies largely between different systems under test that support different transactional throughput rates. An alternative approach would be not to measure peak transactional and analytical performance, but to measure how much analytical throughput can be achieved while a fixed transactional throughput is fulfilled. Moreover, a mixed workload benchmark could measure resource requirements or energy consumption while maintaining fixed transactional and analytical performance. These alternative approaches are out of the scope of this paper, but seem to be an interesting direction for future work.

References

1. Bog, A., Sachs, K., Zeier, A.: Benchmarking Database Design for Mixed OLTP and OLAP Workloads. In: Second Joint WOSP/SIPEW International Conference on Performance Engineering (2011)
2. Bog, A., Schaffner, J., Krüger, J.: A Composite Benchmark for Online Transaction Processing and Operational Reporting. In: IEEE Symposium on Advanced Management of Information for Globalized Enterprises (2008)

3. Cole, R., Funke, F., Giakoumakis, L., Guy, W., Kemper, A., Krompass, S., Kuno, H., Nambiar, R., Neumann, T., Poess, M., Sattler, K.-U., Seibold, M., Simon, E., Waas, F.: The mixed workload CH-benCHmark. In: ACM International Workshop on Testing Database Systems (ACM DBTEST), ACM Special Interest Group on Management of Data (ACM SIGMOD) Conference Workshops (2011)
4. Doppelhammer, J., Höppler, T., Kemper, A., Kossmann, D.: Database Performance in the Real World - TPC-D and SAP R/3. In: ACM SIGMOD International Conference on Management of Data (1997)
5. Plattner, H.: A common database approach for OLTP and OLAP using an in-memory column database. In: ACM SIGMOD International Conference on Management of Data (2009)
6. Poess, M., Nambiar, R.: Building Enterprise Class Real-Time Energy Efficient Decision Support Systems. In: Fourth International Workshop on Enabling Real-Time Business Intelligence (BIRTE), International Conference on Very Large Data Bases (VLDB) Workshops (2010)
7. Transaction Processing Performance Council. TPC-C specification (2010), www.tpc.org/tpcc/spec/TPC-C_v5-11.pdf
8. Transaction Processing Performance Council. TPC-H specification (2011), http://www.tpc.org/tpch/spec/tpch2.14.0.pdf
9. VoltDB. TPC-C-like Benchmark Comparison - Benchmark Description, http://community.voltdb.com/node/134

Appendix: Queries

This section contains the SQL code of all 22 analytic queries of the TPC-H-like query suite.[2] All dates, strings and ranges in the queries are examples only.

Q1: Generate orderline overview

```
select  ol_number ,
        sum( ol_quantity ) as sum_qty ,
        sum( ol_amount ) as sum_amount ,
        avg( ol_quantity ) as avg_qty ,
        avg( ol_amount ) as avg_amount ,
        count(∗) as count_order
from  orderline where ol_delivery_d > '2007−01−02_00:00:00.000000'
group by ol_number order by ol_number
```

Q2: Most important supplier/item-combinations (those that have the lowest stock level for certain parts in a certain region)

```
select  su_suppkey , su_name , n_name , i_id , i_name , su_address , su_phone , su_comment
from  item , supplier , stock , nation , region ,
      ( select  s_i_id as m_i_id , min( s_quantity ) as m_s_quantity
        from  stock , supplier , nation , region
        where  mod(( s_w_id ∗ s_i_id ) ,10000)=su_suppkey
        and  su_nationkey=n_nationkey
        and  n_regionkey=r_regionkey
        and  r_name like 'Europ%'
        group by s_i_id ) m
where  i_id = s_i_id
and  mod(( s_w_id ∗ s_i_id ), 10000) = su_suppkey
and  su_nationkey = n_nationkey
and  n_regionkey = r_regionkey
and  i_data like '%b'
and  r_name like 'Europ%'
and  i_id=m_i_id
and  s_quantity = m_s_quantity
order by n_name , su_name , i_id
```

Q3: Unshipped orders with highest value for customers within a certain state

```
select  ol_o_id , ol_w_id , ol_d_id , sum( ol_amount ) as revenue , o_entry_d
from  customer , neworder , orders , orderline
where  c_state like 'A%'
and  c_id = o_c_id
and  c_w_id = o_w_id
and  c_d_id = o_d_id
and  no_w_id = o_w_id
and  no_d_id = o_d_id
and  no_o_id = o_id
and  ol_w_id = o_w_id
and  ol_d_id = o_d_id
and  ol_o_id = o_id
and  o_entry_d > '2007−01−02_00:00:00.000000'
group by ol_o_id , ol_w_id , ol_d_id , o_entry_d
order by revenue desc , o_entry_d
```

Q4: Orders that were partially shipped late

```
select  o_ol_cnt , count(∗) as order_count
from  orders
where  o_entry_d >= '2007−01−02_00:00:00.000000'
and  o_entry_d < '2012−01−02_00:00:00.000000'
and  exists ( select ∗
              from  orderline
              where  o_id = ol_o_id
              and  o_w_id = ol_w_id
              and  o_d_id = ol_d_id
              and  ol_delivery_d >= o_entry_d )
group by o_ol_cnt
order by o_ol_cnt
```

---

[2] The SQL code for all 22 queries can be found at
http://www-db.in.tum.de/research/projects/CH-benCHmark/.

Q5: Revenue volume achieved through local suppliers

```
select n_name, sum(ol_amount) as revenue
from customer, orders, orderline, stock, supplier, nation, region
where c_id = o_c_id
and c_w_id = o_w_id
and c_d_id = o_d_id
and ol_o_id = o_id
and ol_w_id = o_w_id
and ol_d_id=o_d_id
and ol_w_id = s_w_id
and ol_i_id = s_i_id
and mod((s_w_id * s_i_id),10000) = su_suppkey
and ascii(substr(c_state,1,1)) = su_nationkey
and su_nationkey = n_nationkey
and n_regionkey = r_regionkey
and r_name = 'Europe'
and o_entry_d >= '2007-01-02_00:00:00.000000'
group by n_name
order by revenue desc
```

Q6: Revenue generated by orderlines of a certain quantity

```
select sum(ol_amount) as revenue
from orderline
where ol_delivery_d >= '1999-01-01_00:00:00.000000'
and ol_delivery_d < '2020-01-01_00:00:00.000000'
and ol_quantity between 1 and 100000
```

Q7: Bi-directional trade volume between two nations

```
select su_nationkey as supp_nation,
       substr(c_state,1,1) as cust_nation,
       extract(year from o_entry_d) as l_year,
       sum(ol_amount) as revenue
from supplier, stock, orderline, orders, customer, nation n1, nation n2
where ol_supply_w_id = s_w_id
and ol_i_id = s_i_id
and mod((s_w_id * s_i_id), 10000) = su_suppkey

and ol_w_id = o_w_id
and ol_d_id = o_d_id
and ol_o_id = o_id
and c_id = o_c_id
and c_w_id = o_w_id
and c_d_id = o_d_id
and su_nationkey = n1.n_nationkey
and ascii(substr(c_state,1,1)) = n2.n_nationkey
and (
      (n1.n_name = 'Germany' and n2.n_name = 'Cambodia')
      or
      (n1.n_name = 'Cambodia' and n2.n_name = 'Germany'))
and ol_delivery_d between '2007-01-02_00:00:00.000000' and '2012-01-02_
    00:00:00.000000'
group by su_nationkey, substr(c_state,1,1), extract(year from o_entry_d)
order by su_nationkey, cust_nation, l_year
```

Q8: Market share of a given nation for customers of a given region for a given part type

```
select extract(year from o_entry_d) as l_year,
     sum(case when n2.n_name = 'Germany' then ol_amount else 0 end) / sum(ol_amount)
       as mkt_share
from item, supplier, stock, orderline, orders, customer, nation n1, nation n2, region
where i_id = s_i_id
and ol_i_id = s_i_id
and ol_supply_w_id = s_w_id
and mod((s_w_id * s_i_id),10000) = su_suppkey
and ol_w_id = o_w_id
and ol_d_id = o_d_id
and ol_o_id = o_id
and c_id = o_c_id
and c_w_id = o_w_id
and c_d_id = o_d_id
and n1.n_nationkey = ascii(substr(c_state,1,1))
and n1.n_regionkey = r_regionkey
and ol_i_id < 1000

and r_name = 'Europe'
and su_nationkey = n2.n_nationkey
and o_entry_d between '2007-01-02_00:00:00.000000' and '2012-01-02_00:00:00.000000'
```

```
and i_data like '%b'
and i_id = ol_i_id
group by extract(year from o_entry_d)
order by l_year
```

Q9: Profit made on a given line of parts,broken out by supplier nation and year

```
select n_name, extract(year from o_entry_d) as l_year, sum(ol_amount) as sum_profit
from item, stock, supplier, orderline, orders, nation
where ol_i_id = s_i_id
and ol_supply_w_id = s_w_id
and mod((s_w_id * s_i_id), 10000) = su_suppkey
and ol_w_id = o_w_id
and ol_d_id = o_d_id
and ol_o_id = o_id
and ol_i_id = i_id
and su_nationkey = n_nationkey
and i_data like '%BB'
group by n_name, extract(year from o_entry_d)
order by n_name, l_year desc
```

Q10: Customers who received their ordered products late

```
select c_id, c_last, sum(ol_amount) as revenue, c_city, c_phone, n_name
from customer, orders, orderline, nation
where c_id = o_c_id
and c_w_id = o_w_id
and c_d_id = o_d_id
and ol_w_id = o_w_id
and ol_d_id = o_d_id
and ol_o_id = o_id
and o_entry_d >= '2007-01-02_00:00:00.000000'
and o_entry_d <= ol_delivery_d
and n_nationkey = ascii(substr(c_state,1,1))
group by c_id, c_last, c_city, c_phone, n_name
order by revenue desc
```

Q11: Most important (high order count compared to the sum of all order counts) parts supplied by suppliers of a particular nation

```
select s_i_id, sum(s_order_cnt) as ordercount
from stock, supplier, nation
where mod((s_w_id * s_i_id),10000) = su_suppkey
and su_nationkey = n_nationkey
and n_name = 'Germany'
group by s_i_id
having sum(s_order_cnt) >
    (select sum(s_order_cnt) * .005
     from stock, supplier, nation
     where mod((s_w_id * s_i_id),10000) = su_suppkey
     and su_nationkey = n_nationkey
     and n_name = 'Germany')
order by ordercount desc
```

Q12: Determine whether selecting less expensive modes of shipping is negatively affecting the critical-priority orders by causing more parts to be received late by customers

```
select o_ol_cnt,
        sum(case when o_carrier_id = 1 or o_carrier_id = 2 then 1 else 0 end) as
            high_line_count,
        sum(case when o_carrier_id <> 1 and o_carrier_id <> 2 then 1 else 0 end) as
            low_line_count
from orders, orderline
where ol_w_id = o_w_id
and ol_d_id = o_d_id
and ol_o_id = o_id
and o_entry_d <= ol_delivery_d
and ol_delivery_d < '2020-01-01_00:00:00.000000'
group by o_ol_cnt
order by o_ol_cnt
```

Q13: Relationships between customers and the size of their orders

```
select c_count, count(*) as custdist
from (select c_id, count(o_id)
      from customer left outer join orders on (
            c_w_id = o_w_id
            and c_d_id = o_d_id
            and c_id = o_c_id
            and o_carrier_id > 8)
      group by c_id) as c_orders (c_id, c_count)
group by c_count
order by custdist desc, c_count desc
```

Q14: Market response to a promotion campaign

```
select 100.00 *
      sum(case when i_data like 'PR%' then ol_amount else 0 end) / 1+sum(ol_amount) as
            promo_revenue
from orderline, item
where ol_i_id = i_id and ol_delivery_d >= '2007-01-02-00:00:00.000000'
and ol_delivery_d < '2020-01-02-00:00:00.000000'
```

Q15: Determines the top supplier

```
with revenue (supplier_no, total_revenue) as (
      select mod((s_w_id * s_i_id),10000) as supplier_no,
            sum(ol_amount) as total_revenue
      from orderline, stock
      where ol_i_id = s_i_id and ol_supply_w_id = s_w_id
      and ol_delivery_d >= '2007-01-02-00:00:00.000000'
      group by mod((s_w_id * s_i_id),10000))
select su_suppkey, su_name, su_address, su_phone, total_revenue
from supplier, revenue
where su_suppkey = supplier_no
and total_revenue = (select max(total_revenue) from revenue)
order by su_suppkey
```

Q16: Number of suppliers that can supply parts with given attributes

```
select i_name,
      substr(i_data, 1, 3) as brand,
      i_price,
      count(distinct (mod((s_w_id * s_i_id),10000))) as supplier_cnt
from stock, item
where i_id = s_i_id
and i_data not like 'zz%'
and (mod((s_w_id * s_i_id),10000)) not in
      (select su_suppkey
       from supplier
       where su_comment like '%bad%')
group by i_name, substr(i_data, 1, 3), i_price
order by supplier_cnt desc
```

Q17: Average yearly revenue that would be lost if orders were no longer filled for small quantities of certain parts

```
select sum(ol_amount) / 2.0 as avg_yearly
from orderline, (select i_id, avg(ol_quantity) as a
                 from item, orderline
                 where i_data like '%b'
                 and ol_i_id = i_id
                 group by i_id) t
where ol_i_id = t.i_id
and ol_quantity < t.a
```

Q18: Rank customers based on their placement of a large quantity order

```
select c_last , c_id o_id , o_entry_d , o_ol_cnt , sum(ol_amount)
from customer , orders , orderline
where c_id = o_c_id
and c_w_id = o_w_id
and c_d_id = o_d_id
and ol_w_id = o_w_id
and ol_d_id = o_d_id
and ol_o_id = o_id
group by o_id , o_w_id , o_d_id , c_id , c_last , o_entry_d , o_ol_cnt
having sum(ol_amount) > 200
order by sum(ol_amount) desc , o_entry_d
```

Q19: Machine generated data mining (revenue report for disjunctive predicate)

```
select sum(ol_amount) as revenue
from orderline , item
where ( ol_i_id = i_id
        and i_data like '%a'
        and ol_quantity >= 1
        and ol_quantity <= 10
        and i_price between 1 and 400000
        and ol_w_id in (1,2,3))
or ( ol_i_id = i_id
     and i_data like '%b'
     and ol_quantity >= 1
     and ol_quantity <= 10
     and i_price between 1 and 400000
     and ol_w_id in (1,2,4))
or ( ol_i_id = i_id
     and i_data like '%c'
     and ol_quantity >= 1
     and ol_quantity <= 10
     and i_price between 1 and 400000
     and ol_w_id in (1,5,3))
```

Q20: Suppiers in a particular nation having selected parts that may be candidates for a promotional offer

```
select su_name, su_address
from supplier , nation
where su_suppkey in
      (select mod(s_i_id * s_w_id , 10000)
       from stock , orderline
       where s_i_id in
             (select i_id
              from item
              where i_data like 'co%')
       and ol_i_id=s_i_id
       and ol_delivery_d > '2010-05-23_12:00:00 '
       group by s_i_id , s_w_id , s_quantity
       having 2*s_quantity > sum(ol_quantity))
and su_nationkey = n_nationkey
and n_name = 'Germany '
order by su_name
```

Q21: Suppliers who were not able to ship required parts in a timely manner

```
select su_name, count(*) as numwait
from supplier , orderline l1 , orders , stock , nation
where ol_o_id = o_id
and ol_w_id = o_w_id
and ol_d_id = o_d_id
and ol_w_id = s_w_id
and ol_i_id = s_i_id
and mod((s_w_id * s_i_id),10000) = su_suppkey
and l1.ol_delivery_d > o_entry_d
and not exists (select *
                from orderline l2
                where l2.ol_o_id = l1.ol_o_id
                and l2.ol_w_id = l1.ol_w_id
                and l2.ol_d_id = l1.ol_d_id
                and l2.ol_delivery_d > l1.ol_delivery_d)
and su_nationkey = n_nationkey
and n_name = 'Germany '
group by su_name
order by numwait desc , su_name
```

Q22: Geographies with customers who may be likely to make a purchase

```
select  substr(c_state,1,1) as country,
        count(*) as numcust,
        sum(c_balance) as totacctbal
from    customer
where  substr(c_phone,1,1) in ('1','2','3','4','5','6','7')
and  c_balance > (select avg(c_BALANCE)
                  from customer
                  where c_balance > 0.00
                  and substr(c_phone,1,1) in ('1','2','3','4','5','6','7'))
and not exists (select *
                from orders
                where o_c_id = c_id
                and o_w_id = c_w_id
                and o_d_id = c_d_id)
group by substr(c_state,1,1)
order by substr(c_state,1,1)
```

Towards an Enhanced Benchmark Advocating Energy-Efficient Systems

Daniel Schall[1], Volker Hoefner[1], and Manuel Kern[2]

[1] Database and Information Systems Group
University of Kaiserslautern, Germany
{schall,hoefner}@cs.uni-kl.de
[2] SPH AG
Stuttgart, Germany
m.kern@sph-ag.com

Abstract. The growing energy consumption of data centers has become an area of research interest lately. For this reason, the research focus has broadened from a solely performance-oriented system evaluation to an exploration where energy efficiency is considered as well. The Transaction Processing Performance Council (TPC) has also reflected this shift by introducing the TPC-Energy benchmark. In this paper, we recommend extensions, refinements, and variations for such benchmarks. For this purpose, we present performance measurements of real-world DB servers and show that their mean utilization is far from peak and, thus, benchmarking results, even in conjunction with TPC-Energy, lead to inadequate assessment decisions, e.g., when a database server has to be purchased. Therefore, we propose a new kind of benchmarking paradigm that includes more realistic power measures. Our proposal will enable appraisals of database servers based on broader requirement profiles instead of focusing on sole performance. Furthermore, our energy-centric benchmarks will encourage the design and development of energy-proportional hardware and the evolution of energy-aware DBMSs.

1 Introduction

The TPC-* benchmarking suites are widely used to assess the performance of database servers. To consider a sufficiently wide spectrum of practical demands, various benchmarks were developed for simulating different kinds of applications scenarios. To illustrate the application and hardware dimensions of these benchmarks, a short overview is given.

TPC-C is an on-line transaction processing (OLTP) benchmark that measures transaction throughput of order processing on a single database instance. Typical systems under test (SUT) consist of multiple database nodes, each having several multi-core CPUs with plenty of DRAM attached (up to 512 GB per

R. Nambiar and M. Poess (Eds.): TPCTC 2011, LNCS 7144, pp. 31–45, 2012.

node). Additionally, a huge storage array of several thousand disks (or, recently, SSDs) is used.[1]

TPC-E is another OLTP benchmark – simulating the workload of a brokerage firm – with similar hardware requirements as TCP-C. At the time this paper was written, the fastest SUT consisted of a single server with 8 processors (80 cores) and 2 TB DRAM. For storage, 16 SAS controllers and more than 800 disk drives were used.

TPC-H is an ad-hoc decision support benchmark processing a set of OLAP queries. Although the query types are different compared to OLTP, the hardware requirements are equally demanding. For example, the fastest server running this benchmark (for the 30 TB benchmark configuration) consists of a single node, equipped with 64 processors, 1 TB of DRAM, and more than 3,000 hard disk drives.

Obviously, the huge amount of hardware is consuming a lot of power – for all three benchmarks. As an example, the top TPC-E system mentioned earlier is consuming up to 4,500 watts at peak performance. Despite such substantial energy needs, power consumption was ignored by TPC in the past. However, the newly created benchmark *TPC-Energy* is approaching the emerging demand for energy-related measures. While TPC-[C,E and H] are reporting performance only, TPC-Energy is introducing measures for the energy consumption during query processing. TPC-Energy additionally regulates how power measurements must be performed, e.g., what measurement devices should be used and what measurement precision must be maintained. The metrics defined by TPC-Energy is *Energy Consumption* over *Work done* expressed in *Joule* per *transactions*, which translates to *Power Consumption* over *Work delivered* expressed in *Watts* per *tps*.

Although TPC-Energy made a first step towards energy-related measures compared to the former performance-centric TCP benchmarks, we advocate appropriate measures which are still missing to get meaningful insights into the servers' energy consumption behavior, e.g., power usage over system utilization. For this reason, we propose a new benchmarking paradigm which extends the already existing TPC-Energy.

This paper is structured as follows: In Section 2, we introduce some definitions regarding power consumption and energy and pinpoint the influence of the server load to the power consumption. In Section 3, we will briefly review related energy-centric benchmarks, whereas we will revisit TPC-Energy and point out its limitations by showing measurements of real-world servers in Section 4. We will argue that servers are usually not running at peak load and discuss the implications on the power consumption. Based on our findings in the preceding sections, we propose a new kind of benchmarking paradigm in Section 5. Our proposal will overcome the limitations we identified earlier. Finally, in Section 6, we conclude our contribution and give an outlook, how a new benchmarking paradigm can change both the way systems are built and the customers' view on new systems.

---

[1] For detailed TPC-C results, see
http://www.tpc.org/tpcc/results/tpcc_perf_results.asp

2   Energy Efficiency and Other Measures

Energy consumption of data centers is steadily growing due to the ascending number of server installations and due to the increasing power consumption of each server. At the same time, energy costs are rising continuously. For an average utilization period (~5 years), energy costs have now drawn level with the server's acquisition cost [3]. The total cost of ownership is therefore heavily influenced by the energy footprint of the devices. Further costs, over and above the plain energy cost of powering the servers, come to play, i.e., cooling cost, additional batteries, and amply dimensioned power switches.

In recent years, a lot of efforts have been made to limit the spendings on energy. Some of these efforts include the building of data centers in regions, where power can be cheaply acquired, or the augmented utilization of servers by virtualization techniques [7]. Nevertheless, the best approach is reducing the power consumption of the hardware in the first place. As the power consumption of a server does not scale linearly with its utilization, overdimensioned hardware has a huge impact on its overall energy consumption. Figure 1 charts the power consumption at various compute loads. As the load level drops, the power consumption does not scale well. Even at idle, the system uses about 50 % of its peak power.

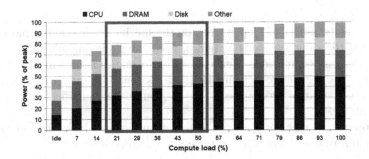

Fig. 1. Power by component at different activity levels, from [6]

Due to the growing influence of the energy consumption on buyers' decisions, it is crucial to provide sound energy measurement results besides the performance data for servers. It is especially necessary to provide energy measurements that cover the whole operating area of a database server. Hence, not only the peak performance and respective power consumption are important to buyers. The average energy consumption expected for a certain machine has much more influence on the anticipated spendings during the next years and are therefore equally relevant. Because the power consumption of servers is not linear to the delivered performance, it is important to know the load curve and the resulting energy consumption of a system. The relation between consumed power and delivered work relative to their peak is called *Energy Proportionality* and will be explained in the following definitions.

2.1 Definitions

In this paper, we will use the term *power* (or power consumption) to denote the current consumption of electricity; hence, the unit of power is *Watt*. The power consumption of a server/component over time is called *energy* (or energy consumption). Energy consumption is expressed in *Joule*:

$$energy = \int power\ dt$$

$$1\ Joule = 1\ Watt \cdot 1\ second$$

To quantify the amount of computational work done on a server, different hardware-related measures can be employed, e.g. *MIPS, FLOPS, IOPS*, or more complex, often application-related measures. In the database community, and for the TPC-* benchmarks as well, the number of transactions – defined as specific units of work in the application environments addressed by the TPC-* workloads – has prevailed as an application-related measure for the quantity of computations. We are using the same (generic) measure referring to *transactions per time unit*, in particular, *transactions per second (tps)* here:

$$1\ tps = \frac{1\ transaction}{1\ second}$$

Because of the transactions' dependency on the specific application scenario, only results from the same benchmark, hence, with the same dataset and the same set of queries, are comparable. Hence, such performance figures must always be qualified by the respective benchmark (such as *tpmC* or *tpsE*). In this paper, performance measures are expressed in *tps*, but other qualifiers can be used exchangeably.

To express how efficiently a certain set of queries can be processed using a given amount of energy, we use the term *energy efficiency*:

$$energy\ efficiency = \frac{\#\ of\ transactions}{energy\ consumption}$$

which can be transformed to the amount of work done per time unit when a certain amount of power is given:

$$energy\ efficiency = \frac{tps}{Watt}$$

The higher the energy efficiency, the better a given system transforms electricity into "work". Note, this is the inverse of the formula used in TPC-Energy which applies $\frac{Watt}{tps}$ as its metrics. The rationale of the TPC for choosing the inverse was the desire to be similar to the traditional TPC metrics *price over throughput* and, furthermore, to allow a secondary metrics for each of the subsystems. To conform with already established practices, we will use $\frac{Watt}{tps}$ as well.

In addition to that absolute measure, we are using the term *energy proportionality*, coined by [1], when we want to reference the power consumption of a server (at a given level of system utilization) *relative* to its peak consumption. Ideally, the power consumption of a system should be determined by its utilization [2]. Hence, energy proportionality describes the ability of a system to scale its power consumption linearly with the utilization.

Therefore, energy proportionality can not be expressed using a scalar value. Instead, a function or graph is needed to display the characteristics of a system. For each level x, $0 \leq x \leq 1$, of system utilization[2], we can measure the power used and denote this value as the actual power consumption at load level x . To facilitate comparison, we use relative figures and normalize the actual power consumption at peak load ($x = 1$) to 1, i.e., $PC_{act}(x = 1) = 1$. Using this notation, we can characterize a system whose power consumption is constant and independent of the actual load by $PC_{act}(x) = 1$.

Note, we obtain by definition true energy proportionality at peak load, i.e., $PC_{ideal}(x = 1) = 1$. In turn, a truly energy-proportional system would consume no energy when it is idle (zero energy needs), i.e., $PC_{ideal}(x = 0) = 0$. Due to the linear relationship of energy proportionality to the level of system utilization, we can express the ideal power consumption at load level x by $PC_{ideal}(x) = x$.

With these definitions, we can express the energy proportionality $EP(x)$ of a system as a function of the load level x:

$$EP(x) = \frac{PC_{ideal}(x)}{PC_{act}(x)} = \frac{x}{PC_{act}(x)} \tag{1}$$

This formula delivers EP values ranging from 0 to 1. Note, for $x < 1$ in a real system, $PC_{act}(x) > x$. According to our definition, each system is perfectly energy proportional at $x = 1$. If a system reaches $EP(x) = 1$, it is perfectly energy proportional for all load levels x. In turn, the more $EP(x)$ deviates from 1, the more it loses its ideal characteristics.

Using the results of Figure 1 as an example, we yield $EP(x = 0.5) = 0.55$, $EP(x = 0.3) = 0.35$, and $EP(x = 0.01) = 0.02$. Special care must be taken for defining $EP(x = 0)$ to avoid having a zero value in the numerator of the formula. In this paper, we have agreed to define $EP(x = 0) := EP(x = 0.01)$. Therefore, this value should be taken with care. Nevertheless, the worst EP figure is provided by a constant-energy-consuming system in idle mode: $EP(x = 0) = 0$.

Obviously, assessing energy proportionality is a lot more expressive than mere energy consumption. While the latter only captures a single point of the system's energy characteristics, the former reveals the ability of the system to adapt the power consumption to the current load.

---

[2] By multiplying x by 100%, the percentage of system utilization can be obtained.

3   Related Benchmarks

In this section, we will give a short overview of existing benchmarks and their relation to energy measurements. Poess et al. provide a more detailed summary in [4].

As the first observation, the TPC-[C, E, H] benchmarks are not considering energy consumption at all. These benchmarks are purely performance-centric. The TPC-Energy benchmark – an extension to any of the three benchmarks – is defining measurements for energy consumption. It gives advice how to measure the power consumption while the benchmark is running and provides additional guidelines how to measure the power consumption of the idle system.

SPEC (the Standard Performance Evaluation Corporation) has introduced the *SPECpower_ssj2008* benchmark for measuring the performance and energy consumption of a system running Java-based workloads. In contrast to TPC-Energy, the SPEC benchmark does measure power consumption at 11 load levels (from 0% load to 100% load) and aggregates the measurements by the geometric mean to form a single result. Additionally, newer releases of the SPEC benchmark like *SPECweb_2009* and *SPECvirt_sc2010* incorporate the power measurement methodologies from SPECpower.

Apart from benchmarks specified by benchmark-centric organizations, the database community itself moved forward to propose an energy-related benchmark to evaluate the energy efficiency of computer systems. The *JouleSort* [5] benchmark is a sort benchmark, whose idea is to account the energy consumed for sorting a given input size. Instead of benchmarking *sorted records per $*, JouleSort is reporting *sorted records per Joule*. Thus, this benchmark reveals the energy efficiency of a computer system close to 100% load, but the scenario (just focusing on sorting) is rather narrow and differing from real-world database workloads.

In addition, the SPC (Storage Performance Council), whose benchmarks are targeted on evaluating storage components, defined energy-related extensions for their benchmarks. These extensions do not track the power consumed at peak load, but measure it at 80% (denoted as heavy) and 50% (denoted as moderate) of the peak performance as well as in idle mode. Furthermore, they introduce the weighted average power consumption based on three different usage patterns (low, medium, and high).

4   Server Load Profiles

In contrast to the assumptions made for existing benchmarks, i.e., testing a system at peak performance, real-world applications do not utilize servers that way. Typically, the hardware of database servers is designed to handle peak load; hence, it is overprovisioned for the average daily work. In the rare events of peak load, the servers reach their processing limits, but most of the time, their hardware is heavily underutilized. In the following, we will outline two studies that analyzed the energy consumption and load of servers.

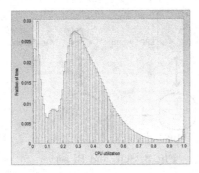

Fig. 2. Average CPU utilization of Google's servers, from [1]

4.1 Google Study

In 2007, Louiz Barroso and Urs Hölzle published a study that revealed performance data of Google's MapReduce server cluster [1]. According to this study, the servers are typically operating at 10% to 50% of their maximum performance. That way, servers are barely idle but, as well, barely fully utilized. Figure 2 charts the aggregate histogram for the CPU utilization of 5,000 servers hosted at Google.

4.2 SQL- and BI-Server Data

SPH AG monitored the performance of some of the database and analysis servers of its customers – data we use to visualize typical utilization and workload behavior of SQL and Business Intelligence (BI) applications. SPH AG is a mid-sized ERP-developing company that specializes in the branches mail order and direct marketing. Its ERP products are based on IBM System i5 or (in the considered case) on Microsoft Dynamics AX. For some of its customers, SPH AG is hosting the ERP servers in-house, including SQL servers and BI servers. The SQL servers are used to store the ERP data, such as customer, sales order, and invoice information. For the ERP system, 24/7 availability is also needed, because on-line shops are connected to the ERP systems. The BI servers are used to process data of the SQL servers for the preparation of reports for the company management. This data is updated by a nightly job. On all servers, a thorough performance and load monitoring is installed.

Every customer gets its own SQL and BI server to isolate the user data of different customers at hardware level. Figure 3 shows a sketch of the systems' layout. The OLTP server on the left-hand side is processing transactional workloads issued by an upstream ERP system. The BI server at the right-hand side is pulling all tables of interest in a nightly job from the OLTP server. After the new data has arrived, the BI server starts building indexes and running OLAP queries. The results are stored on the BI server and can be accessed by the management. Both servers consist of two Intel Xeon E5620 2.4 GHz with 8 cores

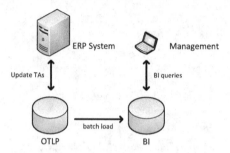

Fig. 3. SQL and BI server

per CPU and 32 GB DRAM in total. They have two hard disk drives attached, one for the database files which has 800 GB, and the second one for the log files (300 GB). The servers are interconnected via Ethernet. One may argue that this hardware configuration is not very powerful for servers typically benchmarked with TPC-*, but it delivers sufficient power for these tasks. As we will see, even this configuration is overprovisioned for the average daily load.

We analyzed the performance-monitoring log files from SPH and charted the servers' CPU and disk utilization for some customer. The overall disk and pro-

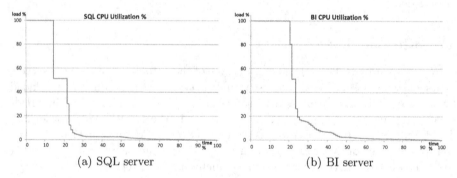

      (a) SQL server   (b) BI server

Fig. 4. CPU utilization histograms

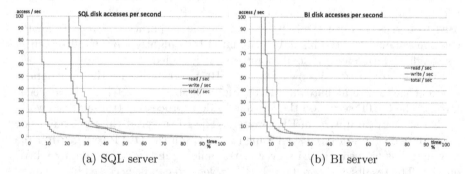

      (a) SQL server   (b) BI server

Fig. 5. Disk utilization histograms

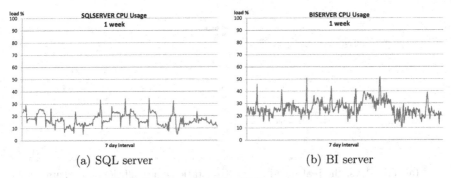

(a) SQL server   (b) BI server

Fig. 6. Weekly CPU usage

cessor utilization histograms of the servers are depicted in figures 4(a), 4(b), 5(a), and 5(b). For an arbitrary day in the data set, the graphs show the probability distribution of the CPU utilization sorted from 100% to 0% (idle) and the disks' utilization by *accesses/second*, respectively. As the graphs indicate, the servers spend most of their time idle.

A weekly breakdown of the servers CPU load is depicted in figures 6(a) and 6(b). At night, the BI starts its update cycle and gathers daily transaction data from the SQL server. During some rush hours, the SQL server is processing most of the transactional workload, while customers and employees are accessing the ERP system. During the rest of the day, the servers are heavily underutilized.

Overall, it gets obvious that the claims made by Barroso and Hölzle apply to these servers as well. As the figures 6(a) and 6(b) show, the servers are utilized about 25% of the time and very rarely at peak.

5   Proposal

Based on the observations in the previous section, it is easy to see that current server installations do not behave like the systems measured in traditional benchmarks. While benchmarks usually measure peak performance, typical servers operate far away from that point during most of the time. Nevertheless, benchmark results are comparable and meaningful when it comes to performance only. As long as attention is not turned to energy consumption, the mismatch between benchmarking and real usage of servers does not carry weight. Performance measurements under peak utilization can be easily broken down to lower load situations. Hence, a system, able to process x *tps per second* at peak, can also process *0.5x tps per second*.

In contrast, energy-related measurements obtained at some point of utilization are not transferable to other load situations because of the non-linear scaling of energy consumption of todays computer hardware. Therefore, the whole span of different load situations should be measured separately to obtain meaningful energy data for customers.

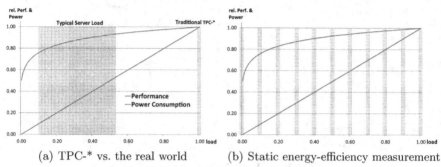

(a) TPC-* vs. the real world   (b) Static energy-efficiency measurement

Fig. 7. Comparing benchmark paradigms

As an analogy from a well-known field, automobiles are benchmarked similarly with additional "energy-related" measures. Hence, the power of a car is estimated by its horse power and its top speed, like database servers are classified by their hardware and their peak $tpmC$ / $QphH$ / $tpsE$. On the other hand, the gas consumption of a car, estimated at top speed, is meaningless for the average driver, because the measurement does not reveal the gas consumption for average usages. Therefore, a car's mileage is measured by driving the car through a set of standardized usage profiles which reflect the typical use of the vehicle. The same paradigm should be applied to database benchmarks as well, where energy consumption measured at peak utilization is no indicator for the average use case.

Figure 7(a) depicts the point that all TPC-* benchmarks measure compared to the typical working region of a server. Note the mismatch in energy efficiency between both regions. To cope with the limitations we have outlined previously and to keep the TPC benchmarking suite up to date, we propose a new paradigm in benchmarking.

5.1 Static Weighted Energy Proportionality

Nowadays, the measurement paradigm for the TPC benchmarks strictly focuses on performance results, i.e., to get the most (in terms of units of work) out of the SUT. Hence, this methodology collides with the desire to get a meaningful energy-efficiency metrics for the system. Therefore, we propose a sequence of small benchmarks that utilize the SUT at different load levels, instead of a single run at peak load. Figure 7(b) depicts a feasible set of benchmark runs at different utilization ratios. First, a traditional TPC-* run will be performed, i.e., at full utilization. That run is used as a baseline to get the maximum possible performance the SUT can handle (see equation 2). Next, based on the results from the first run, the number of queries per second issued for the other runs is calculated using equation 3, where x denotes the system utilization between 0 and 1.

$$baseline := \frac{transactions}{second} @100\% \tag{2}$$

$$\frac{transactions}{second} @x := baseline \cdot x \tag{3}$$

Of course, depending on the type of benchmark, the characteristics and knobs for throttling can differ, e.g., for TPC-C increasing the think time seems reasonable while for TPC-H a reduction of concurrent streams is the only possibility. We call this a *static weighted energy-proportionality benchmark*, because the workload does not change in between and, therefore, the system does not have to adapt to new load situations. To allow the system adapting to the current workload, a preparation phase of a certain timespan is preceding each run. During the preparation time, the SUT can identify the workload and adapt its configuration accordingly. It is up to the system whether and how to adapt to the workload, e.g., the system can power down unused CPU cores or consolidate the workload on fewer nodes in order to save energy. After the preparation phase, the overall energy consumption during the run is measured. In other words, instead of measuring the performance of the SUT, we are now measuring the power consumption for a certain system usage.

At each load level, the system's energy proportionality (according to equation 1) is calculated. By multiplying each result with the relative amount of time the system is running at that load level, we can estimate the overall energy proportionality under realistic workloads.

Formula. Let EP_i be the energy proportionality at load level i, and let T_i be the relative time, the system operates at that level. Then, the static weighted energy proportionality of the system ($= SWEP$) can be calculated as:

$$SWEP = \int_{i=0.0}^{1.0} EP_i \cdot T_i \, di \tag{4}$$

We can estimate the power consumption ($= PC$) of the SUT during the measured interval by multiplying the (absolute) power consumption of each interval (PC_i) with the relative time, the system operates in that load interval:

$$PC = \int_{i=0.0}^{1.0} PC_i \cdot T_i \, di \qquad [Watts] \tag{5}$$

Furthermore, by adding the system's performance to the formula (denoted as *tps* in the following), we can estimate the overall energy efficiency.

$$EE = \int_{i=0.0}^{1.0} \frac{PC_i}{tps_i} \cdot T_i \, di \qquad \left[\frac{Watts}{tps}\right] \tag{6}$$

Table 1. Example calculation of the SWEP

load	rel. time	rel. PC	EP	EP · time rel.	rel. PC	EP	EP · time rel.
		real system			energy-proportional system		
idle	0.11	0.47	0.00	0.00	0.0	1.0	0.11
0.1	0.08	0.7	0.14	0.01	0.1	1.0	0.08
0.2	0.19	0.78	0.26	0.05	0.2	1.0	0.19
0.3	0.23	0.84	0.36	0.08	0.3	1.0	0.23
0.4	0.18	0.88	0.45	0.08	0.4	1.0	0.18
0.5	0.10	0.91	0.55	0.05	0.5	1.0	0.10
0.6	0.05	0.93	0.65	0.03	0.6	1.0	0.05
0.7	0.02	0.94	0.74	0.01	0.7	1.0	0.02
0.8	0.01	0.98	0.82	0.01	0.8	1.0	0.01
0.9	0.01	0.99	0.91	0.01	0.9	1.0	0.01
1.0	0.02	1.00	1.00	0.02	1.0	1.0	0.02
SWEP (= $\sum$)				0.37			1.00

In a practical application, the integrals in the formulas 4, 5, and 6 are approximated by the sum of load situations measured, e.g., by eleven measurements of loads from 0% to 100% using a 10% increment.

Example. To clarify the calculation of the weighted average, we will give an example using the load and energy measurements provided by Google (see Figures 1 and 2). Table 1 shows the (relative) average power consumption and time fractions of a hypothetical server for 11 utilization levels. The data is derived from the two studies done by Google. For comparison, the relative energy footprint of a theoretical, perfectly energy-proportional system is shown.

This static approach has certain drawbacks: First, the measurements are rather coarse grained in reality, i.e., "reasonable" static measurements will be employed at 0, 10, 20, ..., 100% load, but not in greater detail. And second, this calculation does not take transition times from one load/power level to another into account.

5.2   Dynamic Weighted Energy Efficiency

To design an energy-related benchmark that overcomes the drawbacks of the static approach, we are proposing a refinement of the previous benchmark, called *dynamic weighted energy-efficiency benchmark* (DWEE). In order to simulate an even more realistic workload on the SUT, the static measurements at various load levels of the SWEP benchmark are replaced by continuous sequences of different length and different load situations (so called *Scenes*), followed by each other without interruption or preparation times. In contrast to the static approach, all scenes run consecutively, thus transition times are measured as well in this benchmark. That enables us to test the systems ability to dynamically adapt (if possible) while running.

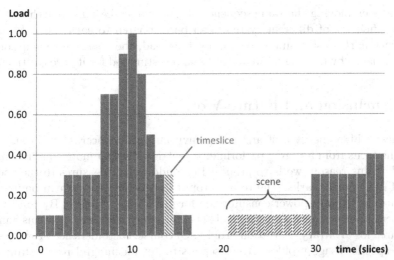

Fig. 8. Dynamic weighted energy-efficiency benchmark – sample load pattern

Every scene will run for a defined timespan T, as sketched in Figure 8. A *timespan* is always a cardinal multiple of a constant *time slice* t, thus, all scenes run for a multiple of that time slice.

The dynamic energy-efficiency benchmark should simulate a typical workload pattern, hence, the sequence of load levels should reflect the intended usage pattern of the SUT.

Influence of the Length of the Time Slice t. By adjusting the cardinal time slice t to smaller values, all benchmarking scenes will be shorter, hence, the system must react faster to changing loads. Such a course of action enables testing the SUTs ability to quickly react to changes. Of course, when benchmarking different systems, the results for a specific benchmark can only be compared by choosing the same time slice t and the same sequence of scenes.

The minimum length of the time slice should not go below 10 minutes, because real-world utilization usually does not change faster than that.

Formula. Calculating the result of the DWEE benchmark is simpler than calculating the SWEP results, because the weighting of the utilization is determined by the selection of scenes. Because we are measuring the overall throughput and energy consumption, we do not have to aggregate several measurements. To obtain comparable results, benchmark runs will be characterized by $Watt/tps$. Hence, the overall result of the dynamic weighted energy-efficiency benchmark, short $DWEE$, is:

$$DWEE = \frac{overall\ Energy\ Consumption}{overall\ \#\ of\ Transactions} \qquad \left[\frac{Joule}{transactions} = \frac{Watt}{tps}\right]$$

Hence, by employing the same sequence of scenes and the same length of t, the energy efficiency of different systems can be compared to each other. Because the benchmark closely simulates a daily workload, the energy consumption to be anticipated by the system under test can be estimated for its prospective use.

6   Conclusion and Future Work

In times of high energy cost and rising environmental concerns, it is crucial to shift the focus from a purely performance-centric view to a more comprehensive look. For this reason, we have proposed two additional measures to the widely used TPC-* benchmarks. The results from the benchmark runs can be used to estimate the average power consumption for given usage profiles. By comparing the overall performance and the load-specific energy efficiency, systems can be compared for arbitrary utilization profiles. Of course, customers need to be aware of the specific usage profile of their servers to get meaningful results from the benchmarks.

We have explained, why high throughput as sole optimization criterion and $/tps$ (or $/tpmC$, $/tpsE$, etc.) as the solitary driver for purchase decisions are no longer up to date. Therefore, we proposed a paradigm shift for the TPC benchmarks: the same shift that has already moved *SPEC* and *SPC* to energy-related benchmarks. This paper introduced more sophisticated energy measures to allow a more detailed view of the systems' energy efficiency. By comparing the *static weighted energy proprtionality* of two servers, one can easily derive, which server is the more energy proportional one. Additionally, if the usage pattern of the server is known, the servers real energy consumption can be estimated. Finally, for getting more realistic, energy-related results, the *DWEE benchmark* can be run with workloads, that reflect the estimated usage for a customer. These workloads could stem from historical performance data provided by the customer to enable tailor-made comparisons of different systems. Alternatively, a workload specified by the TPC would enable standardized benchmarking as usual, with respect to energy.

Since customers are slowly becoming energy-aware also as far as their computer equipment is concerned, measures revealing energy-related characteristics of servers are gaining increasing attention. Our benchmark proposal will help comparing the energy profile of different systems.

Our approach focuses on the overall power consumption of the SUT. We do not make restrictions regarding the power consumption of individual components. Therefore, it is up to the system designers how to improve the energy footprint of their systems. Some of the possibilities include powering down redundant, but underutilized components, e.g., disks in a storage array, CPU cores, or networking adapters. Other approaches could focus on the hardware level, i.e., choosing more energy-efficient components while building the system. Typical servers can widely vary in power consumption, depending on the DRAM sizes and modules used. Finally, the software driving the hardware can have a great impact on the behavior of the system. Todays database systems do not consider energy consumption as a first-class optimization goal, e.g., the use of energy-efficient algorithms. Nevertheless, we expect future generations of database servers to show an increasing awareness of energy-related characteristics. Energy-aware operating systems and database management software can leverage energy efficiency of the plain hardware significantly.

For the future, we encourage researchers and benchmarking enthusiasts to focus on energy as well as performance. This proposal exposes a first concept how a comprehensive energy benchmark should look like. As the details have to be worked out yet, we expect our contribution to influence the design of future benchmarks.

Acknowledgements. We thank our anonymous reviewers for their insightful comments. We'd also like to thank SPH AG, Stuttgart[3] for providing very useful performance data to us.

References

1. Barroso, L.A., Hölzle, U.: The Case for Energy-Proportional Computing. Computer 40, 33–37 (2007)
2. Härder, T., Hudlet, V., Ou, Y., Schall, D.: Energy Efficiency Is Not Enough, Energy Proportionality Is Needed! In: Xu, J., Yu, G., Zhou, S., Unland, R. (eds.) DASFAA Workshops 2011. LNCS, vol. 6637, pp. 226–239. Springer, Heidelberg (2011)
3. Poess, M., Nambiar, R.O.: Energy Cost, The Key Challenge of Today's Data Centers: A Power Consumption Analysis of TPC-C Results. PVLDB 1(2), 1229–1240 (2008)
4. Poess, M., Nambiar, R.O., Vaid, K., Stephens Jr., J.M., Huppler, K., Haines, E.: Energy Benchmarks: A Detailed Analysis. In: Proceedings of the 1st International Conference on Energy-Efficient Computing and Networking, E-Energy 2010, pp. 131–140. ACM, New York (2010)
5. Rivoire, S., Shah, M.A., Ranganathan, P., Kozyrakis, C.: JouleSort: A Balanced Energy-Efficiency Benchmark. In: SIGMOD Conference, pp. 365–376 (2007)
6. Spector, A.Z.: Distributed Computing at Multi-dimensional Scale (Keynote). In: Proceedings of Int. Middleware Conference (2008)
7. Weiss, A.: Computing in the Clouds. Networker 11, 16–25 (2007)

---

[3] www.sph-ag.com

Optimization of Analytic Data Flows for Next Generation Business Intelligence Applications

Umeshwar Dayal, Kevin Wilkinson, Alkis Simitsis, Malu Castellanos, and Lupita Paz

HP Labs, Palo Alto, CA,USA
{umeshwar.dayal,kevin.wilkinson,alkis.simitsis,
malu.castellanos,lupita.paz}@hp.com

Abstract. This paper addresses the challenge of optimizing analytic data flows for modern business intelligence (BI) applications. We first describe the changing nature of BI in today's enterprises as it has evolved from batch-based processes, in which the back-end extraction-transform-load (ETL) stage was separate from the front-end query and analytics stages, to near real-time data flows that fuse the back-end and front-end stages. We describe industry trends that force new BI architectures, e.g., mobile and cloud computing, semi-structured content, event and content streams as well as different execution engine architectures. For execution engines, the consequence of "one size does not fit all" is that BI queries and analytic applications now require complicated information flows as data is moved among data engines and queries span systems. In addition, new quality of service objectives are desired that incorporate measures beyond performance such as freshness (latency), reliability, accuracy, and so on. Existing approaches that optimize data flows simply for performance on a single system or a homogeneous cluster are insufficient. This paper describes our research to address the challenge of optimizing this new type of flow. We leverage concepts from earlier work in federated databases, but we face a much larger search space due to new objectives and a larger set of operators. We describe our initial optimizer that supports multiple objectives over a single processing engine. We then describe our research in optimizing flows for multiple engines and objectives and the challenges that remain.

Keywords: Business Intelligence, Data Flow Optimization, ETL.

1   Introduction

Traditionally, Business Intelligence (BI) systems have been designed to support off-line, strategic "back-office" decision making, where information requirements are satisfied by periodical reporting and historical queries. The typical BI architecture (Fig. 1) consists of a data warehouse that consolidates data from several operational databases and serves a variety of querying, reporting, and analytic tools. The back end of the architecture is a data integration pipeline for populating the data warehouse by periodically extracting data from distributed, often heterogeneous, sources such as online transaction processing (OLTP) systems; cleansing, integrating and transforming the data; and loading it into the data warehouse. The traditional data integration

R. Nambiar and M. Poess (Eds.): TPCTC 2011, LNCS 7144, pp. 46–66, 2012.
© Springer-Verlag Berlin Heidelberg 2012

pipeline is a batch process, usually implemented by extract-transform-load (ETL) tools [26]. Designing and optimizing the ETL pipeline is still a challenging problem [e.g., 6, 21, 23]. After the data is cleansed and loaded into the data warehouse, it is then queried and analyzed by front-end reporting and data mining tools.

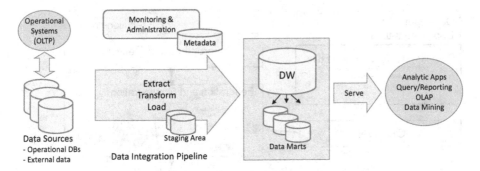

Fig. 1. Traditional business intelligence architecture

As enterprises become more automated, real-time, and data-driven, the industry is evolving toward Live BI systems that support on-line, "front-office" decision making integrated into the operational business processes of the enterprise. This imposes even more challenging requirements on the information pipeline. The data sources and data types are much more diverse: structured, unstructured, and semi-structured enterprise content, external data feeds, Web and Cloud-based data, sensor and other forms of streaming data. Faster decision making requires eliminating latency bottlenecks that exist in current BI architectures.

In this new architecture, as shown in Fig. 2, the back-end integration pipeline and the front-end query, reporting, and analytics operations are fused into a single analytics pipeline that can be optimized end-to-end for low latency or other objectives; for instance, analytics operations can be executed on "in-flight" streaming data before it is loaded into a data warehouse. Integration into the business processes of the enterprise requires fault tolerance, with little or no down-time. In general, optimizing the end-to-end pipeline for performance alone is insufficient. New quality objectives entail new tradeoffs; e.g., performance, cost, latency, fault-tolerance, recoverability, maintainability, and so on. We refer to these as *QoX objectives* [22]. Instead of a "one size fits all" engine, there may be many choices of engine to execute different parts of the pipeline: column and row store DBMSs, map-reduce engines, stream processing engines, analytics engines. Some operations are more efficiently executed in specific engines, and it may be best to move the data to the engine where the operation is most efficiently executed (*data shipping*). Other operations may have multiple implementations, optimized for different engines, and it may be better to leave data *in situ* and move the operation to the data (*function shipping*). The ETL flows, followed by querying, reporting, and analytics operations, are thus generalized to analytic data flows that may span multiple data sources, targets, and execution engines.

In this paper, we describe the problem of physical design and optimization of analytic data flows for the next generation BI applications. We model such flows as data flow graphs, whose nodes are data sources, targets, or operations on intermediate data. Given (a) a logical data flow graph, (b) optimization objectives for the flow, and (c) a physical infrastructure (data stores, processing engines, networks, compute nodes), the physical design problem is to create a graph that implements the logical flow on the physical infrastructure to achieve the optimization objectives.

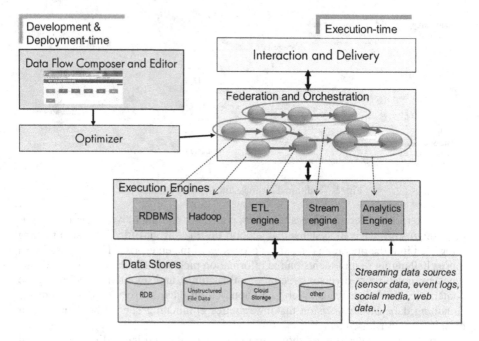

Fig. 2. Live BI system architecture

Example Scenario. We present a simple, example scenario to illustrate our approach. The scenario presumes a nationwide marketing campaign is conducted that promotes a small set of products. At the end of the campaign, a report is required that lists product sales for each product in the campaign. The input to the report is a modified version of the Lineitem fact table of TPC-H. This table lists, for each item in a purchase order, the quantity sold and the unit price. We also assume a dimension table that lists attributes for a marketing campaign. A synopsis of the database schema is shown below:

```
Lineitem:        orderKey, productKey, quantity, unitCost
Orders:          orderKey, orderDate
CmpmDim:         cmpnKey, productKey, dateBeg, dateEnd
RptSalesByProdCmpn:  productKey, cmpnKey, sales
```

The logical data flow to generate the report is shown in Fig. 3. We assume that the Lineitem table itself is created by periodically extracting recent line-item rows from OLTP databases in the various stores, taking their union, and then converting the production keys to surrogate keys. Similar extracts are needed for the Orders table and the dimension tables, but these are not shown. We acknowledge that a real-world flow would be much more complicated, e.g., multiple data sources and targets, extensive data cleaning, and so on. However, our purpose here is to illustrate our approach to optimization, so we have abstracted away many details in the flow.

To illustrate the new demands posed by Live BI, we augment our scenario by adding semi-structured content. We assume a Twitter feed is filtered for references to the enterprise's products and the resulting tweets are stored in the distributed file system of a Map-Reduce engine such as Hadoop. We perform a sentiment analysis on those Twitter feeds to obtain feedback on the public reaction to the campaign products and add that analysis to the campaign sales report.

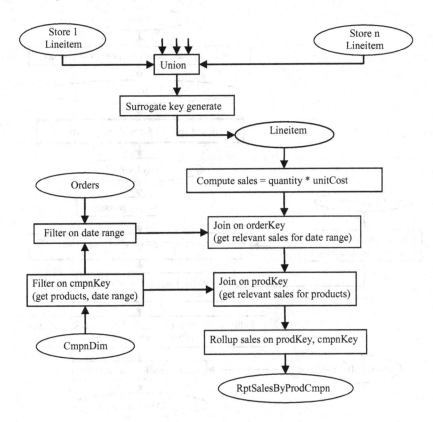

Fig. 3. Flow for RptSalesByProdCmpn

In this scenario, the Twitter feed includes any tweet that mentions the enterprise's products, and these tweets are passed to the sentiment analysis part of the flow. The logical data flow for this example is in Fig. 4. The sentiment analysis computation is shown here as a black box (later, in Section 2, we will expand this black box to show details of the sentiment analysis operations). The result of sentiment analysis is, for each tweet, a sentiment score for each *attribute* of a *topic*. For example, a tweet might have a weakly positive sentiment for the quality of a printer but a strongly negative sentiment for its price. To simplify, we assume a topic identifies a particular product, but in general a topic hierarchy or lattice could be used, e.g., a tweet might reference a particular printer model, a class of printers, or all printers sold by the enterprise. After sentiment analysis, the product identifiers in the tweets are replaced by their surrogate keys. The sentiment scores per tweet are then aggregated per product and time period so that they can be joined with the campaign sales report. In the rollup operation, the computation to aggregate the sentiment scores by attribute is assumed to be some user-defined function (defined by the marketing department) that assigns weight to the various sentiment values (e.g., the weight may depend on the influence score of the tweeter).

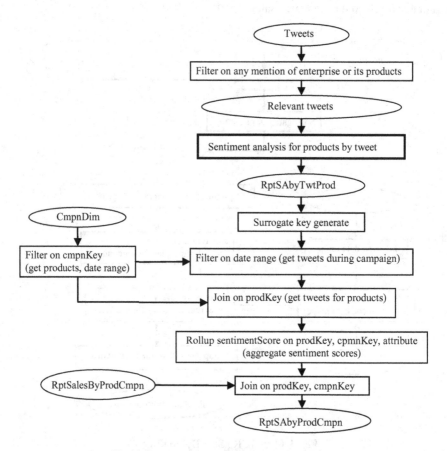

Fig. 4. Expanded Flow for RptSAByProdCmpn

A synopsis of the additional tables used by this expanded flow is shown below.

Tweet: tweetKey, tweetUser, timestamp, tweetText
RptSAbyTwtProd: tweetKey, timestamp, productKey, attribute, sentimentScore
RptSAbyProdCmpn: productKey, cmpnKey, sales, attribute, sentimentScore

In Section 2, we describe our framework for optimizing analytic data flows. Given a logical data flow graph of the kind shown in Fig. 3 and Fig. 4, and a set of QoX objectives, the optimizer produces a physical data flow that is optimized against those objectives. The optimizer assigns fragments of the flow graph to possibly different engines for execution. Since the choices made by the optimizer are cost driven, we have to characterize the execution of the fragments on different engines with respect to the different quality objectives. Our approach is to use micro-benchmarks to measure the performance of different engines on the various operators that occur in the analytic data flows. Section 3 describes some of our work on such micro-benchmarks. There are many remaining challenges in developing an optimizer for analytic data flows. After describing related work in Section 4, we list some of these challenges in Section 5.

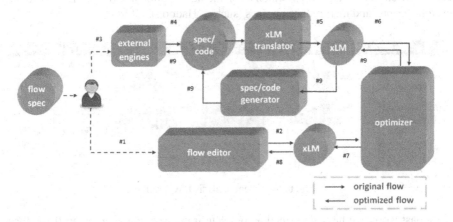

Fig. 5. QoX-driven optimization

2 Our Optimization Approach

Our optimization approach takes as input a flow graph, a system configuration, and some QoX objectives and produces as output a physical flow graph that is optimized according to the objectives (see Fig. 5).

The input logical data flow graph represents data sources, targets, and logical operations, together with annotations representing QoX objectives. Typical data sources are OLTP systems, flat files, semi-structured or unstructured repositories, sensor data, Web portals, and others. Typical targets are OLAP and data mining applications, decision support systems, data warehouse tables, reports, dashboards, and so on. The flows may contain a plethora of operations such as typical relational operators (e.g., filter, join, aggregation), data warehouse-related operations (e.g., surrogate key assignment, slowly changing dimensions), data and text analytics operations (e.g., sentence detection, part of speech tagging), data cleansing operations (e.g., customer de-duplication, resolving homonyms/synonyms), and others. How to design such a flow from SLAs and business level objectives is itself a challenging research and practical problem. Some work has been done in the past (e.g., [28]), but we do not elaborate further on this topic in this paper. Internally, each flow is represented as a directed acyclic graph that has an XML encoding in an internal language we call xLM.

A flow graph may be designed (edge #1 in Fig. 5) in a flow editor which directly produces xLM (edge #2) or in an external engine (edge #3); e.g., an ETL flow may be designed in a specific ETL engine and exported in some XML form (edge #4) (most modern ETL engines store flow metadata and execution information in proprietary XML files). An xLM parser translates these files (edge #5) and imports them into the QoX Optimizer (edge #6). The optimizer produces an optimized flow (edge #7) that is displayed back on the editor (edge #8), so that the user can see –and even modify– the optimized flow. In addition, an optimized file is translated into requests to the target execution engines (edges #9), which may include relational DBMSs, ETL engines, custom scripts, and map-reduce engines (such as Hadoop).

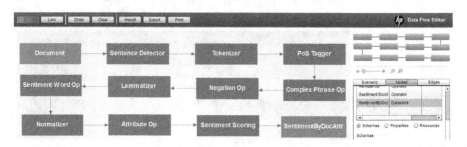

Fig. 6. Sentiment analysis flow graph

In past work, we have described a complete framework for optimizing flows for a variety of QoX objectives such as performance and fault tolerance [6]. Our approach to flow optimization involves both the logical and physical levels. For example, to optimize the logical flow in Fig. 3 for performance, the optimizer would compare the two joins over Lineitem (with the order keys and the product keys) and perform the most selective join first. It might also eliminate the sales computation task by combining it with the rollup task. At the physical level, if the Lineitem, Orders, and CmpnDim tables are all stored within the same RDBMS, the optimizer might perform the joins and rollup in the RDBMS rather than use an ETL engine.

To optimize the logical flow in Fig. 4 for fault tolerance, a recovery point might be inserted after the surrogate key generation, since sentiment analysis and surrogate key generation are time-consuming tasks that would have to be repeated in the event of a failure. As a more complicated example, suppose the combined flows of Fig. 3 and Fig. 4 were to be optimized for freshness. Then, it might be desirable to filter on the campaign dimension very early in the flow to significantly reduce the amount of useless data transferred. In this case, the lineitem extracts and the tweet stream could be filtered by campaign, product key, and date range. Note that the tweet dataset would then be much smaller. Hence, at the physical level, rather than storing it on the map-reduce engine, the optimizer may choose to extract it to a single compute node where the sentiment analysis could be performed faster, avoiding the higher overhead of the map-reduce engine.

Additional choices involve the granularity at which operations are considered by the optimizer. For example, sentiment analysis can be seen as a complex operator that in turn is composed by a flow of lower level operators corresponding to the different tasks in the analysis. Fig. 6 shows a flow graph for the sentiment analysis operation that was represented by a single node in Fig. 3, displayed on the canvas of the Flow Editor.

Treating this complex operation as a composition of other lower-level operators makes it possible for the optimizer to consider the possibility of executing the component operations on different engines. In our sentiment analysis flow, there is a Normalization operator (to reduce all variations of a word to a standard form) that does a look-up operation into a dictionary to retrieve the standard form of a given word. This kind of operation can be implemented in different ways: as a relational join, as a Unix script, as an ETL look-up operator, or as a program in Java (or some other programming language). Similarly, the Sentiment Word operator looks up a word in a lexicon to determine if the word is an opinion word. Assuming that different implementations exist for these look-up operators, the issue is to determine the best execution engine for each operator. Other operators in the sentiment analysis flow, for instance those which perform shallow natural language processing (NLP) tasks (sentence detection, tokenization, parts-of-speech tagging, lemmatization, and complex noun phrase extraction), are typically implemented as functions in NLP libraries.

2.1 QoX-Driven Optimizer

The QoX optimizer first works on a logical data flow graph and tries to optimize it for the specified QoX objectives. Then, the optimized flow can be further refined, and specific physical choices are made. There are several ways to optimize such a flow, even at the logical level. The most obvious objective is to meet an execution time window and produce accurate and correct results. Typically, optimizing a flow for objectives other than performance – e.g., fault tolerance, maintainability, or recoverability – might hurt performance. For example, for adding a recovery point we may have to pay an additional I/O cost. Thus, in general, we optimize first for performance and then consider strategies for other optimization objectives: adding recovery points, replication, and so on.

At the physical level, the optimized logical flow is enriched with additional design and execution details. For example, a logical operation (such as the join on prodKey) may have alternative physical implementations (nested loops, sort-merge, hash join). A specific algorithm may have different incarnations based on the execution engine; e.g., surrogate key assignments can have a sequential implementation on an ETL engine or a highly parallel implementation on a Hadoop engine. At this level, we need to specifically describe implementation details such as bindings of data sources and targets to data storage engines, and binding of operators to execution engines. Still, the physical plan should be independent of any specific execution engine. However, the optimization may use specific hooks that an engine provides in order to optimize better for that specific engine.

Internally, the QoX Optimizer formulates the optimization problem as a state space search problem. The states in this state space are flow graphs. We define an extensible set of transitions for producing new states. When a transition is applied to a state, a new, functionally equivalent, state is produced. Based on an objective function, we explore the state space in order to find an optimal or near optimal state. We have a set of algorithms to prune the state space and efficiently find an optimized flow satisfying a given set of objectives; i.e., an objective function.

An example objective function can be as follows:

$$OF(F, n, k, w): minimize\ c_{T(F)},\ where\ time(F(n, k)) < w$$

which translates to: minimize the execution cost, 'c', of a flow, 'F', such that its execution time window should be less than a specified size 'w' time units, its input dataset has a certain size, 'n', and a given number, 'k', of failures should be tolerated (see [23]).

The execution cost of a flow is a function of the execution costs of its operations. The choice of this function depends on flow structure. For example, the execution cost of a linear flow (i.e., a sequence of unary operations) can be calculated as the sum of the costs of its operations. Similarly, the execution cost of a flow consisting of a number of parallel branches is governed by the execution cost of the slowest branch. Cost functions for each operator capture resource cost, selectivity, processing rate, cost of data movement, and so on. Simple formulae for the execution cost of an operation can be determined based on the number of tuples processed by the operation; e.g., the execution cost of an aggregator may be $O(n\ log n)$, where n is the size of the input dataset. More complex and accurate cost functions should involve output sizes (e.g., based on the operation's selectivity), processing time (e.g., based on throughput), freshness, and so on. Deriving cost formulae for non-traditional operations (e.g., operations on unstructured data or user-defined analytic operations) that can appear in analytic data flows is a challenging problem. Section 3 describes an approach based on micro-benchmarks for obtaining cost formulae for individual operators. However, the optimization process is not tied to the choice of a cost model.

The set of state space transitions depends on the optimization strategies we want to support. For improving performance, an option is flow restructuring. With respect to the example of Fig. 3, we already mentioned pushing the most selective join early in the flow. Alternatively, one could consider partitioning the flow, grouping pipeline operations together, pushing successive operators into the same engine, moving data across engines or data stores, and so on. Typical transitions for improving performance are: swap (interchange the position of two unary operations), factorize/distribute (push a unary operation after/before an n-ary operation), and partition (add a router and a merger operations and partition the part of the flow between these two into a given number of branches). Example transitions for achieving fault tolerance are adding recovery points and replicating a part of the flow. Other transitions may be used as well so long as they ensure flow correctness. In [6], we described several heuristics for efficiently searching the state space defined by these transitions.

2.2 Extending the Optimizer to Multiple Engines

Our earlier work had focused on optimizing back-end integration flows, which we assumed were executed primarily on a single execution engine (typically, an ETL engine or a relational DBMS). We are now interested in optimizing analytic data flows that may execute on a combination of engines (ETL engines, relational DBMSs, custom code, Hadoop, etc.). This requires extending the physical level of the QoX Optimizer.

As an example, consider the flow depicted in Fig. 4. We can imagine three different execution engines being used to process this flow. The tweets are loaded into a map-reduce engine to leverage its parallel execution capabilities for the sentiment analysis task. The campaign dimension and campaign sales reports are stored in an RDBMS and must be retrieved for processing. Imagine the remaining flow (surrogate key, filter, joins, rollup) being processed by an ETL engine. The optimizer might choose to push some filtering tasks from the ETL engine down into the RDBMS (filter on campaign) and the map-reduce engine (filter on date range). As described earlierr, the sentiment analysis task is itself a series of sub-tasks and so the optimizer may choose to move some of its sub-tasks from map-reduce to the ETL engine.

In general, there are several engine options for executing an analytic data flow, and a particular task may have implementations on more than one execution engine. In order to automate the choice of an engine, first we need to characterize the execution of operations on different engines. For that, we perform an extensive set of micro-benchmarks for a large variety of operations.

Our use of micro-benchmarks is motivated by tools used to calibrate database query optimizers. Such tools measure the time and resource usage of various operators needed for query processing, such as comparing two character strings, adding two integers, copying a data buffer, performing random I/O, performing sequential I/O. The tools are run on each platform on which the database system will be deployed. The individual measurements are combined to estimate the cost of higher-level operations such as expression evaluation, table scans, searching a buffer, and so on. Section 3 provides an overview of our current work on micro-benchmarks.

Applying the micro-benchmark concept to our framework presents two challenges. First, our micro-benchmarks are high-level operations with parameters that create a large, multi-dimensional space (e.g., sort time might be affected by input cardinality, row width, sort key length, etc.). The benchmark cannot cover the entire parameter space, so point measurements must be taken. For an actual flow, it is likely that an operator's parameters will not exactly match a measured benchmark. So, interpolation is required, but it may reduce the accuracy of the estimate.

A second challenge is that the ultimate goal is to estimate the cost of a data flow, not the cost of individual operators. The operators are coupled through the data flow and may interact in complex ways. A method is needed to compose the micro-benchmarks for individual operators to estimate the cost of a flow. We previously mentioned how the cost of a parallel flow is determined by the slowest branch. As another example, consider a flow of two operators, one producer and one consumer. If producer and consumer process data at similar rates and do not share resource, then the cost of the flow is a simple linear combination. However, if they run at different rates, the slower operator meters the flow. Additionally, if they share resources, the interaction must be considered when composing the individual micro-benchmark results. Addressing these challenges is a current area of research.

3   Micro-benchmarks for Performance

As described in Section 2, the goal of the optimizer at the physical level is to decide on the appropriate execution engine to process fragments of a flow graph in order to achieve the QoX objectives for the entire flow. The optimizer considers both the storage location of data (and the associated execution engine, e.g., RDBMS for tables, map-reduce for DFS, etc.) as well as the execution engines available for processing a flow graph (e.g., ETL engines, custom scripts, etc.). The optimizer may choose to perform data shipping, in which data is moved from the storage system of one execution engine to another, or it may choose to perform function shipping, in which a task is pushed down to be performed in the execution engine where the data is stored. A task that has multiple implementations is said to be polymorphic, and the optimizer must evaluate each implementation relative to the flow objectives.

In this section, we describe how the optimizer characterizes the implementation of a task relative to an objective. The approach is to use micro-benchmarks to measure the performance of a task at various points in the parameter space. The focus here is just on performance but the same approach can be used for other objectives. The performance curves generated from the micro-benchmarks can then be compared to choose the best implementation of a task for a specific flow graph configuration. In the first sub-section, we describe how micro-benchmarks are applied for conventional (ETL, relational) operators. In the second sub-section, we describe how the same approach can be extended for the new types of operators of Live BI. In particular, we show how micro-benchmarks can be used for the text analytics operators that comprise the sentiment analysis flow.

3.1   Micro-benchmarks for Conventional Operators

We study how several parameters of the flow and the system configuration affect the design choice. Example flow parameters to consider are: data size, number and nature of operations (e.g., blocking vs. non-blocking), flow and operation selectivity, QoX objectives such as degree of replication vs. desired fault-tolerance and freshness, input data size and location (e.g., if a mapping table is in a file or in the database). Example system configuration parameters include: network load and bandwidth, cluster size and resources, cluster node workload, degree of parallelism supported by the engine, and so on.

Knowing how each operation behaves on different engines and under various conditions, we may determine how a combination of operations behaves, and thus, we may decide on how to execute a flow or different segments of the flow. To illustrate our approach, we discuss example alternative designs for a sequence of blocking operations typified by the sort operation. Due to their blocking nature, as we increase the number of such operations, on a single-node, the flow performance linearly decreases. We experimented with different parallel implementations for improving the performance of the flow. Candidate choices we compared are: Unix shell scripts (os-sort), an ETL engine (etl-sort), a parallel dbms (pdb-sort), and Hadoop (hd-sort). Due to space considerations, we discuss the os-sort and hd-sort methods and present example tradeoffs among os-sort, hd-sort, and pdb-sort.

We implemented os-sort as a combination of C code and shell scripts in Unix, running directly on the operating system. First, the data file is split in equal-sized chunks based on the formula: *file size / #nodes* (any possible leftover is added to the first chunk). Then, each chunk is transferred to a different remote node, where it is sorted. Assuming we have a series of n blocking operators, each sort operator i (where i = 1…n) sorts the i-th data field; if the number of fields is less than n, then the (n + 1)-st operator goes back to the first field. In doing so, we eliminate the impact of cache memory in our experiments. Next, the sorted data chunks are transferred back to a central node and merged back in a hierarchical manner. Intentionally, we tried to avoid pipelining as much as we could, in order to make a fair comparison with both the etl-sort and hd-sort, where there is no pipelining between blocking operators. In practice, therefore, os-sort could perform better than our results show; however, the trends shown in our findings do not change. hd-sort is executed as Hadoop code. We tested different variations namely in-house developed user-defined functions (udf), Pig scripts, and JAQL scripts. Although we did observe differences in terms of absolute numbers, the behavior of this approach compared against the other strategies is not affected much. Comparing different Hadoop implementations is not amongst our goals; so here, we just present the generic trend (based on average numbers) and explain the functionality using only the Pig language. As an example of a series of blocking operators, we may write the following script in Pig:

```
sf$sf = load 'lineitem.tbl.sf$sf'
       using PigStorage('|') as (f1,f2,...,f17);
ord1_$nd = order sf$sf by f1 parallel $nd;
...
ord10_$nd = order ord9_$nd by f10 parallel $nd;
store ord$op_$nd into 'res_sf$sf_Ord$op-$nd.dat'
       using PigStorage('|');
```

Table 1. Statistics for TPC-H lineitem

SF	1	10	100
Size (GBs)	0.76	7.3	75
Rows (x10^6)	6.1	59.9	600

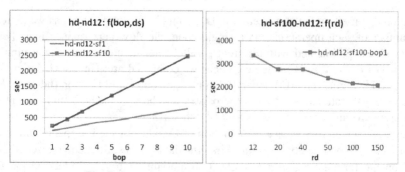

Fig. 7. Execution of blocking operation in Hadoop

The parameters used in this script, $sf, $nd, $op, stand for the scale factor of the lineitem datafile, the number of nodes, and the number of operators (sorters in this example), respectively.

For the experiments, we used synthetic data produced using the TPC-H generator. We experimented with varying data sizes using the scale factors 1, 10, and 100. Example statistics for the lineitem table are shown in Table 1.

Fig. 7 shows how Hadoop implementations behave for blocking operations (hd-sort). The left graph shows that as the number of blocking operations increases, flow performance is negatively affected. In fact, performance becomes worst if at the same time the data size increases too. Thus, for large files, having a series of blocking operations executed one after the other becomes quite costly. One optimization heuristic we can use for improving Hadoop performance is to increase parallelism by increasing the number of reduce tasks. The right graph shows how performance is improved when we increase the number of reducers (up to a certain point) whilst executing a single blocking operation for a SF=100 datafile (~75GBs).

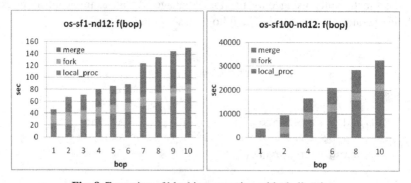

Fig. 8. Execution of blocking operation with shell scripts

Fig. 8 shows performance measures for flows executed as shell scripts in Unix (os-sort). The left and right graphs show an analysis of performance measures for two datafiles sized 0.76 GB and 75 GBs or SF=1 and SF=100, respectively. The blue part of each bar (bottom part) represents the time spent on each remote node, while the green (middle) and red (upper) part of each bar represent the time spent for distributing and merging back, respectively, data on the master node. As we increase the number of blocking operations each remote node has more processing to do. On the master node, distributing data is not affected by the number of remote nodes (each time we need to create the same number of chunks), while the merge time increases as we increase the number of blocking operations. This happens because each blocking operator essentially sorts data on a different field: the first on the first field and the N-th on the N-th field. Thus, each time we have to merge on a field that is placed deeper in the file, and thus merge has to process more data before it reaches that field.

Fig. 9 compares os-sort, hd-sort, and pdb-sort for executing a series of blocking operations (1 to 10). pdb-sort ran on a commercial parallel database engine. Starting from the top-left graph and going clockwise, the graphs show results of the three methods on small-sized (SF=1), medium-sized (SF=10), and large-sized (SF=100) data files. In all cases, pdb-sort is faster than os-sort and hd-sort. Hence, if our data resides inside the database, there is no reason to sort data outside. However, if our data is placed outside the database (e.g., data coming from flows running elsewhere like the results of hadoop operations on unstructured data) we have to take into account the cost of loading this data into our parallel database. This cost increases with data size and for this case, the total time (load+sort) is shown in the graphs as the green line (pdbL). In this scenario, there are some interesting tradeoffs. For large datasets and for a small number of sort operations, it might make sense to use hadoop. For medium sized datasets, it might worthwhile to pay the cost of loading the data into a database. For small datasets, if the data is not in the database, it is too expensive to run pdb-sort; then, it is better to sort outside either using os-sort (e.g., an ETL tool, custom scripts) or even hadoop (up to a certain number of sort operations).

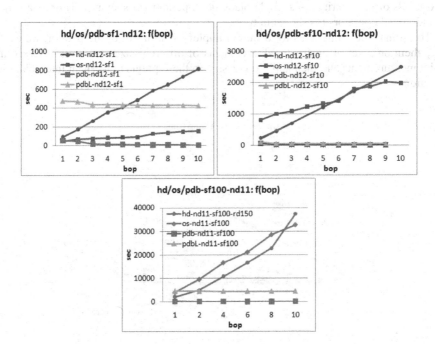

Fig. 9. Comparison of flow execution using Hadoop and shell scripts

Between os-sort and hd-sort, it seems that, for large data files and up to a certain number of blocking operations, it is better to use the hd implementation. After that number, the Hadoop reduce tasks become quite expensive and hd is not the best option any more. On the other hand, the trend changes for smaller data files. For small files, hd-sort is always the worst case, where for medium-sized files there is a crossover point. If we have high freshness requirements, then typically we have to process smaller batches. In such cases, Hadoop may become quite expensive. If we have to process larger batches (e.g., when we have low freshness requirements or the source data is updated less frequently), then Hadoop might be a very appealing solution.

In the same way, we may perform similar micro-benchmarks for other operations. We also need to cover the other parameters mentioned earlier and we need to define and perform micro-benchmarks for other QoX objectives in addition to performance. Using the micro-benchmarks for optimization poses further challenges such as *interpolation* (e.g., micro-benchmark measures 1MB sort and 10MB sort, but the actual flow has 3MB sort) and *composition* (estimating the performance of segments of a flow given the performance of individual operations in the flow).

3.2   Micro-benchmarks for Unconventional Operators

For optimizing data analytic flows for performance and other objectives, we need to consider operations that significantly differ from traditional relational and ETL operations, such as operations used in text analytics flows. This section discusses our approach for benchmarking the operators that occur in the sentiment analysis flow of Fig. 4. As discussed earlier, these operators are complex and can be benchmarked at two levels of granularity: as a single black box operator (as shown in 4) or as a flow of individual operators (as shown in 6).

To estimate cost functions for different implementations of each operator, we execute them on a set of unstructured documents of different sizes to obtain a series of point measurements and then apply regression to these points to learn an interpolation function.

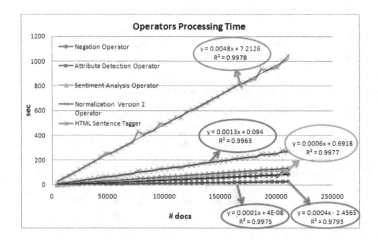

Fig. 10. Linear regression of execution costs

The initial experiments were on a single node and used dataset sizes from a few thousand documents up to 100,000. In all these runs, the operators of the sentiment analysis flow of our sample scenario exhibited a linear behavior. Thus, we used linear regression to approximate the data points to a line with minimum error, as the R-squared values in Fig. 10 show. These functions can be plugged into the QoX Optimizer so that it can interpolate to other values.

Further experiments with larger datasets revealed that an important parameter that affects this linear behavior is memory size. The individual operators have different memory requirements and consequently different sensitivity to the memory size. There is an inflection point at which the linear behavior changes to exponential, due to increased paging. The inflection point at which this change in behavior occurs for a given operator depends on the amount of available memory. In particular, for the sentiment analysis operators implemented in Java, the JVM heap size determines the location of the inflection point, which varies from operator to operator as depicted in the left three charts of Fig. 11 for two example operations, tokenizer and attribute detection, and for the entire sentiment analysis flow. (The bottom-left chart shows the behavior when the entire sentiment analysis is implemented as a single, black-box operator in a single JVM.) However, for the same experiments ran on a 12-node Hadoop cluster, the behavior remained linear past the single-node inflection point range of 150K to 190K documents for the different operators. We went up to 30 million documents and the behavior was still linear as shown in the two middle charts of Fig 12. Consequently, the overall processing time for the entire flow also remained linear.

Another set of experiments focused on a performance comparison among different implementations: (i) a single node implementation; (ii) a distributed implementation on Hadoop, in which the entire sentiment analysis flow was implemented as a single map task that Hadoop could distribute among the nodes of the cluster; and (iii) a distributed implementation without Hadoop.

Fig. 12 shows the results for different dataset sizes and the three different implementations. As for the conventional operators, we observe that for small datasets it is too costly to use Hadoop due to its startup cost. The distributed implementation without using Hadoop outperforms the Hadoop implementation because we partitioned the data set uniformly on all 12 nodes in the cluster. The Hadoop implementation, on the other hand, used the default block size of 64MB, and hence used at most 3 nodes. Fig. 13 illustrates this point. In the left chart of Fig. 13, we can distinguish two regions: one where the execution time of the operator grows linearly in the dataset size and the other, where the execution time stabilizes. For small datasets, a single partition is enough and consequently only one map task in one node is needed. The execution time of the task is proportional to the size of the partition. However, as the datasets get larger, more map tasks are created to process in parallel the various partitions, and the execution time stabilizes, not depending any more on the dataset size. This suggests that if it selects the Hadoop implementation, the optimizer will need to control the block size depending on the dataset size. The right graph shows that within the stable region, as the dataset size gets larger, more map tasks are needed to process the larger number of partitions.

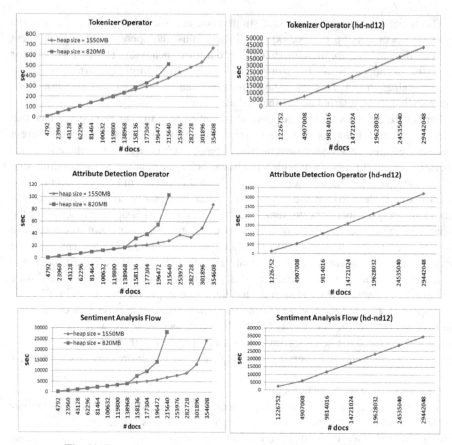

Fig. 11. Execution cost inflection point sensitiveness to JVM heap size

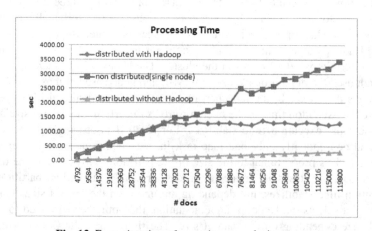

Fig. 12. Execution times for sentiment analysis operator

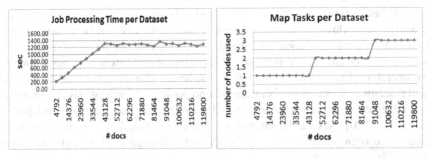

Fig. 13. Performance of sentiment analysis operator implemented in Hadoop

4   Related Work

To the best of our knowledge, there is no prior work on optimizing end-to-end analytic data flows, and very little work even on optimizing back-end integration flows. Off-the-shelf ETL engines do not support optimization of entire flows for multiple objectives (beyond performance). Some ETL engines provide limited optimization techniques such as pushdown of relational operators [10]) but it is not clear if and how these are tied to optimization objectives. Beyond our own QoX approach to integration flow optimization, research on ETL processes and workflows has not provided optimization results for multiple objectives. An optimization framework for business processes focuses on one objective and uses a limited set of optimization techniques [27]. Query optimization focuses on performance and considers a subset of operations typically encountered in our case [e.g. 9, 13, 18, 19]. Also, we want the optimizer to be independent of the execution engine; in fact, we want to allow the optimized flow to execute on more than one engine. Research on federated database systems has considered query optimization for multiple execution engines, but this work, too, was limited to traditional query operators and to performance as the only objective; for example, see query optimization in Garlic [8,16], Pegasus [7], and Multibase [5].

   Several research projects have focused on providing high-level languages that can be translated to execute on a map-reduce engine (e.g., JAQL [3], Pig [15], Hive [24]). These languages offer opportunities for optimization. Other research efforts have generalized the map-reduce execution engine to create a more flexible framework that can process a large class of parallel-distributed data flows (e.g. Nephele [2], Dryad [11], CIEL [14]). Such systems typically have higher-level languages that can be optimized and compiled to execute on the parallel execution engine (for example, see PACTs in Nephele, DryadLINQ in Dryad, SCOPE [4], Skywriting in CEIL). None of these projects addresses data flows that span different execution engines. HadoopDB is one example of a hybrid system in which queries span execution engines [1]. HadoopDB stores persistent data in multiple PostgreSQL engines. It supports SQL-like queries that retrieve data from PostgreSQL and process the data over Hadoop. However, it is not designed as a general framework over multiple engines.

Several benchmarks do exist, but so far, none is specifically tailored for generalized analytic data flows. TPC has presented a successful series of benchmarks. TPC-DS provides source and target schemas, but the intermediate integration process is quite simplistic (it contains a set of insert and delete statements mostly based on relational operators) [25]. TPC-ETL is a new benchmark that TPC is currently working on and it seems to focus on performance, but no further information has been released yet. Another effort proposes an ETL benchmark focusing on modeling and performance issues [20]. Several benchmarking and experimental efforts on map-reduce engines have been presented, but so far, these focus mainly on performance issues [e.g., 12, 17].

5   Conclusions and Future Work

In this paper, we have addressed the challenges in optimizing analytic data flows that arise in modern business intelligence applications. We observe that enterprises are now incorporating into their analytics workflows more than just the traditional structured data in the enterprise warehouse. They need event streams, time-series analytics, log file analysis, text analytics, and so on. These different types of datasets are best processed using specialized data engines; i.e., *one size does not fit all*. Consequently, analytic data flows will span execution engines. We sketched our previous work on QoX-driven optimization for back-end information integration flows, where the quality objectives include not just performance, but also freshness, fault-tolerance, reliability, and others. This paper outlines how this approach can be extended to optimizing end-to-end analytic data flows over multiple execution engines. We described the results of initial micro-benchmarks for characterizing the performance of both conventional (ETL and database) operations and unconventional (e.g., text analytic) operations, when they are executed on different engines.

Many challenges remain, and we hope to address these in future work. These include:

- defining and implementing micro-benchmarks for additional representative operations, including event and stream processing, front-end data mining and analytic operations;
- developing interpolation models and interaction models for estimating the cost of complete flows;
- optimization strategies at the physical level for assigning segments of the flow to execution engines; and
- extending the benchmarks, cost models, objective functions, and optimization strategies to QoX objectives other than performance.

References

1. Abouzeid, A., Bajda-Pawlikowski, K., Abadi, D.J., Rasin, A., Silberschatz, A.: Hadoop DB: An Architectural Hybrid of Map Reduce and DBMS Technologies for Analytical Workloads. PVLDB 2(1), 922–933 (2009)

2. Battré, D., Ewen, S., Hueske, F., Kao, O., Markl, V., Warneke, D.: Nephele/PACTs: a Programming Model and Execution Framework for Web-Scale Analytical Processing. In: SoCC, pp. 119–130 (2010)
3. Beyer, K., Ercegovac, V., Gemulla, R., Balmin, A., Eltabakh, M., Kanne, C.C., Ozcan, F., Shekita, E.: Jaql: A Scripting Language for Large Scale Semistructured Data Analysis. In: VLDB (2011)
4. Chaiken, R., Jenkins, B., Larson, P.-Å., Ramsey, B., Shakib, D., Weaver, S., Zhou, J.: SCOPE: Easy and Efficient Parallel Processing of Massive Data Sets. PVLDB 1(2), 1265–1276 (2008)
5. Dayal, U.: Processing Queries over Generalization Hierarchies in a Multidatabase System. In: VLDB, pp. 342–353 (1983)
6. Dayal, U., Castellanos, M., Simitsis, A., Wilkinson, K.: Data Integration Flows for Business Intelligence. In: EDBT, pp. 1–11 (2009)
7. Du, W., Krishnamurthy, R., Shan, M.-C.: Query optimization in heterogeneous DBMS. In: VLDB, pp. 277–291 (1992)
8. Haas, L., Kossman, D., Wimmers, E.L., Yang, J.: Optimizing Queries across Diverse Data Sources. In: VLDB, pp. 276–285 (1997)
9. Han, W.-S., Kwak, W., Lee, J., Lohman, G.M., Markl, V.: Parallelizing query optimization. PVLDB 1(1), 188–200 (2008)
10. Informatica. PowerCenter Pushdown Optimization Option Datasheet (2011), http://www.informatica.com/INFA_Resources/ds_pushdown_optimization_6675.pdf
11. Isard, M., Budiu, M., Yu, Y., Birrell, A., Fetterly, D.: Dryad: Distributed Data-Parallel Programs from Sequential Building Blocks. In: EuroSys (2007)
12. Jiang, D., Chin Ooi, B., Shi, L., Wu, S.: The Performance of MapReduce: An In-depth Study. PVLDB 3(1), 472–483 (2010)
13. Lohman, G.M., Mohan, C., Haas, L.M., Daniels, D., Lindsay, B.G., Selinger, P.G., Wilms, P.F.: Query Processing in R*. In: Query Processing in Database Systems, pp. 31–47 (1985)
14. Murray, D.G., Schwarzkopf, M., Smowton, C., Smith, S., Madhavapeddy, A., Hand, S.: CIEL: A Universal Execution Engine for Distributed Data-flow Computing. In: USENIX NSDI (2011)
15. Olston, C., Reed, B., Srivastava, U., Kumar, R., Tomkins, A.: Pig Latin: a Not-so-foreign Language for Data Processing. In: SIGMOD, pp. 1099–1110 (2008)
16. Roth, M.T., Arya, M., Haas, L.M., Carey, M.J., Cody, W.F., Fagin, R., Schwarz, P.M., Thomas II, J., Wimmers, E.L.: The Garlic Project. In: SIGMOD, p. 557 (1996)
17. Schad, J., Dittrich, J., Quiané-Ruiz, J.-A.: Runtime Measurements in the Cloud: Observing, Analyzing, and Reducing Variance. PVLDB 3(1), 460–471 (2010)
18. Sellis, T.K.: Global Query Optimization. In: SIGMOD, pp. 191–205 (1986)
19. Sellis, T.K.: Multiple-Query Optimization. TODS 13(1), 23–52 (1988)
20. Simitsis, A., Vassiliadis, P., Dayal, U., Karagiannis, A., Tziovara, V.: Benchmarking ETL Workflows. In: Nambiar, R., Poess, M. (eds.) TPCTC 2009. LNCS, vol. 5895, pp. 199–220. Springer, Heidelberg (2009)
21. Simitsis, A., Vassiliadis, P., Sellis, T.K.: Optimizing ETL Processes in Data Warehouses. In: ICDE, pp. 564–575 (2005)
22. Simitsis, A., Wilkinson, K., Castellanos, M., Dayal, U.: QoX-driven ETL design: Reducing the Cost of ETL Consulting Engagements. In: SIGMOD, pp. 953–960 (2009)
23. Simitsis, A., Wilkinson, K., Dayal, U., Castellanos, M.: Optimizing ETL Workflows for Fault-Tolerance. In: ICDE, pp. 385–396 (2010)

24. Thusoo, A., Sen Sarma, J., Jain, N., Shao, Z., Chakka, P., Zhang, N., Anthony, S., Liu, H., Murthy, R.: Hive - a Petabyte Scale Data Warehouse Using Hadoop. In: ICDE, pp. 996–1005 (2010)
25. TPC. TPC-DS specification (2011),
    http://www.tpc.org/tpcds/spec/tpcds1.0.0.d.pdf
26. Vassiliadis, P., Simitsis, A.: Extraction, Transformation, and Loading. In: Encyclopedia of Database Systems, pp. 1095–1101 (2009)
27. Vrhovnik, M., Schwarz, H., Suhre, O., Mitschang, B., Markl, V., Maier, A., Kraft, T.: An Approach to Optimize Data Processing in Business Processes. In: VLDB, pp. 615–626 (2007)
28. Wilkinson, K., Simitsis, A., Castellanos, M., Dayal, U.: Leveraging Business Process Models for ETL Design. In: Parsons, J., Saeki, M., Shoval, P., Woo, C., Wand, Y. (eds.) ER 2010. LNCS, vol. 6412, pp. 15–30. Springer, Heidelberg (2010)

Normalization in a Mixed
OLTP and OLAP Workload Scenario

Anja Bog[1], Kai Sachs[2], Alexander Zeier[1], and Hasso Plattner[1]

[1] Hasso Plattner Institute, University of Potsdam, 14482 Potsdam, Germany
{anja.bog,alexander.zeier,hasso.plattner}@hpi.uni-potsdam.de
[2] SAP AG, 69190 Walldorf, Germany
kai.sachs@sap.com

Abstract. The historically introduced separation of online analytical processing (OLAP) from online transaction processing (OLTP) is in question considering the current developments of databases. Column-oriented databases mainly used in the OLAP environment so far, with the addition of in-memory data storage are adapted to accommodate OLTP as well, thus paving the way for mixed OLTP and OLAP processing. To assess mixed workload systems benchmarking has to evolve along with the database technology. Especially in mixed workload scenarios the question arises of how to layout the database. In this paper, we present a case study on the impact of database design focusing on normalization with respect to various workload mixes and database implementations. We use a novel benchmark methodology that provides mixed OLTP and OLAP workloads based on a real scenario.

Keywords: Combined OLTP and OLAP Workloads, Database Design, Normalization, Workload Mix, Benchmarking.

1 Introduction

Online transaction processing (OLTP) systems are the backbone of today's enterprises for daily operation. They provide the applications for the business processes of an enterprise and record all business movements, e.g. sales and purchase orders, production, billing, and payments. For strategic insights to make business decisions for the future and to monitor the performance of their business, enterprises utilize online analytical processing (OLAP) systems. Since OLTP and OLAP present very different challenges for database architectures and transaction throughput is essential for OLTP, they have been separated into different systems in the mid 1990s to avoid impairments. The business data used in both domains is the same, however, stored in differently optimized structures. The separation implies several drawbacks, for example, keeping redundant versions of the same data, data staleness for analytics, as data in the OLAP system is updated only periodically, or having only a selected data set available for analytics.

Hardware development, that is, multi-core technology and systems with large main memory provide more powerful systems as a basis for business processing.

R. Nambiar and M. Poess (Eds.): TPCTC 2011, LNCS 7144, pp. 67–82, 2012.

In [26], Nambiar and Poess analyze Moore's law [24] directly with respect to transaction processing systems and show that it holds true even on this higher level. They show that systems have been (and most probably will be) capable of running ever larger transaction processing workloads with a growth that closely resembles Moore's predictions. In combination with recent developments of database systems, especially column-oriented storage in addition to lightweight compression techniques, the question arises if the historically grown separation of the two domains is still necessary. Plattner [28] states that in-memory column-oriented databases are capable of running OLTP and OLAP applications in one and the same system in a mixed mode.

Running OLTP and OLAP in a mixed mode directly leads to the question of how to design the database. Database design is a major distinguishing characteristic between the OLTP and OLAP domains and has conflicting goals for optimization. So far, efforts to optimize database design have been focused on one or the other domain, but not considering a mixed workload of both. Using a methodology to benchmark composite OLTP and OLAP systems that enables the simulation of mixed workloads, we present a case study of the impact of database design for different workload mixes and different database storage architectures. Regarding the database design, our focus in this study lies on different degrees of normalization of the database schema. In this paper, we report our results for the behavior of databases with primary storage on disk, in main memory as well as row and column-orientation. A brief announcement of this case study was presented in [4]. In this paper, we give a complete introduction to the schema variants analyzed in the case study and present results for a wide range of mixed workloads and database architectures.

In the following section, we discuss the background of our study by giving examples for applications that do not clearly fit either into the OLTP or OLAP domain. Further, we provide a short introduction of OLTP and OLAP database design and its normalization in particular and we review related work in the area of database benchmarking and optimizing database design for OLTP and OLAP. In Section 3 we introduce our database design variants related to normalization. We apply these variants in a comprehensive case study in Section 4, discuss the results of the study and finally, we summarize our findings.

2   Background

In this section we present applications which do not clearly fit either into the OLTP or OLAP domain, we observe that database architectures exist that already cater for mixed OLTP and OLAP workloads and we present an overview of the benchmarks for OLTP and OLAP systems. Further, we discuss database design in general and optimization of database design in detail and we point out work related to database optimization as our case study aims at optimizing databases regarding mixed workloads.

2.1   Applications Spanning Across Domains

Applications are classified to belong to one or the other domain based on their data processing characteristics. French [10] characterizes the OLTP workload as simple mixed queries of inserts, updates, and deletes that are relatively short running, retrieve a large number of columns of a table and touch only a small set of rows. In contrast, OLAP operations are characterized as complex, read-mostly queries that touch a small number of columns, but a large number of rows. According to Abolhassani [1] applications exist in either domain that show the application characteristics typical for the other domain. As a result, although a line is drawn between OLTP and OLAP, it is not always obvious from the characteristics of an application which domain it belongs to.

Krueger et al. [21] point out several examples, e.g., dunning and available-to-promise (ATP), where this classification is not clear. Dunning and ATP are categorized as OLTP operations, which need the latest business data in order to determine the right results. Dunning runs, for example, are triggered for entire sales areas or customer groups, and therefore touch a relatively large data set. To avoid long run times in relation to typical OLTP operations and to avoid queuing other OLTP operations, workarounds have been introduced. For dunning runs it means that they are triggered only periodically, e.g. during times of low system load. To further reduce the impact of long response times through reading large amounts of data on the OLTP system, secondary tables, e.g., holding information about unpaid bills for dunning or materialized aggregates, i.e., time lines for availability-to-promise are created and kept up-to-date in synchronization with the business transactions.

2.2   Combined OLTP and OLAP Database Architectures

Because of the need of OLAP to analyze ever fresher and more complete OLTP data, database architectures and systems that allow a combined workload of OLTP and OLAP are proposed. Röhm [29] introduced his unified architecture for OLTP and OLAP to allow OLAP clients the access to up-to-date data. He proposes a middleware-based database cluster with OLTP and OLAP nodes side by side where each OLAP node holds its own copy of the data with a varying degree of freshness. In contrast to this middleware-based approach, HyPer [18] handles OLTP and OLAP using hardware assisted replication mechanisms. This achieves consistent and up-to-date snapshots of the transaction data. Other prototypes such as OctopusDB [8] and Hyrise [12] aim to avoid keeping multiple copies of data and instead adapting the storage layout of the data according to usage patterns in the workload.

2.3   Related Work in Benchmarking OLTP and OLAP

The methodology we use in our case study is targeted as a new benchmark for mixed OLTP and OLAP workloads. However, it is not a standard and we briefly discuss why it is desirable to introduce a new benchmark and note where its benefits lie regarding our case study.

As transactional and analytical benchmarking have been treated as separate domains so far, being able to use the existing benchmarks only limited statements can be made concerning the ability of data management systems to handle a mixed workload. Running an OLTP and an OLAP benchmark in parallel, is a valid approach to create a mixed workload. However, with the current benchmarks only a partial picture of the actual performance of a hybrid system will be achieved, measuring the effects of hardware resource contention. Because the benchmarks still run on their dedicated data sets, conflicts arising from data access to the same data set are not observed. Harmonizing the different requirements for the design of the data set for optimal access are a characteristic of particular interest for a mixed workload.

Regarding combined OLTP and OLAP workloads, we are aware of two non-standard benchmarking approaches, one is the composite benchmark for transaction processing and operational reporting (CBTR) [3] and the other is TPC-CH [11]. CBTR is based on the order-to-cash process of a real enterprise system that is widely applicable in many industries and TPC-CH is derived from the standard benchmarks TPC-C [31] and TPC-H [32].

Both benchmark proposals include workload mix as a new parameter that is of importance in the mixed OLTP/OLAP scenario. Workload is defined by the types of actions that take place and their frequency of execution. The contribution of the OLTP and OLAP-style workloads to the total workload should not be constant because transactional and analytical processing follow conflicting optimization goals and consequently the share of OLTP and OLAP-style actions has an impact on the decisions to optimize a combined system. TPC's transactional web e-Commerce benchmark TPC-W [30], which has been marked as obsolete since 2005, but is still in use, explicitly models different workloads of its basic transactions in order to reproduce diverse user behavior. These are browsing, shopping and ordering. Similar to the mix of OLTP and OLAP actions these mixes cover conflicting optimization goals, e.g. fast access of a large amount of data during browsing versus providing hassle-free insertion of data during ordering. For our study of the impact of database design, workload mix is of particular interest.

In our case study we used CBTR because its data schema and the included data are the most realistic concerning data found in real enterprise systems and we believe our results concerning the impact of database design decisions under varying workloads to be more accurate. In [3], we provide a detailed description of the scenario, database design and statements used in CBTR.

2.4 OLTP and OLAP Database Design

For both, OLTP and OLAP, basic rules for the creation of optimized database designs exist. The resulting database schemas, however, differ to a great extend and the design goals for optimizing OLTP and OLAP systems are in conflict, meaning that a design which is optimized for OLAP performance degrades OLTP performance and vice versa [9].

The borders between the OLTP and OLAP domain are increasingly blurring when observing the characteristics of the involved data set. The data set of OLAP systems, though part of it is highly optimized for multi-dimensional queries and aggregation, increasingly bears similarity with the OLTP data set. According to Inmon [15] operational data stores (ODS), which are part of the OLAP environment hold almost fresh OLTP data on the transactional level of detail, i.e., the same or a very similar logical schema as in the OLTP system. The freshness of the data within the ODS ranges from updates appearing in the ODS only seconds later to 24 hours or more, depending on the ODS class. As data in the ODS ages, it passes into the data warehouse.

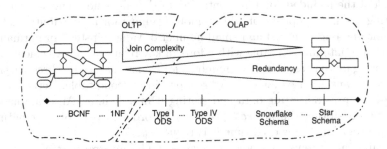

Fig. 1. Analytical vs. Transaction Processing Schemas

In Figure 1 we illustrate the database schema variants used in OLTP and OLAP systems. They are ordered according to the join complexity, a fixed query occurs if the underlying schema is varied. With the decreasing complexity of joins, the level of redundancy within the data set increases.

2.5 Normalization in Database Design

In this section we focus on normalization as this is the main differentiating factor when comparing OLTP and OLAP database schemas.

To achieve a sound logical database design and in particular to reduce redundancy within data that can cause false relationships and inconsistencies, the principles of normalization were developed [13]. In [6], Codd introduces the objectives of normalization, that include obtaining a powerful retrieval capability by simplifying the set of relations, removing undesirable insertion, update and deletion anomalies, and reducing the need for restructuring when adding new types of data, thus increasing the life span of application programs.

However, for an increased level of normalization of a set of relations a penalty towards data retrieval has to be accepted. Data that could have been retrieved from one tuple in a denormalized design may have to be retrieved from several tuples in a normalized design. Kent [19] acknowledges, that the highest level of normalization need not be enforced, where performance requirements have to be taken into account. Mullins [25] enforces normalization by pointing out that a normalized schema should never be denormalized unless a performance need arises which cannot be solved in any other way.

Denormalization can be observed in the data schemas of productive systems for analytical processing as well as in transaction processing. Bock and Schrage [2] discuss and give examples how denormalization can be used to improve system response times for transaction processing, while avoiding redundant storage and without incurring prohibitive data maintenance. Furthermore, Mullins [25] names different types of denormalization techniques, of which the types *redundant data*, *repeating groups*, and *derivable data* can still be observed in today's transactional systems. Redundant data means adding columns of a table B to table A if they are always queried in combination with table A. This is only advisable if the included columns contain data that does not change frequently. Repeating groups comprises of adding more columns for an attribute that can have multiple, but a limited and small number of values, instead of normalizing this attribute into an own table with a foreign key relationship. A typical example is storing up to three telephone numbers for a customer. Here, three *telephone number* columns are used instead of three rows in a second table. Derivable data comprises of pre-computing data and storing it in a column. An example is an extra column storing the *net sales value* of an order instead of aggregating it from the order line items each time it is requested.

In analytical systems, the types *pre-joined tables* and *report tables* are common. In pre-joined tables, as the name says, two or more tables are stored in their joined form, omitting redundant columns. Report tables are tables that already represent the report based on the data that is otherwise stored in several tables and can only be retrieved via complex SQL statement. Thus, the report can be built using simple SQL queries. The star and snowflake schemas are members of this category. In our study, we particularly focus on the denormalization type pre-joined tables under mixed workload conditions.

According to Martyn [23], the denormalization found in the star schema in the data warehouse is acceptable because of the read-only character of the data warehouse and the opportunity of addressing potential update anomalies during the ETL process. Kimball expresses a similar opinion, writing that the "use of normalized modeling in the data warehouse presentation area defeats the whole purpose of data warehousing, namely, intuitive and high-performance retrieval of data." [20] In contrast, Date [7], when discussing relational models in general which applies to OLTP as well as OLAP schemas, views denormalization in a critical fashion and believes "that anything less than a fully normalized design is strongly contraindicated" and that denormalization should only be used as a last resort if all other strategies to improve performance fail.

2.6   Related Work in Optimizing the Database Design for OLTP and OLAP

Structures for optimized query performance like indexes, views, or precomputed aggregates introduce redundancy, which adds overhead to the insertion of new data, updates, and deletes [22]. They are relativized with a growing share of read access or the increasing size of tables while access patterns, e.g. queried time windows, are constant. A variety of prototypes and tools exist that propose configurations for indexes and materialized views, for example, AutoAdmin for Microsoft SQL Server [5], or to automate partitioning, see Autopart for large scientific databases [27]. Zilio et al. [33] introduced DB2 Design Advisor, which additionally takes into account clustering and partitioning. All optimization approaches are, however, focused on either OLTP or OLAP workloads. Furthermore, they utilize only structures of physical database design, while a difference between OLTP and OLAP data schemas can also be found on the logical level of database design, that is, normalization. Our case study provides insights on the performance of different database schemas with respect to normalization under a mixed workload.

The development of ODSs shows how a mixed workload can be handled by one system. There are four types of ODS (cf. [17]). Three of them are copies of transactional data and can be categorized according to data freshness. The fourth type of ODS additionally includes strategic information. Data created from a report in the data warehouse environment is transported back into the ODS [14]. The different types of users producing the mixed workload are characterized by Inmon as "farmers" and "explorers" [16]. Whereas farmers repeat the same task over and over again and exactly know what they are looking for, i.e. benefit from clearly structured data like it is the case in OLTP, explorers exhibit unpredictable behavior. They skim through a large data set to search for patterns and relationships similar to OLAP workloads.

The reason why these diverse loads could be integrated within the ODS as one system are that farmers and explorers operate on only a limited amount of data copied into the ODS to produce reports concerned only with a short period of time, e.g. totals sales of the day or the number of new customers. Our focus, however, lies on systems which contain the entire operational data set of a company for analytics and not just a snapshot.

3 Database Design Variants Focusing on Normalization

In this section, we exemplify database design variation in the case of normalization. Database systems expose a very individual behavior, which heavily depends on the specific queries, underlying data schema, and physical optimizations. For a hybrid workload of OLTP and OLAP-like queries the task of choosing an optimal database design and optimizations according to a specific mix of queries becomes vital due to the wide range of data access behavior of the operations in a combined OLTP and OLAP system.

Figure 2 gives an overview of the levels relevant in database design. The top layer represents the abstract or conceptual definition of involved entities, attributes and their relations. OLTP and OLAP queries are defined based on these definitions and should be oblivious to changes of the database design on the lower layers. The lower two layers, logical and physical, show the possible variations of the database design. Normalization as a transformation of the tables resides in the logical layer.

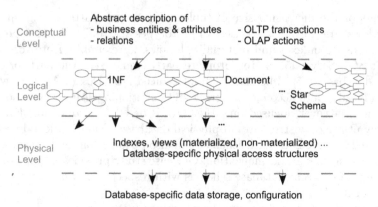

Fig. 2. Data Model Variation Levels

The logical layer in Figure 2 depicts the schema variations applied in our case study. 1NF is the extracted part of a data schema of a real enterprise system, which is modeled in CBTR. Document and star schema are its variations to analyze the impact of normalization under varying workloads and in different types of databases. These will be introduced in Section 3.2.

3.1   The Base Schema

Our starting point is an original database schema taken from a real-world OLTP database, modeled in CBTR [3]. Figure 3 depicts the database schema that is the basis for an order-to-cash scenario. This scenario covers sales order processing, deliveries, billing and payment processing as the related functions of accounting.

18 tables support this scenario, seven of them containing master data and 11 tables for transactional data. Master data is visualized in gray shading and transactional data is shown with a black header. Primary keys of tables are marked in bold face. Foreign keys are displayed by additional connections that start at the foreign key and point to the table and attribute that is referenced. In this schema only the most important attributes and relationships are illustrated for easier understanding. The complete schema contains 2316 columns that are distributed over the shown tables. The columns are not evenly distributed. Thus, table widths vary between 5 and a maximum of 327 columns.

The mapping of the conceptual design to the tables of this schema is not trivial. Business partner data is represented by three customer master tables and product data respectively by three product master tables. The order entity is split up into sales header, sales item, sales conditions, and sales partner. The delivery, billing, and accounting information entities are each split up in header and item tables respectively.

This schema is optimal for the OLTP operations taking place in the order-to-cash scenario, i.e., order entry, delivery scheduling, billing, and payment recording. Only a small set of transactional tables have to be touched during any of

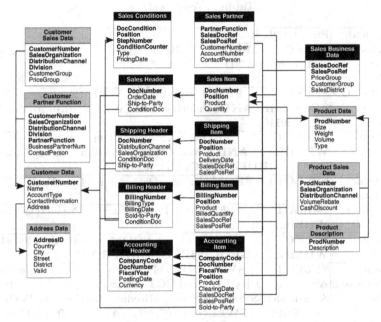

Fig. 3. Original OLTP Schema

these actions and no joins are needed. However, the access pattern looks completely different for the OLAP operations. Customer payment behavior, order processing time, and order completion access data from several transactional tables and joining over four header and item tables is common. These joins are particularly problematic since the header and item tables have the largest cardinality. For the measurements, the OLTP and OLAP actions as defined in the CBTR benchmark are used. Table 1 gives an overview of the transaction profiles for the benchmark actions. We refer to [3] for the detailed profiles and SQL statements.

Table 1. Overview of CBTR Transaction Profiles and SQL Statements

Type	Action	Profile/SQL Statement
wOLTP	Sales Order	Header: Select [Cust. Data, Sales Data, Partner Function, Address Data], Insert [Sales Header]; Per Item: Select [Product Data, Description, Sales Data], Insert [Sales Item, Business Data, Business Partner]
	Shipping	Header: Insert [Shipping Header]; Per Item: Select [Sales Item], Insert [Shipping Item]
	Billing	Header: Insert [Billing & Accounting Header, Sales Conditions]; Per Item: Select [Sales & Shipping Item], Insert [Billing & Accounting Item]
	Payment	Select [Accounting Header]; Per Item: Update [Accounting Item]

Table 1. (continued)

Type	Action	Profile/SQL Statement
rOLTP	Sales Order by Key	**SELECT** [...] **FROM** SalesHeader, SalesItem **WHERE** OrderID = @DocNum **AND** [...];
	Sales Order by Period	**SELECT** [...] **FROM** SalesHeader **WHERE** CustomerID = @CustomerID **AND** (OrderDate **BETWEEN** '01.10.2011" **AND** "31.10.2011");
	Open Items	**SELECT** [...] **FROM** AccountingItem, AccountingHeader **WHERE** [...] **AND** AccountType = "Debitor" **AND** Clearing-Date= "" **ORDER BY** CustID, AccID;
	Customer Details	**SELECT** [...] **FROM** CustomerData, AddressData **WHERE** [...];
	Product Details	**SELECT** [...] **FROM** ProductData, ProductDescription **WHERE** [...];
OLAP	Daily Flash	**SELECT** [...] **SUM**(Quantity) **FROM** SalesHeader, SalesItem **WHERE** [...] **GROUP BY** [...] **ORDER BY** [...];
	Order Processing Time	**SELECT** [...], **AVG**(DATEDIFF(T.DeliveryDate, T.OrderDate)) **AS** Days **FROM** (**SELECT DISTINCT** [...] **FROM** SalesHeader, SalesItem, ShippingHeader, ShippingItem **WHERE** OrderDate **BETWEEN** "01.07.2011" **AND** "30.09.2011", [...])T **GROUP BY** [...] **ORDER BY** Days **DESC**;
	Order Delivery Fulfillment	**SELECT** [...] **SUM**(DeliveredQuantity), (**SELECT** **SUM**(OrderQuantity) **FROM** SalesItem, SalesHeader **WHERE** [...]) **AS** Expected **FROM** SalesHeader **AS** sdh, SalesItem, ShippingHeader **AS** sh, ShippingItem **WHERE** sh.DeliveryDate ¦= sdh.DeliveryDate **AND** [...] **GROUP BY** [...] **ORDER BY** DeliveredQuantity **DESC**;
	Days Sales Outstanding	**SELECT** [...], (1 - **SUM**(Amount) / (**SELECT SUM**(NetValue + TaxAmount) **FROM** BillingHeader **WHERE** [...])*91 **AS** DSO **FROM** AccountingItem, BillingHeader **WHERE** ClearingDate <> "" **AND** AccountType = "Debitor" **AND** [...] **GROUP BY** Currency **ORDER BY** DSO **DESC**;

3.2   Normalization Variants of the 1NF Schema

Figures 4 and 5 illustrate schema variations to optimize the performance of OLAP operations by avoiding the joins. Through pre-joining the tables, that is denormalization, the level of redundancy within the data set is increased. This adds effort for the OLTP operations that insert data.

To assess the impact of normalization for the specific OLAP operations the tables are denormalized as follows: In Figure 4 header and item tables are joined, because header and item information is mostly requested in combination by the OLAP operations. From a business perspective the data about the line items of an order is never queried without accessing the order header. Even in contexts where *top n sold products* are analyzed the header information is necessary to provide the time dimension, as such queries always reference a certain time frame, such as last quarter. This schema variant will be called *Document* in the

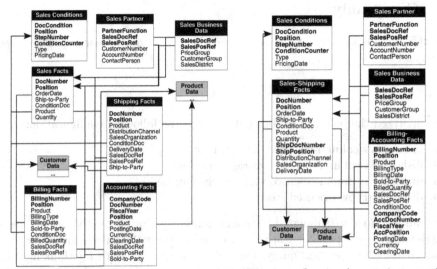

Fig. 4. Header-Item Join

Fig. 5. Invoice-Accounting and Order-Shipping Fact Tables

following because it provides the join between header and item information as would be reflected in a complete order document.

The schema variant in Figure 5 further increases the level of denormalization by joining together the sales and delivery information on one hand and the billing and accounting entities on the other hand. Thus, joins between transactional data tables can be completely avoided in the OLAP operations. This schema variant resembles a star schema with shared dimension tables and will be called *Denormalized* in the following. It represents the maximum level of denormalization that fits the set of OLAP operations given in CBTR. No changes are applied to the master data, therefore only stubs are depicted that represent the same master data tables and relations between them as shown in Figure 3.

According to the changes in the tables the actions needed to be adapted. This means for the OLAP queries and read-only OLTP transactions mainly exchanging the tables to be accessed and removing joins for the Document and Denormalized schemas. Insert OLTP transactions become bulkier with a higher degree of denormalization. For example, new sales order transactions insert one sales order header line and one or more sales order item lines into the tables depending on the number of items ordered. In the Document schema, the single header insert is removed, instead the header data is inserted together with each line item, redundantly storing the information of the sales order header. Besides increased storage space consumption additional complexity is introduced to updates of header information as multiple line item tuples have to be updated.

4   Case Study

In this section we present the setup and the results of our normalization case study.

4.1   Setup

We analyzed the behavior of four databases of the following configuration:

1. in-memory column-oriented data storage
2. disk-based column-oriented storage (System A)
3. disk-based column-oriented storage (System B)
4. disk-based row-oriented storage

For our workload we simulated 100 concurrently running clients that fire requests to the database in parallel. Each client upon receiving the answer for its request, immediately fires the next query. Thus, clients do not simulate any thinking time between requests. The OLTP and OLAP workload mix is controlled via the share of client types within the set of the 100 clients. Clients can be of type OLAP and OLTP, with OLAP clients sending only OLAP requests to the database, OLTP clients behave respectively. OLTP clients execute either read-only (rOLTP) or modifying statements (wOLTP) each with a share of approximately 50%. For example, in the workload (OLTP,OLAP) = (80,20) the share of workload types is (wOLTP,rOLTP,OLAP) = (40%, 40%, 20%).

For each database, nine workload configurations (OLTP,OLAP) $\in$ ((100,0), (80,20), (75,25), (60,40), (50,50), (40,60), ...,(0,100)) were tested for the above introduced three schema variants (1NF, Document, and Denormalized).

4.2   Results

The results of our experiments are shown in Figure 6. Each row depicts the results for one database. The workload configuration is shown on the x-axis[1], and the schema variants are depicted as series. The average response time is depicted for each workload type on a scale, which is normalized per database for easier comparison of the schemas for one database. For better comparison of those schema variants with very fast response times, some graphs are magnified.

From the tests we can see that independent of the the database the performance of some schemas varies when the workload mix is changed, particularly in the cases of the read-only statements. Especially in the OLAP cases, increasing response times are an indicator for the system becoming clogged with too many requests touching large datasets and being processed independent of each other's context. In the memory-column case we can observe that response times are decreasing with increasing OLAP workload for the Denormalized schema.

---

[1] For better readability in some graphs the axis description is omitted. The x-axes are the same for all graphs of a workload type and the y-axes are the same for all non-magnified graphs. Thus, axis descriptions on the bottom/left are applicable.

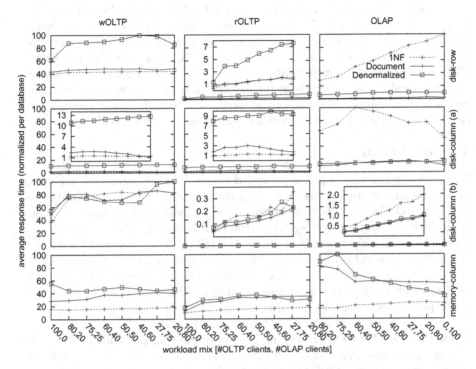

Fig. 6. Database Schema Performance for Varying Database Implementations and Workloads

This shows the impact of reusing intermediate results. As requests concentrate on few tables in the Denormalized schema, the probability of reusing existing results increases.

Depending on the workload, the schema which allows top performance differs. As was expected, for example, for the OLAP cases, the pre-joined schemas are advantageous, except in the case of the memory-column database, which is the only system tested that is being developed for a mixed workload. Here we can see, that 1NF as the schema with the highest degree of normalization tested, is the top candidate for all workload types. Thus, Date's view on normalization mentioned in Section 2.5 is enforced, which emphasizes denormalization as a strategy to be used for performance improvement as the last resort.

Depending on the database, different schemas allow top performance. In the disk-row case, we can see that for OLTP 1NF offers the best query performance closely followed by the Document schema. However, for OLAP the 1NF schema performs increasingly worse than Document or Denormalized with greater numbers of OLAP clients running concurrently. The conclusion for this database would be to use the Document schema as it achieves the best response times for all workload types. Taking a look at the results for the disk-column (a) database, the same conclusion in favor of the Document schema can be drawn. The average response times of the schemas for the disk-column (a) database are lowest for 1NF for OLTP, but clearly not for OLAP. Since 1NF is in favor for OLTP, but not in the OLAP case, a decision in favor of the Document schema would be made, which is close to the optimum for OLTP, is the optimum in the OLAP case, and performs much better for the OLAP queries compared with 1NF. For the disk-column (b) database making a decision between Document and Denormalized is hard without further knowledge of priorities and workload specifications. Only in the case of the memory-column database, one schema, i.e., 1NF outperforms all other variants regardless of the workload type.

5   Conclusion

The increasing need of up-to-date and detailed data for enterprise analytical processing and strategic decision making counteracts the current separation of OLTP and OLAP into two separate domains. Drawing them back into one domain, however, requires new system architectures that are able to mediate between the conflicting demands of OLTP and OLAP. The resulting new domain of a combined workload requires benchmarking activities to evolve in order to accompany and drive the further development of database systems and they need more effort than just extending existing benchmarks, as workload mix as a new parameter is brought into play.

Next, the question of database design has to be answered. Efforts so far are focused on OLTP or OLAP and mainly on optimizing physical database design using indexes, partitioning, clustering or views. Another aspect, however, is added when uniting OLTP and OLAP, which is their difference on the logical database design layer. Normalization is the main distinguishing factor when comparing typical OLTP and OLAP database designs. To our knowledge no study exists on the variation of database designs on the logical level under a mixed OLTP and OLAP workload. Therefore, we measured the impact of logical database design with the focus on normalization on various workload mixes. We analyzed four databases: one mainly used in the OLTP domain, two from the OLAP domain and one designed to handle mixed workloads and found that only for the database developed for a mixed workload one schema is optimal for all workload types under all tested workload mixes, which is the one with the highest degree of normalization. Thus, denormalization as the highly disputed weapon of last resort for performance improvement is not required.

Normalization is only one dimension of logical schema variation as mentioned in Section 3. More redundant data can be observed in real enterprise data models, i.e. materialized aggregates. In future work the impact of removing these and computing them on-the-fly will be analyzed. Further future work includes the consideration of basic service levels for operations, e.g., *99% of all billing insertion OLTP operations should have a response time of less than 5ms*. With a set of such rules and priorities the database design could be adapted automatically.

Acknowledgements. The authors would like to thank Franziska Häger for her contribution on improving the benchmark definitions and her support in running the database tests.

References

1. Abolhassani, M.: Business Objects and Enterprise Applications. In: Managing Information Technology in a Global Environment, IRMA 2001, pp. 240–242. Idea Group Publishing, Hershey (2001)
2. Bock, D.B., Schrage, J.F.: Denormalization Guidelines for Base and Transaction Tables. ACM SIGCSE Bulletin 34(4), 129–133 (2002)
3. Bog, A., Plattner, H., Zeier, A.: A mixed transaction processing and operational reporting benchmark. Information Systems Frontiers 13, 321–335 (2010), http://dx.doi.org/10.1007/s10796-010-9283-8
4. Bog, A., Sachs, K., Zeier, A.: Benchmarking database design for mixed oltp and olap workloads. In: Proceeding of the Second Joint WOSP/SIPEW International Conference on Performance Engineering, ICPE 2011, pp. 417–418. ACM, New York (2011)
5. Chaudhuri, S., Narasayya, V.R.: An efficient cost-driven index selection tool for microsoft sql server. In: Proceedings of the 23rd International Conference on Very Large Data Bases, VLDB 1997, pp. 146–155. Morgan Kaufmann Publishers Inc., San Francisco (1997)
6. Codd, E.F.: Normalized data base structure: a brief tutorial. In: Proceedings of the 1971 ACM SIGFIDET (now SIGMOD) Workshop on Data Description, Access and Control, SIGFIDET 1971, pp. 1–17. ACM, New York (1971)
7. Date, C.J.: Database in Depth: Relational Theory for Practitioners. O'Reilly (2005)
8. Dittrich, J., Jindal, A.: Towards a One Size Fits All Database Architecture. In: Outrageous Ideas and Vision Track, 5th Biennial Conference on Innovative Data Systems Research, CIDR 2011, January 9-12 (2011)
9. French, C.D.: "One size fits all" database architectures do not work for DSS. In: SIGMOD 1995: Proceedings of the 1995 ACM SIGMOD International Conference on Management of Data, pp. 449–450. ACM, New York (1995)
10. French, C.D.: Teaching an OLTP Database Kernel Advanced Data Warehousing Techniques. In: ICDE 1997: Proceedings of the 13th International Conference on Data Engineering, pp. 194–198. IEEE Computer Society Press, Washington, DC (1997)
11. Funke, F., Kemper, A., Neumann, T.: Benchmarking hybrid oltp&olap database systems. In: Härder, T., Lehner, W., Mitschang, B., Schöning, H., Schwarz, H. (eds.) 14. GI-Fachtagung Datenbanksysteme für Business, Technologie und Web (BTW). LNI, vol. 180, pp. 390–409. GI (2011)
12. Grund, M., Krüger, J., Plattner, H., Zeier, A., Cudre-Mauroux, P., Madden, S.: Hyrise: a main memory hybrid storage engine. Proceedings of the VLDB Endowment 4(2), 105–116 (2010)
13. Haderle, D.J.: Database Role in Information Systems: The Evolution of Database Technology and its Impact on Enterprise Information Systems. In: Blaser, A. (ed.) Database Systems of the 90s. LNCS, vol. 466, pp. 1–14. Springer, Heidelberg (1990)
14. Imhoff, C.: A New Class of Operational Data Store. Intelligent Solutions. Information Management Magazine (July 2000)
15. Inmon, W.H.: The Operational Data Store. In: InfoDB, pp. 21–24 (February 1995)
16. Inmon, W.H.: The Operational Data Store. Designing the Operational Data Store. Information Management Magazine (July 1998)
17. Inmon, W.H.: ODS Types. Information Management: Charting the Course. Information Management Magazine (January 2000)

18. Kemper, A., Neumann, T.: HyPer: A hybrid OLTP&OLAP main memory database system based on virtual memory snapshots. In: Abiteboul, S., Böhm, K., Koch, C., Tan, K.-L. (eds.) IEEE 27th International Conference on Data Engineering, ICDE, Hannover, pp. 195–206. IEEE Computer Society (April 2011)
19. Kent, W.: A simple guide to five normal forms in relational database theory. Communications of the ACM 26(2), 120–125 (1983)
20. Kimball, R., Ross, M.: The Data Warehouse Toolkit: The Complete Guide to Dimensional Modeling. Wiley (2002)
21. Krueger, J., Tinnefeld, C., Grund, M., Zeier, A., Plattner, H.: A Case for Online Mixed Workload Processing. In: 3rd International Workshop on Testing Database System (2010)
22. Lightstone, S.S., Teorey, T.J., Nadeau, T.: Physical Database Design: The Database Professional's Guide to Exploiting Indexes, Views, Storage, and more. Morgan Kaufmann Publishers (2007)
23. Martyn, T.: Reconsidering Multi-Dimensional schemas. ACM SIGMOD Record 33(1), 83–88 (2004)
24. Moore, G.E.: Cramming More Components onto Integrated Circuits. Electronics 38(8), 114–117 (1965)
25. Mullins, G.: Database Administration: The Complete Guide to Practices and Procedures. Addison-Wesley (2002)
26. Nambiar, R., Poess, M.: Transaction Performance vs. Moore's Law: A Trend Analysis. In: Nambiar, R., Poess, M. (eds.) TPCTC 2010. LNCS, vol. 6417, pp. 110–120. Springer, Heidelberg (2011)
27. Papadomanolakis, E., Ailamaki, A.: Autopart: Automating schema design for large scientific databases using data partitioning. In: Proceedings of the 16th International Conference on Scientific and Statistical Database Management, pp. 383–392. IEEE Computer Society (2004)
28. Plattner, H.: A common database approach for oltp and olap using an in-memory column database. In: Proceedings of the 35th SIGMOD International Conference on Management of Data, SIGMOD 2009, pp. 1–2. ACM, New York (2009)
29. Röhm, U.: OLAP with a Database Cluster. In: Database Technologies: Concepts, Methodologies, Tools, and Applications, pp. 829–846. IGI Global, Hershey (2009)
30. TPC. TPC-W, Version 1.8. Technical report, Transaction Processing Performance Council (Febuary 2002)
31. TPC. TPC Benchmark C, Standard Specification, Revision 5.9. Technical report, Transaction Processing Performance Council (June 2007)
32. TPC. TPC Benchmark H (Decision Support), Standard Specification, Revision 2.7.0. Technical report, Transaction Processing Performance Council (February 2008)
33. Zilio, D.C., Rao, J., Lightstone, S., Lohman, G., Storm, A., Garcia-Arellano, C., Fadden, S.: Db2 design advisor: integrated automatic physical database design. In: Proceedings of the 30th International Conference on Very Large Data Bases, VLDB 2004, vol. 30, pp. 1087–1097. VLDB Endowment (2004)

Measuring Performance of Complex Event Processing Systems

Torsten Grabs and Ming Lu

Microsoft StreamInsight, Microsoft Corp., One Microsoft Way, Redmond, WA 98052
{Torsteng,milu}@microsoft.com

Abstract. Complex Event Processing (CEP) or stream data processing are becoming increasingly popular as the platform underlying event-driven solutions and applications in industries such as financial services, oil & gas, smart grids, health care, and IT monitoring. Satisfactory performance is crucial for any solution across these industries. Typically, performance of CEP engines is measured as (1) *data rate*, i.e., number of input events processed per second, and (2) *latency*, which denotes the time it takes for the result (output events) to emerge from the system after the business event (input event) happened. While data rates are typically easy to measure by capturing the numbers of input events over time, latency is less well defined. As it turns out, a definition becomes particularly challenging in the presence of data arriving out of order. That means that the order in which events arrive at the system is different from the order of their timestamps. Many important distributed scenarios need to deal with out-of-order arrival because communication delays easily introduce disorder.

With out-of-order arrival, a CEP system cannot produce final answers as events arrive. Instead, time first needs to progress enough in the overall system before correct results can be produced. This introduces additional latency beyond the time it takes the system to perform the processing of the events. We denote the former as *information latency* and the latter as *system latency*. This paper discusses both types of latency in detail and defines them formally without depending on particular semantics of the CEP query plans. In addition, the paper suggests incorporating these definitions as metrics into the benchmarks that are being used to assess and compare CEP systems.

Keywords: Complex Event Processing, CEP, Performance Evaluation, Benchmark Definition, Data Rate, Latency, System Latency, Information Latency.

1 Introduction

Many application scenarios today rely on complex event processing (CEP) for event-driven near real-time analytics of data that are typically digitally born. Such application scenarios include web click analysis for more targeted online advertisement delivery [1], smart grid monitoring to balance power grids and avoid power outages [2, 3], or monitoring of financial markets in near real-time for trading opportunities and regulatory compliance.

R. Nambiar and M. Poess (Eds.): TPCTC 2011, LNCS 7144, pp. 83–96, 2012.
© Springer-Verlag Berlin Heidelberg 2012

CEP Systems. Complex event processing systems typically receive continuous input in the form of events from underlying data sources. The processing of the input is performed by so-called standing queries that continuously and incrementally produce output as new input events arrive.

CEP system vendors and practitioners currently face the challenge how to validate that their CEP systems satisfy the performance requirements of the application. Besides the input *data rate* that captures system throughput in terms of input events processed per second, latency is a key performance metric for any near real-time system. *Latency* describes the time it takes for results to emerge after their corresponding input events have arrived at the system. Depending on the application scenario, users care about worst case latency, average latency or different quantiles of latency.

Contributions. This paper takes a fresh look at latency and the different components that contribute to latency in CEP systems. An important distinction here is between system latency and information latency. *System latency* is well understood and it is easy to explain as the delays that are introduced by the processing of the events, i.e., the time it takes a CEP system to do its work. *Information latency* in turn is a component of latency that has received little attention so far. Information latency is caused by delays that the CEP system spends waiting for additional input. An important example is out of order arrival of events where a CEP system may need to wait for late coming input events before it can proceed with its processing and produce a final result set [9, 19]. In this paper, we discuss definitions of information latency and introduce ways how to measure and compare information latency between different CEP systems. We propose to include information latency comparisons into the existing benchmark metrics used to compare CEP system performance.

2 Related Work

Efficient processing of events has been an important topic for research in data processing and middleware systems. Database research for instance has developed benchmarks such as BEAST (BEnchmark for Active database SysTems) to assess and compare performance of active database systems [24]. A popular benchmark for message-oriented middleware is SPECjms2007 defined by the Standard Performance Evaluation Corporation (SPEC) [25]. Workload parameters such as message or event rate in these benchmarks are closely related to data rate with CEP systems.

Current benchmarking efforts for CEP, however, rely on both data rate and latency as performance metrics. Most benchmark workloads so far have focused on specific industries. For instance, the set of benchmarks developed by the Securities Technology Analysis Center (STAC) provides a compelling set of performance metrics and workloads for use cases in financial services [4]. The linear road benchmark in turn is a popular workload focused on the traffic and transportation verticals [17]. Prior work in research on data stream processing in turn has focused on defining key performance metrics, making them measurable with low overhead and providing a feedback loop to the CEP system to continuously adapt and improve performance [5, 6, 7, 8, 18].

The challenges arising from out-of-order arrival of messages have been researched in earlier work on time management in distributed simulation systems [21]. Similar to CEP systems such as [9, 14, 19], optimistic time management in distributed simulation aims to proceed with the simulation without blocking. Although this may lead to incorrect intermediate results, it reduces latency since the computation does not stall waiting for additional input. Approaches such as Time Warp eventually produce the correct result by rolling back incorrect intermediate results and replacing them with the correct ones [22].

3   Complex Event Processing Systems

This section provides a brief overview of CEP systems and some of their underlying concepts.

CEP systems process events. Processing events means consuming and producing events from the input and on the output of the system, respectively. An *event* is typically characterized by a time stamp and a payload. The event thus indicates that the payload has been observed at the point in time denoted in the time stamp. Note that this separates *application time* – the time that the events carry – from *system time* – the time at which events arrive at the CEP system [9, 14]. Some systems also allow for events with a start and an end time stamp besides the payload, e.g. [9]. In this case, the time span between the start and end time stamp indicates the duration during which the corresponding payload is valid.

When new events become available, CEP systems then apply *processing logic* to the new input events as described by the CEP application. Depending on the underlying CEP system, application developers can implement the processing with rules, e.g. [10], pattern languages or declarative relationally-influenced operations [9, 11, 12, 20]. An important ingredient across different CEP systems is their ability to express *temporal processing* that relates to the time stamps attached to the events. Time windows for example accumulate events over time and then perform an operation such as an aggregate over event payloads within each window incarnation.

Events arrive at a CEP system as streams. A *stream* denotes a potentially infinite sequence of events. A stream is characterized by the shapes of events that it produces, the timestamps and payloads that the events carry and the order in which the events arrive from the stream at the CEP system. A particularly challenging situation for CEP systems is what we call *out-of-order arrival* [19]. With out-of-order arrival, the sequence in which events arrive is different from the order of their time stamps.

Out-of-order arrival makes it difficult to produce final results as the CEP system has to ensure that no more events will arrive subsequently that impact a result that the CEP system is about to output. CEP systems therefore introduce the concept of *advancement of time, heartbeat* or *punctuation* which indicate that time has progressed to a certain point and no more events before that point will arrive [9, 14, 19]. CEP systems with out-of-order arrival need to advance time regularly to finalize results.

4 Performance Requirements

Many real-world scenarios for event processing are characterized by multiple assets that are instrumented to produce event data which in turn is sent to a CEP system for analysis. Examples for assets are pieces of equipment such as a transformer in an electric power grid, users browsing the web generating click-stream data, or stocks traded at a stock exchange from which we receive a ticker feed. We denote assets that produce event data as *data sources*. The data source emits events as a potentially infinite sequence over time.

With regard to its data sources, various parameters characterize a CEP deployment:

- **Number of data sources:** How many data sources are connected?
- **Event rate per data source:** How many events does a data source generate?
- **Event size:** How large are the events?

The combination of these parameters defines the aggregate input load or input *data rate* of the CEP system. Depending on the scenario, the aggregate input load may fluctuate over time. Solutions based on CEP systems need to be able to scale to the required input loads. This indicates one dimension of performance analysis for CEP systems that we will discuss in more detail below when introducing performance metrics.

While CEP-based solutions need to be able to process the input from the data sources, they also need to deliver results to the users in a timely fashion. This requirement is typically measured by the time span between an input event arriving at the CEP system and its corresponding result events emerging in the output. This time span is denoted as *latency*. Real-world scenarios employ various techniques to keep latency small:

- **Reduce delays:** Delays can occur in many forms. Communication delays for instance may delay events on their way from the data sources to the CEP system. This can introduce significant delays for overall results of the system. Think of an aggregate computed across all assets monitored by the CEP system. The finalized result for such an aggregate requires input from all data sources and has to wait until the input events from all sources have arrived at the CEP system.
  Further delays can occur in the CEP system when processing the incoming events. A prominent source of such delays is when there are not enough resources (e.g. CPU, memory) available and incoming events have to wait until resources free up.
- **Speculation:** Besides producing finalized results as discussed above, some CEP systems also produce intermediate ("speculative") results that are not yet final but that may already be acted upon by the user [9]. Since the results are speculative the CEP system may need to revise them as additional input data is received.

Depending on the scenario and the vertical, requirements for data rates and latency vary:

- **Manufacturing:** Monitoring a complex production process with different pieces of equipment typically requires processing more than 10,000 input events per second.

- **Oil and gas:** In proof of concepts with our oil & gas customers, we had to demonstrate that the system can handle more than 100,000 input events per second [23].
- **Power utilities:** In smart grid scenarios, households install smart meters that produce meter readings with power consumption information every couple of seconds. For large power utilities with millions of households, the aggregate data rate on the input to the CEP system can easily reach 100,000 events per second. We expect this number to grow as power utilities want to react more quickly to changes in demand and grid stability.

  Besides data rates, smart grid scenarios also have strict latency requirements. Phasor measurement use cases for instance target end-to-end delays to be smaller than a few seconds. During that time, the system has to aggregate and analyze events from geographically distributed phasor management units where each unit produces an event up to 60 times a second [2].
- **Finance:** Finance scenarios present challenging requirement for both data rate and latency for CEP systems. For instance, subscribing to the full OPRA feed from the Options Price Reporting Authority generated about a million messages per second in 2008 and the data rate of the OPRA feed has been increasing since [13]. Trading scenarios usually require latency to be less than a millisecond. For high frequency trading, latency requirements are in the tens of microseconds and tend to become increasingly stricter as hardware and software advance.
- **IT monitoring:** Monitoring computer systems can also lead to challenging event rates depending on the level of instrumentation of the systems. With Event Tracing for Windows (ETW), event categories such as context switches on the processor can reach above 100k events per second on each computer with ETW turned on.

Data rates and event sizes are easy to measure and compare. We will revisit those in Section 6 when defining benchmarking metrics, and now focus on latency in the following section.

5   Latency

In Section 4, we identified low latency as a key requirement for CEP systems. Latency was characterized as the delay that events experience on their way from the data source to the consumer of the results of the CEP system. To design performance metrics and benchmarks for CEP systems, it helps to understand the different ways in which CEP systems can introduce additional and sometimes even unnecessary delays. Latency in CEP systems consists of two components: (1) system latency, and (2) information latency. The following paragraphs discuss both kinds of latency in more detail.

5.1   System Latency

One obvious cause for delays is the processing that is required to produce results from the CEP system. For instance, it takes CPU resources (and time) to perform an aggregation over thousands of input events. We denote the delays that are caused by the activity in the CEP system to process events as *system latency*.

5.2   Information Latency

Different kinds of delays though are caused by the CEP system waiting for input. Think for instance of an aggregation that computes average temperature across several temperature sensors over a certain period of time. In order to compute the aggregate, the CEP system needs to receive the input events from all the participating sensors. In addition, it also needs to receive the information that no more sensor readings are expected from any of the participating sensors before the CEP system can produce a final result of the aggregate. In more general terms, these delays are characterized by the CEP system waiting for additional data before proceeding. As in the example with the temperature sensors, the additional data can be events or information about the advancement of time from the data sources. We call the delays caused by waiting as *information latency*.

The example above illustrates information latency that is introduced between the data sources and the CEP system. However, these delays can also be introduced between other components of the CEP solution. If the CEP system is following the popular data flow engine architecture, any component within the CEP system can cause information latency based on its semantics and implementation. While the first kind of information latency is caused by components external to the CEP system, we particularly want to understand, measure and improve the second kind where the latency is introduced by the CEP system.

Hopping Window Example. Consider a CEP query with a hopping window that accumulates incoming events in windows and outputs aggregates over the event payloads in the window as time progresses. Events arrive over time and can arrive out of order as **Fig. 1** shows.

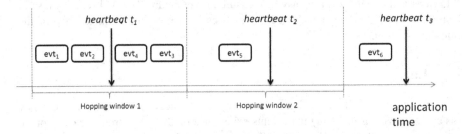

Fig. 1. Hopping Window Query

In the figure, the numbers in the subscript of the events indicate arrival order while their position over the time axis denotes their application time stamp, i.e., the time stamps that the events carry. As the figure shows, event 4 arrives out of order: event 3 with a higher time stamp has been received before event 4. To accommodate late events (i.e. out of order arrival), data sources communicate the advancement of time with the heartbeats shown in the figure. Heartbeat t_1 in the figure, for instance, advances time to t_1, indicating all events prior to t_1 have arrived. With heartbeats trailing the arrival of events, this provides slack to allow for late comers. In the figure, for ease of presentation, a heartbeat collectively advances application time for all data sources. Having received a heartbeat for time t, the CEP system can now finalize all output up to t since it is guaranteed that no events with time stamps before t can arrive and no revisions to the results are needed for everything that ends before t. One would therefore expect that a CEP system running a hopping query like the one in the figure would produce the output for *Hopping window 1* once it has received the heartbeat for t_2. Earlier versions of Microsoft StreamInsight however had to delay the result for *a* hopping window until a heartbeat beyond the following window incarnation had been received. For instance, the results for *Hopping window 1* in the figure was delayed until a heartbeat like the one at t_3 after *Hopping window 2* had been received. The reasons for this behavior were rooted in the algebraic underpinnings of StreamInsight. In this case, the result was held back to allow for expansions of the window result events although expansions could not possible occur with that query shape. While a detailed discussion of the algebraic causes of the behavior is beyond the scope of this current paper, they significantly increased information latency for this type of CEP queries and put customers at a disadvantage when they wanted to react to the query result as soon as possible.

Event Horizons.
In the above example, a combination of issues led to an unnecessary increase in information latency that delayed results longer than justified by the shape of the query and the nature of the input events. Information latency issues caused by the implementation of a CEP system are difficult to reason about because they require a deep understanding of the system implementation and the semantics of the query given a particular input. In order to make information latency more tractable, consider **Fig. 2** with a pivoted representation of the event input from **Fig. 1**.

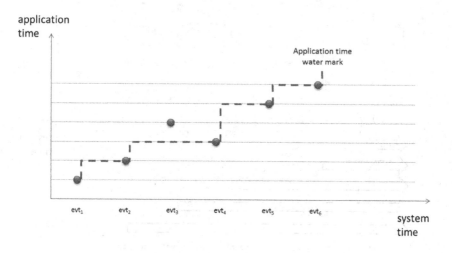

Fig. 2. Event Horizon: Progression of application time water mark for the events in **Fig. 1**

The figure shows events in their arrival order over the system time axis. This defines the *event history* as the sequence in which events arrive over system time. The application time axis in turn plots the application time of the events (or sync time for systems with bi-temporal semantics or speculation [9, 14]).

The figure now shows a water mark as the dashed line that follows the events and their timestamps. More formally, at any given point in the event history, the water mark at that point is the maximum application time that is smaller or equal to any application time of events that arrive later in the event history. Intuitively, the water mark indicates the *event horizon* or the most aggressive way that application time can advance for a CEP system provided full knowledge about the event history, including all future events. In other words, any input event arriving at system time *st* has an application time stamp *t* on or above the water mark at *st*. Note that event *evt₃* lies above the water mark line since it arrived out of order and the event horizon still has to accommodate event *evt₄* with a smaller time stamp.

Minimizing Information Latency.

Having defined the event horizon with the application time water mark now allows us to reason about information latency and to compare results with regard to information latency. Recall that the event horizon indicates the most aggressive way how application time can advance given complete knowledge of the full event history, i.e., full knowledge of all past and future events and their time stamps.

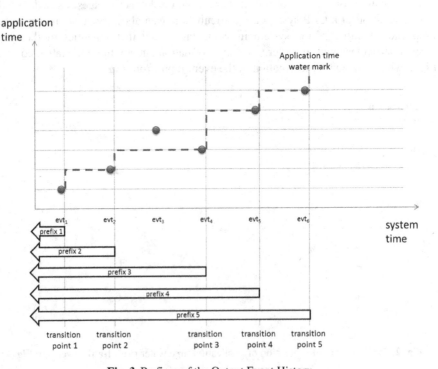

Fig. 3. Prefixes of the Output Event History

To compare information latency between systems, the transition points in the event horizon are particularly interesting. The transition points are the points where the water mark line in **Fig. 2** moves up. A CEP system that has complete knowledge about how time at the data sources will advance can use these transition points to produce output. As transition points occur along the sequence of input events, this defines a sequence of prefixes of the result history. More formally, the prefix of the result history or *result history prefix* for a given transition point *tp* in the input history is the set of result (or output) events produced by a CEP system that has only been provided with input events up to and including the transition point in the input.

Fig. 3 illustrates the sequence of transitions points and their corresponding result history prefixes for the input event history in **Fig. 2**. Note how transition points coincide with the places in the physical input sequence where the event horizon edges up. As the figure shows, prefixes are overlapping such that a given prefix includes the results of all previous prefixes, i.e., its prefixes "to the left" in the figure.

We are now ready to define how to compare and minimize information latency. Given the complete event input history, the definition relies on (1) the full result set of output events over the input history and on (2) the sequence of result history prefixes for all the transition points in the input history. A CEP system exhibits *minimum information latency* if at each transition point its result history prefix for the transition point is maximal with regard to the full result history.

Comparing Information Latency.
Following from this definition, a theoretical lower bound on information latency is a system that reliably predicts all input events and can provide the full result at the first transition point in the event history without consuming the full input. Practical CEP system implementations however produce results over time as events arrive. They do not know about future events. Therefore, we can compare their information latency properties by comparing their result history prefixes.

Intuitively, a CEP system has lower (better) information latency if the system produces larger prefixes early on in the output sequence. We can formalize this with the following definition.

Information Latency Comparison: Given a CEP query Q and two CEP systems S1 and S2 with identical result event histories for Q. System S1 has lower (better) information latency if none of S1's prefixes is smaller than the corresponding prefix from S2 and at least one of S1's prefixes is larger than the corresponding prefix in S2's result history.

Fig. 4 illustrates comparing of information latencies for our running example with the hopping window query in **Fig. 1**. As the figure shows, we are comparing CEP System 1 against CEP System 2. With CEP System 1, *prefix 3* already produces the result for *Hopping window 1* while it takes until *prefix 5* for CEP System 2 to produce the result for the same hopping window. Hence, with CEP System 2, users have to wait longer to see results for *Hopping window 1*.

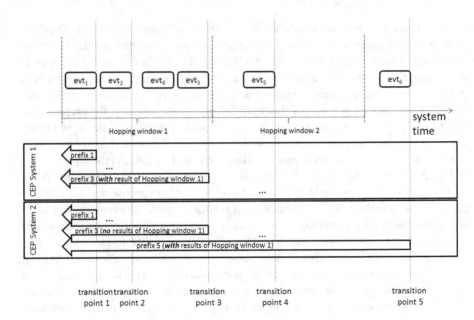

Fig. 4. Comparing information latency between CEP systems

The following sections will use this observation to define metrics for benchmarking CEP systems based on their information latency.

6   Metrics for CEP System Benchmarking

CEP solutions across different verticals do not necessarily put the same emphasis on all dimensions of CEP performance. CEP in financial services scenarios such as high frequency trading for instance favor low latency. End-of-day billing for smart grids in turn has stricter demands on throughput. Vendors with platform CEP offerings that target different industries therefore have to cater to the different demands in a single implementation while vendors with specific CEP solutions can optimize for the demands of their solution and vertical.

The following definitions aim to provide metrics that allow both assessing CEP systems along a single dimension and combinations of the metrics to asses overall performance of CEP systems.

6.1   Single Dimension Metrics

Input Data Rate. Data rate is expressed by the number of aggregate input events arriving at the CEP system per second. With varying data rates on the input, both average data rate and maximum data rate are important metrics that are also easy to capture. Note that the input data rate also constitutes a compelling dimension to define different scale factors for CEP benchmarks.

Input Event Size. Event sizes are described in terms of bytes per event. With varying event sizes both average event size and maximum event size are meaningful metrics and easy to measure.

System Latency. As discussed in [5], system latency can easily be measured by adding stimulus time, i.e., wall clock event arrival time, as an additional payload field to incoming events. Stimulus times are updated while events flow through the processing in the CEP system [5]: the new stimulus time of an event produced by an operation in the system is the maximum time stamp across all source events in its lineage [15]. Latency for a given event is the difference between its stimulus time and current wall clock time. Note, however, that this latency only includes system latency. In particular for system latency, quantiles are also meaningful. Ideally, a scatter plot of events output and corresponding latency is provided as part of the disclosure report.

Fig. 5 illustrates a scatter plot of event latencies taken from performance tests during the development of Microsoft StreamInsight. The figure shows that sometimes it is beneficial to track latencies for individual events. In this case, most events took between 100 and 200 microseconds to process. Some events however had surprisingly large latencies. As the figure shows, a few events took about one millisecond to process while some events took even a few hundred milliseconds. For a financial services scenario, these latencies could have exposed a trading strategy to significant risk for a long time in the market. Scatter plots help to identify outliers and understand the root causes for them and improve systems accordingly.

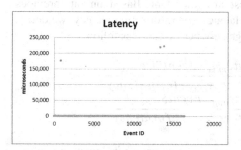 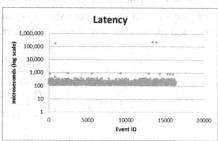

Fig. 5. Scatter plots of latency: (a) linear scale, (b) log scale

Information Latency. As discussed in Section 5, information latency can be measured by how much a given result deviates from the theoretical optimum where all results are produced at the first transition point. Let j be the number of transition points in a given input event history with a total of n result events in the output history. With the theoretical optimum, each prefix has exactly n events since the first prefix already outputs the full result.

Now let k_i denote the size of the result history prefix produced by the system under test for transition point i. We then define information latency as the following ratio between the optimal result prefixes and the prefixes from the system under test:

$$\text{Information Latency} := 1 - \prod_{i=1}^{j} \frac{k_i + 1}{n + 1} = 1 - \frac{1}{(n+1)^j} \cdot \prod_{i=1}^{j} (k_i + 1)$$

Since $k_i \leq n$ for all i, information latency is between 0 and 1. The optimal case is an information latency of 0 where all k_i equal n.

To benchmark systems using information latency, we need a practical way to compute result history prefixes. Assuming that we record the input event history, this can be done by the following simple iterative process over the input history prefixes defined by the transition points of the history:

For all transition points tp_i in the input event history with i ranging from 1 to j, perform the following steps:

- Replay the event input from the beginning of the input event history up to tp_i.
- Advance application time on the input up to the event horizon defined by tp_i.
- Wait for the CEP system to drain all result events.
- The set of result events collected for tp_i constitutes the prefix for tp_i.

6.2 Combined Metrics

While individual results for the performance dimensions discussed in the previous section are of interest, benchmarks typically aggregate those into a single metric that can then be related to price. For CEP systems, worst case and average performance over a given run for a system under test are important. Based on our previous definitions of data rate, event size, system latency and information latency, we define combined metrics for worst case and average case performance as follows:

$$Perf_{worst} := \frac{DataRate_{max} \cdot EventSize_{max}}{SystemLatency_{max} \cdot InfoLatency}$$
$$Perf_{avg} := \frac{DataRate_{avg} \cdot EventSize_{avg}}{SystemLatency_{avg} \cdot InfoLatency}$$

Note how improvements to information latency, i.e., decreasing information latency, in the definitions above help improve overall system performance. Besides the metrics for worst case and average case performance shown here, similar metrics for different quantiles can be defined along the same lines.

6.3 Pricing

More or better hardware will typically lead to better performance regarding both data rates and latency. For instance, faster and more processor cores will lead to lower system latency. More memory in turn will allow the system to accommodate larger event sizes. However, hardware improvements will obviously also make the system more expensive. As it is common practice with the benchmarks of the TPC, any of the metrics discussed above can be weighed by the price of the system under test to define a performance per price metric as for instance in the TPC-H benchmark [16].

7   Conclusions and Outlook

CEP performance so far focused on data rates and system latency. Information latency in turn has received much less attention. For CEP systems that allow for out-of-order arrival of events, however, information latency constitutes a critical component of overall system performance. As we have shown in this paper, sub-optimal performance due to unnecessary information latency can lead to significant delays of output which causes customer frustration as end users unnecessarily have to wait for their results.

To address these shortcomings, this paper presented a framework that allows CEP system vendors to assess system performance with regard to data rate and latency – the key performance metrics for CEP systems. As opposed to previous approaches, our definition of latency includes both system and information latency into the overall performance assessment. A key contribution from this paper is a practical framework that allows CEP vendors to assess and compare their products based on information latency. The framework proposed in this paper builds on the experiences of the StreamInsight product group to improve information latency for Microsoft StreamInsight.

While performance evaluation and benchmarking of CEP systems are not new, we are not aware of any other efforts to include information latency into these evaluations. However, information latency is a key component of the user experience for a CEP system which the industry needs to incorporate into the performance tuning and benchmarking practice for complex event processing. We look forward to working with other CEP vendors to augment existing and new benchmarks by including information latency metrics.

Acknowledgments. We are much indebted to the StreamInsight team at Microsoft for fruitful discussions of CEP performance and in particular information latency. Special thanks to Anton Kirilov for helpful comments on earlier versions of this paper.

References

1. Ali, M.H., et al.: Microsoft CEP Server and Online Behavioral Targeting. PVLDB 2(2), 1558–1561 (2009)
2. Consortium for Electric Reliability Technology Solutions: Phasor Technology and Real-Time Dynamics Monitoring System,
   http://www.phasor-rtdms.com/downloads/guides/RTDMSFAQ.pdf
3. Microsoft Corp.: Smart Energy Reference Architecture,
   http://www.microsoft.com/enterprise/industry/power-utilities/solutions/smart-energy-reference-architecture.aspx
4. Securities Technology Analysis Center, http://www.stacresearch.com/

5. Chandramouli, B., Goldstein, J., Barga, R.S., Riedewald, M., Santos, I.: Accurate latency estimation in a distributed event processing system. In: ICDE 2011, pp. 255–266 (2011)
6. Babcock, B., Babu, S., Datar, M., Motwani, R.: Chain: Operator Scheduling for Memory Minimization in Data Stream Systems. In: SIGMOD Conference 2003, pp. 253–264 (2003)
7. Cammert, M., Krämer, J., Seeger, B., Vaupel, S.: A Cost-Based Approach to Adaptive Resource Management in Data Stream Systems. IEEE Trans. Knowl. Data Eng. 20(2), 230–245 (2008)
8. Tatbul, N., Çetintemel, U., Zdonik, S.B., Cherniack, M., Stonebraker, M.: Load Shedding in a Data Stream Manager. In: VLDB 2003, pp. 309–320 (2003)
9. Barga, R.S., Goldstein, J., Ali, M.H., Hong, M.: Consistent Streaming Through Time: A Vision for Event Stream Processing. In: CIDR 2007, pp. 363–374 (2007)
10. Progress Software: Apama,
    http://web.progress.com/en/apama/index.html
11. StreamBase, http://streambase.com/
12. SQLStream, http://sqlstream.com/
13. Options Price Reporting Authority, http://www.opradata.com/, also see,
    http://en.wikipedia.org/wiki/
    Options_Price_Reporting_Authority
14. Microsoft Corp.: Microsoft CEP Overview,
    http://download.microsoft.com/download/F/D/5/FD5E855C-D895-
    45A8-9F3E-110AFADBE51A/Microsoft%20CEP%20Overview.docx
15. Cui, Y., Widom, J., Wiener, J.L.: Tracing the lineage of view data in a warehousing environment. ACM Trans. Database Syst. 25(2), 179–227 (2000)
16. Transaction Processing Performance Council: TPC-H,
    http://www.tpc.org/tpch/default.asp
17. Arasu, A., et al.: Linear Road: A Stream Data Management Benchmark. In: VLDB 2004, pp. 480–491 (2004)
18. Oracle Corp.: Oracle Complex Event Processing Performance,
    http://www.oracle.com/technetwork/middleware/complex-event-
    processing/overview/cepperformancewhitepaper-128060.pdf
19. Li, J., Tufte, K., Shkapenyuk, V., Papadimos, V., Johnson, T., Maier, D.: Out-of-order processing: a new architecture for high-performance stream systems. PVLDB 1(1), 274–288 (2008)
20. Sybase Inc.: Sybase Aleri Streaming Platform,
    http://www.sybase.com/products/financialservicessolutions/
    aleristreamingplatform
21. Fujimoto, R.M.: Distributed Simulation Systems. In: 35th Winter Simulation Conference 2003, 124–134 (2003)
22. Jefferson, D.R.: Virtual Time. ACM Trans. Program. Lang. Syst. 7(3), 404–425 (1985)
23. Grabs, T., Bauhaus, C.: Building Operational Intelligence Solutions with Microsoft SQL Server and StreamInsight. Microsoft TechEd Europe 2010,
    http://channel9.msdn.com/Events/TechEd/
    Europe/2010/DAT301-LNC
24. Geppert, A., Berndtsson, M., Lieuwen, D.F., Roncancio, C.: Performance Evaluation of Object-Oriented Active Database Systems Using the BEAST Benchmark. TAPOS 4(3), 135–149 (1998)
25. Sachs, K., Kounev, S., Bacon, J., Buchmann, A.: Performance evaluation of message-oriented middleware using the SPEC jms 2007 benchmark. Performance Evaluation 66(8) (2009)

Benchmarking with Your Head in the Cloud

Karl Huppler

IBM MS XQK, 3605 Highway 52 North
Rochester, MN 55901 USA
huppler@us.ibm.com

Abstract. Recent advances in Cloud Computing present challenges to those who create and manage performance benchmarks. A performance benchmark tends to rely on physical consistency – a known hardware configuration, a known software configuration and consistent measurements from run to run. These aspects are not typically present in Cloud Computing. Other aspects change, too. For the consumer, the computation of Total Cost of Ownership shifts to a computation of ongoing expense. Concepts of service and reliability also change from the end-user perspective.

For an organization like the Transaction Processing Performance Council, the expansion of clouds into the commercial, run-your-business space presents new challenges that must be addressed if viable benchmarks are to be created in this important sector of the computing industry. This paper explores these challenges and proposes methods for addressing them.

Keywords: Cloud Computing, Price/Performance, TCO, Total Cost of Ownership, Benchmark, TPC.

1   Introduction

Before one creates a benchmark to measure performance of a cloud, it might be reasonable to ask the question "Just what is cloud computing?" The first answer might be "Cloud computing is the use of shared resources that are physically outside of your control to accomplish your work. You are allocated a specific amount of resource from the larger pool of resources available and your work is tracked to see how much resource you actually use."

This answer appears to be very reasonable, until the questioner responds,

- "How is that different from when, in 1974 I submitted my deck of cards to the operations desk for the University of Wisconsin Univac 1108, knowing that I had to complete my assignments within a specific allocation of compute time?"
- Or perhaps the reply would be "How does that differ from the Service Bureau I worked for in the early 80's, where the business rented a mainframe and customers would contract for time to run their weekly inventory control jobs?"

R. Nambiar and M. Poess (Eds.): TPCTC 2011, LNCS 7144, pp. 97–110, 2012.
© Springer-Verlag Berlin Heidelberg 2012

- Or perhaps the reply question would be "How does that differ from the PROFS application that I ran in the late '80s from my 3270 display running a VM on the System390, appearing as if I had a private computer but being fully aware that I was sharing resources with hundreds of others running similar applications?"
- Or perhaps, "How does that differ from the concepts of 'The Grid' that I heard about a decade ago, where computing resources would be treated the same way that electrical and telephone technologies are, with users unaware of where their actual compute resources are located, but know that they will be billed on the basis of the amount of resources that they consume?"
- Or the simple question might be "Isn't that the same as what we use the web for?"

To all of these questions, the answer is "All of these concepts are embodied in cloud computing." Cloud computing might be considered to be the natural progression of technology that enables end users or even whole corporations to apply shared resources for dedicated purposes. Perhaps what differentiates cloud computing from prior shared resource solutions is that the progression of technology in hardware, firmware and software enables the shared resources to be distant, reapportioned on the fly and migrated from physical resource to physical resource – in ways that are transparent to the actual user and using methods that are stable enough that the option is viewed as a cost-effective alternative to the use of dedicated resources to accomplish computing tasks.

Full System

For performance benchmarks, the growing importance of cloud computing poses some difficult challenges. Most performance benchmarks focus on determining, for some business model, the capacity of a whole system to accomplish work. In the cloud, what is important is the capability of a fractional subsystem to accomplish work. Traditional performance benchmarks often have a set of functional criteria that must be satisfied to qualify for benchmark publication, including such things as the ACID properties used to define transactional integrity requirements for TPC benchmarks. These qualities are important in cloud environments, but are often defined in different terms. Particular to the TPC, the benchmarks assume the price quoted is for the complete purchase of all hardware and all software licenses, with maintenance payments over some period of time. Although this could apply to private clouds, in public clouds the concept of making an initial capital investment is in direct contrast to the cloud model.

Fractional Subsystem

Of course, for all benchmarks it is important to establish a business model for which the benchmark will be targeted. One could no more say "I'm going to create a benchmark to represent all cloud computing" than "I'm going to create a benchmark to represent all multiprocessor computing". It must be clear that the benchmark is addressing only a specific slice of the overall cloud computing pie, with a clear description of the application or computing model that the benchmark hopes to represent.

This paper will explore

- The selection process for determining the physical and logical environments that can be measured in a cloud-oriented benchmark
- The requirements for selection of a valid business model and how this may differ from a traditional system benchmark
- The performance aspects that are of particular interest to cloud users, in comparison to those of a traditional, dedicated system
- Features of the benchmark definition that will need to change from those currently employed by the TPC, if a TPC benchmark is to represent a cloud environment.

2   Selection of Cloud Subset for a Target Benchmark

Before designing a benchmark for cloud computing, we must recognize that the space that is "cloud" is massive, and that the benchmark cannot be expected to cover the entire space. Furthermore, there are some areas where performance is a critical component of the compute model and others where it is not. Finally, there are some practical limitations to what can and cannot be included in a general purpose benchmark.

Consider, first, the three primary delivery models services provided by various cloud solutions, as defined by NIST and summarized in the reference materials [1 - 3]:

- **Software as a Service (SaaS):** The entire compute stack is embodied within the cloud. What the end-user sees is that they have access to an application, where the only thing they control is the information that is to be processed. This delivery model is frequently used by individuals for personal needs. Many web-based applications such as photo editors, photo sharing systems and social media applications can be thought of as SaaS applications. Web-based tax preparation applications also fit, here. As the industry matures it is clearly capable of satisfying general business requirements, as well. Certainly, the applications used in a SaaS delivery model could be "benchmarked" for specific tasks – to compare one established cloud offering with another. A web search for "cloud" and "benchmark" typically finds single user tests for this purpose. Such performance characteristics could play a big role in the selection of a service to use. However, in a general purpose benchmark, the application is an integral part of the benchmark and its controls. For this reason, we eliminate SaaS for consideration in this paper.

Cloud service layers

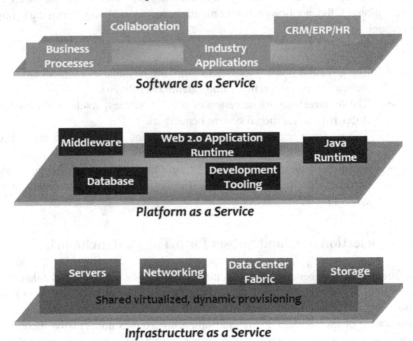

Software as a Service

Platform as a Service

Infrastructure as a Service

- **Platform as a Service (PaaS):** Here, the application to be executed is generally owned and controlled by the consumer of the cloud resources, while the rest of the stack is typically owned and controlled by the cloud service provider. For example, http services, database services and collaborative web application services might be provided by the service supplier – as well as the underlying hardware to support them. The consumer would purchase or author the actual logic that exercises these services – providing a unique web ordering system, or an analysis of consumer habits based on application usage. On line services that provide business support for cataloguing and charging for consumer web sales is a prominent example. Comparing this to a typical TPC benchmark, the benchmark application is under the control of the benchmark sponsor, while the delivery of hardware, operating system, database and middleware functions are under the control of the cloud provider. At first look, this delivery model appears to be closest to today's benchmarks. The "system under test" is comprised of a hardware platform, running a particular OS, using a particular database, and perhaps also using a particular transaction monitor, Java environment, or J2EE provider. The benchmark is the measure of these system components under the stress of the benchmark application.

- **Infrastructure as a Service (IaaS):** For corporate consumers that are first considering migrating to a cloud solution, this may be the natural choice, since they would carry under their own control all of the aspects of the application and the application support software or middleware that it requires. The business model is similar to outsourcing models of the past decade, except that the supplier determines the physical infrastructure in return for guarantees in a service level agreement. The operating system, physical hardware, and the virtualization and provisioning support needed to provide the shared cloud resources are under the control of the cloud provider. Although the vocabulary of the PaaS delivery model may appear to match a public performance benchmark such as the TPC benchmark, the reality of today's public benchmarks is much closer to IaaS. In today's benchmarks, the hardware configuration, the operating system, and the middleware are all tuned explicitly on behalf of the performance of the benchmark application, which is more likely to occur in an IaaS delivery model than a PaaS one, which must support multiple applications simultaneously.

Thus, the target delivery mechanism for a public benchmark for cloud computing would appear to be IaaS, but it is also likely that results from such a benchmark would be used to promote PaaS solutions. In that regard, consideration should be given to defining ways to bring the benchmark definition closer to the PaaS model. Of course, the specific business application must also be taken into account. Some environments are more applicable to a shared resource solution, while others are restricted by regulation or practical reasons [4].

The physical control of the hardware and software components must also be considered: Is the environment Public, Private, or a Hybrid?

- **Public:** The cloud environments that are most highly publicized are those that are offered from both large and moderate sized companies as a service to individuals and other companies. Delivery of consistently strong performance at the contracted level of service is an important aspect of such an offering. Considering its growing popularity, it would be ideal if a public benchmark could be created to measure performance in a public cloud. There are, however, substantial challenges in defining exactly "what" is being benchmarked, since the traditional benchmark is run against a specific configuration of hardware and software. These difficulties should not dissuade the benchmark creators from targeting this environment, but they will mean that the benchmark definition will differ in what is controlled, what is priced and how various functional properties are guaranteed.

- **Private:** A private cloud is more tangible for the "traditional" benchmark developer. The complete physical configuration, the software and middleware, and the associated tuning of these components are all under the control of the owner of the overall system. The challenge, here, is to actually represent cloud computing, instead of a more traditional single application benchmark. In today's public benchmark environment, where test sponsors are typically the vendors who would like the public to consider their overall solution in purchase decisions, the private cloud environment is a reasonable fit.

- **Hybrid:** These environments are becoming more and more common, either because a consumer wants to have complete control of a part of the resources used, such as storage, or because the consumer wants to handle most computing needs privately and contract for public resources to meet high demand. However, the very term "hybrid" connotes uniqueness, making it a difficult environment for a public performance benchmark and a much better candidate for consumer-specific benchmarks to evaluate a particular business need. It is conceivable that a consumer could combine a private-cloud-oriented benchmark with a public-cloud-oriented benchmark to achieve this end, but it is the assertion of the author that hybrid environments should not be the target of public performance benchmarks.

To summarize the above, there is a place for benchmarks that target both public and private cloud solutions, but the goals of the benchmarks and the nature of what is measured and priced will be very different between the two.

The following table summarizes the key points in this section:

	SaaS	PaaS	IaaS
Public	Individual measures possible, not recommended for public benchmark	Excellent target for public benchmark, difficult to define	Reasonable target for public benchmark, but more limited scope than PaaS
Private	Typically not applicable; not recommended for public benchmark	Excellent target for public benchmark, slightly less difficult to define, since there is greater control	Excellent target for public benchmark. Easiest to define. Still some challenges compared to traditional benchmark.
Hybrid	Typically not applicable; not recommended for public benchmark	Not recommended for public benchmark due to uniqueness of each consumer environment	Not recommended for public benchmark due to uniqueness of each consumer environment

3   Business Models and Use Cases for Cloud

The Cloud Computing Use Case Discussion Group [1] has done an excellent job of classifying a variety of use cases and the overall functional requirements associated with them. Each use case is discussed here, with regard to how well it might fit within a public performance benchmark.

3.1   End User to Cloud

This use case is almost always associated with an SaaS delivery model. As mentioned in section 2, this is not thought to be a good model for a general purpose public benchmark, although individual user benchmarks are already available for some applications.

3.2   Enterprise to Cloud to End User

In this scenario, the enterprise likely has an application that is targeted to interact with multiple consumers and enterprise users to generate business for the enterprise. It fits well within either PaaS or IaaS delivery models, and could be a candidate for a public cloud benchmark. It would, however, be difficult to measure, since it would require the simulation of both external and internal users as drivers of the workload. Considering the challenges that would be inherent with the use of a public cloud, this may not be the best candidate as a use case for a general cloud performance benchmark.

3.3   Enterprise to Cloud

Here, the enterprise is essentially outsourcing its internal computing requirements to the cloud. While most likely to fit the IaaS delivery model, this use case could also fit the PaaS model. It has the advantage that it can fit on either a public cloud or a private one. It has the further advantage of being most similar to existing traditional benchmarks. Note, however, that there are many more functional requirements to support this use case in a public cloud than there are for a private cloud, and more for a private cloud than would be required of a single-application server environment. Consequently, while this appears to be a candidate for all of these environments, care should be taken to make sure that results that cross these environments cannot be compared.

3.4   Enterprise to Cloud to Enterprise

Supply chain applications are examples of this use case. Often, these applications are fully automated, so they can be a reasonable use case for a benchmark that measures performance in a public cloud.

3.5   Private Cloud

As discussed above, this can be viewed as a subset of the Enterprise to Cloud use case. There are fewer functional requirements required to maintain user security and business integrity, since many of these controls are inherent within the confines of the enterprise. As such benchmarks in a private cloud should not be compared with public cloud environments. It would not be a fair representation to compare the two different sets of functional requirements, nor would it be representative to require the private cloud to rise to the requirements of the public one.

3.6   Hybrid Cloud

This use case is interesting in the number of functional requirements needed to maintain integrity when some resources are private and some are public. However, as discussed in Section 2, it is difficult to conceiver of a "general purpose" definition for a hybrid cloud, so this case is not recommended for the definition of a public performance benchmark.

4   Performance Criteria Important to Cloud Environments

Performance criteria such as response times and throughput are important in any computing environment – or they become important when they fail to meet expectations. However, there is much more to "business performance" than the measure of transaction response times and overall throughput. This becomes particularly important in a cloud environment, where the resources being used are not under the direct control of the enterprise and where the physical resources being exercised may actually change from day to day, or even moment to moment. Areas of reliability, consistency of service, and the ability to expand and contract allocated resources all play a role in the overall business performance that is delivered by the solution. These areas are important in a dedicated environment, but become key purchase criteria in shared resource environments such as cloud computing.

The following table is adapted from an IBM article on performance considerations for cloud computing [3]. The table was originally used as a list of performance-related items that might be included in a Service Level Agreement. The table has been adjusted by replacing the columns associated with an SLA with the last column that contains comments on the applicability for use as a measure in a general purpose performance benchmark.

Service Level category	Key Performance Indicator	Applicability to a public performance benchmark for cloud computing
Availability	Percentage of time that service or system is available	For public clouds, should be stipulated in the minimum SLA requirements, with transparent or near-transparent fail-over for resources in error and guarantee of data integrity across the migration
	MTBF - Mean time between failure	Covered above
	MTTR - Mean time to repair	Covered above

Performance	Response time for composite or atomic service	Particularly important to set strong criteria for response times in an environment where the physical location of compute resources are not known
	Completion time for a batch or background task	Same as response time, only for long running "transactions"
	Throughput - Number of transactions or requests processed per specified unit of time	Takes on new meaning for cloud. Assumption is that there is always additional resource available to obtain more throughput, so the measure is more likely to be throughput per unit of resource in the SLA
Capacity	Bandwidth of the connection supporting a service	For public clouds, likely a part of the price equation, but should also be a part of the minimum SLA
	Processor speed – Clock-speed of a processor (CPU)	Reported in the benchmark and a contracted part of an SLA. Perhaps a component in the overall throughput measure
	Storage capacity of a temporary or persistent storage medium, such as RAM, SAN, disk, tape	Part of price equation and part of an SLA
Reliability	Probability that service or system is working flawlessly over time	In today's environment, this should be covered by the availability requirement, above
Scalability	Degree to which the service or system is capable of supporting a defined growth scenario	Although a benchmark may be run on a fairly static set of resources, the ability to scale to larger resource use or even to scale to smaller use is a trend that should be included, perhaps even as a dynamic part of the benchmark.

5   Benchmark Requirements for the TPC

For the Transaction Processing Performance Council, there are some special considerations that must be made in the definition of a benchmark that is focused on cloud computing. None of these challenges are insurmountable, and the addressing of them can produce a much richer benchmark than if they are ignored.

5.1   Price

The TPC's Policies document requires that each TPC benchmark have three primary metrics: a performance capacity metric, a price/performance metric, and an availability date. The rules for generating a price to use as the numerator of the price/performance metric are defined in the TPC's Price Specification and the associated TPC Benchmark specifications [5 - 8] and can be summarized as follows:

- Purchase price of the complete hardware configuration
- Purchase price of licenses for software needed to develop and execute the benchmark application
- Price to maintain the hardware and software for a period of three years

For price considerations, we find a significant difference between public and private cloud solutions. The two pricing models are different enough that it may be difficult to achieve comparability between them.

From a benchmark-ability perspective, there are some advantages to using a private cloud model – in that all of the resources are under the control of the benchmark sponsor. However, from a price perspective, and also from a benchmark execution perspective, the need to demonstrate that the benchmark application is only using a fraction of system resources and should only be charged for a fraction of system costs will be a significant challenge.

5.1.1 Pricing Public Cloud Configurations

Particularly for a public cloud, one of the reasons a consumer opts to contract for services is to replace the surge-cost of the purchase of a system that likely has more capacity than is typically needed with more cost-effective expense costs of ongoing monthly service fees for the cloud resources. Instead of up-front payment of the capital equipment costs of the entire configuration, the consumer pays through some combination of three methods that are in contrast to the TPC Pricing Specification's requirements:

- Regular monthly fee for contracted resources, such as X compute cores with Y memory and Z storage ("rental" model)
- Monthly charge for resources used, such as $XX/100GB transfer ("utility" model)
- Fee for specific resource allocation, such as $YY for 25,000 core-seconds of compute time (" prepaid phone" model)

In addition to replacing the items required in current TPC prices (and depending on the service-level-agreement negotiated with the provider), the monthly service fees typically include many of the items that are a part of the overall cost of ownership of compute resources, but are not included in the TPC's price requirements [10]. For public solutions, key items include (some apply to PaaS but not IaaS delivery models):

- Transparent hardware upgrades
- Transparent middleware upgrades
- Database and Middleware administration
- Operational Support
- Electricity

- Floor space and other building costs
- Backup and Recovery services
- Up-time guarantee and associated migration services

By shifting to a 3-year expense cost model for public cloud environments, instead of a purchase + maintenance model, the TPC could accommodate typical cloud pricing models and include these key areas of the total cost of computing that are currently missing in TPC prices. While there are other aspects of benchmarking in public clouds that would be more difficult, this enhancement to pricing requirements could be accomplished by specifying the minimum support required in the contracted Service Level Agreement to ensure that all items are included.

5.1.2 Pricing Private Cloud Configurations

For private cloud configurations, the inclusion of the original TPC price list is possible, but it should be altered to reflect the inclusion above list of items that are missing from current TPC prices and to reflect the fact that cloud solutions are designed to use only a fraction of the total computing power that is available. Including the SLA list from above is more difficult for a private cloud than a public one. For the public configuration, the supplier has completed their own assessment of the collection of costs and has rolled them into the service fee, usually without itemization. For the private cloud, an actual consumer would accomplish something similar, but benchmark rules for establishing a uniform methodology will be a challenge - because it requires some assessment of the cost for administrative and operational support, or for building requirements, which are difficult to define and can change from locale to locale. However, software upgrade support and electricity can certainly be included, as can some requirement for the hardware and software necessary to support fail-over and server migration.

The greater challenge for private cloud configurations is that the price of the configuration in TPC terms is for the entire configuration; as if a single application is using the entire set of resources. However, the same cost savings that attract consumers to public clouds are also what attract them to private ones - - Individual applications do not absorb the entire configuration, so the users of an application get a charge-back only for the resources that they consume.

As a starting point, assume that the total configuration is, on average, used only at 2/3 of the total resources for all possible applications, to ensure sufficient head room for expansion while maintaining appropriate quality of service. Then, a method must be devised to assess what fraction of the configuration the benchmark application is consuming. The ratio of this fraction to 2/3 can be applied to the system costs to derive a benchmark cost. If the total configuration cost is computed using a lease model instead of a purchase model, this method can approximate the method proposed for public clouds. As with public clouds, it will be important to stipulate a minimum set of requirements from the SLA list, above, to ensure that the configuration is a "true" cloud.

5.2   Availability

The TPC's rules for the availability of hardware and software components are also defined in the TPC Pricing Specification. Essentially, the requirement is that all components required for the benchmark be publicly available for delivery within 185 days of the publication of the benchmark result.

For benchmarks that are run on public clouds, the assumption is that the availability date is the date of the benchmark execution, since it is using publicly contracted resources. For private clouds, the TPC's existing requirements can stand as they are.

5.3   Energy

The TPC's Energy Specification [9] has a set of rules to be followed for generating the optional energy metrics for each of the existing TPC benchmarks. The goal is to promote these rules to apply to future TPC benchmarks, as well.

As mentioned in the price section, above, for public clouds, the cost of the energy consumed to support the fractional set of resources in the contract is included in the overall monthly fee that is charged. Although the host of the public cloud certainly has to pay attention to energy consumption, it is not a concern for the consumer and one assumes that the host is providing a price quotation that allows the continuation of payment of these and other costs. Thus, the measure of energy for a public cloud benchmark is likely not required.

For a private cloud, the measure of energy is achievable and likely very important. The challenge is reflective of that described for pricing of private clouds – Assuming the benchmark application is measured on a fraction of the total physical resources available. How does one determine how much of the overall energy consumption should be allocated to the workload? Clearly, the most efficient use of energy is if the system is operating at capacity, but if the benchmark application is using the entire system, it isn't really a cloud. Some rule could be established to observe the fraction of the total capacity that the benchmark application is using and apply some formula to that fraction to arrive at a reasonable energy value.

5.4   ACID Requirements

All TPC benchmarks have data integrity requirements for Atomicity, Consistency, Isolation and Durability. These requirements can and should stand for cloud computing environments, as well – both public and private environments. The nature of the individual tests to ensure these properties may need to be altered.

In the case of Durability, the overall requirement should be altered. As noted earlier, one of the likely requirements for a Service Level Agreement for cloud resources is a guarantee of up-time and migration of services to maintain that up-time in the event of a failure. Thus, the durability requirement for a cloud computing benchmark should not only require that data integrity be maintained after recovery from a failure, but that data integrity be maintained while the application environment is migrated to new physical resources to simulate the loss of the original resources. The migration time and the relative reduction in throughput during and after the migration should be measured and reported as a part of the benchmark metrics.

5.5   System Capacity and Quality of Service (QOS)

TPC benchmarks (and most other industry benchmarks) focus on the capacity of a total configuration to accomplish work under a particular load. If 100% of the system resources are not used to accomplish this, the benchmark sponsor either finds a way to increase the load to use 100% or reduces the scope of resources configured so that 100% are used. Cloud computing is based on the premise that the application will never use 100% of the total system resources – but rather a fraction of the total resource available.

While the overall throughput achievable for the contracted resources is an important measure, there are other performance criteria listed in Section 4 of this article that are also important. Many of them are important in a single-application environment, as well, but become more prominent in cloud computing. Some TPC benchmarks require running within a maximum response time limit, but these requirements are often quite relaxed. In a cloud benchmark, not only the response time component of QOS is important, but overall bandwidth, system availability, resource migration time, resource-on-demand time, and other aspects discussed in section 4 are also important.

TPC Policies require that there be a performance metric for the benchmark, but do not stipulate that it be solely a throughput metric. For cloud computing environments, it is reasonable and advisable to include other components of performance in the overall performance score of the benchmark.

6   Summary Points

Cloud computing is here, and growing. Performance considerations for applications within a cloud environment are an important part of the selection and implementation of a solution, just as they are with a single-application or single-server environment. However, the specific performance criteria for cloud are sometimes different or sometimes treated differently than they are in a more traditional, stand-alone computing environment.

Benchmarking in "the cloud" is desirable and achievable, but is not trivial. To define a public performance benchmark for cloud computing requires changing from a total-system-total-capacity benchmark process to a partial system mind-set in which many of the performance measures will be different than they are with a total system measure.

As with any benchmark, it is important to select an appropriate use case, or business model to target the benchmark towards, and a delivery model that is germane to that business model.

Use cases that are most likely associated with a Software as a Service (SaaS) delivery model are more likely the topic of individual user environments and are not recommended for more general public performance benchmarks. Use cases that fit the Platform as a Service (PaaS) delivery model can be good cases for measures of public clouds. Use cases that fit the Infrastructure as a Service (IaaS) delivery model are more likely candidates for measures of private clouds. Of the variety of use cases that have been defined, the "Enterprise to Cloud" use case is the most likely candidate for an initial attempt at creating a cloud benchmark. There are sufficient differences between public and private clouds that a benchmark should not attempt to span both.

For the TPC, the inclusion of cloud computing in benchmark designs will require rethinking how performance and price are measured, and the way that these metrics are represented to the consumer. A critical component of any cloud benchmark will be the inclusion of minimum service thresholds that will be typical of Service Level Agreements that will be established to bring enterprise solutions to the cloud space.

References

1. Cloud Computing Use Case Discussion Group; Cloud Computing Use Cases White Paper – Version 4 (2010),
   http://opencloudmanifesto.org/Cloud_Computing_Use_Cases_Whitepaper-4_0.pdf
2. Oracle – Anonymous; Oracle Cloud Computing (2011), http://www.oracle.com/us/dm/oracle-cloud-computing-final2-332097.pdf
3. Duijvestijn, Fernnandes, Isom, Jewell, Jowett, Stahl, Stockslager: Performance Implications of Cloud Computing (2010),
   http://www.ibm.com/support/techdocs/atsmastr.nsf/WebIndex/WP101684
4. IBM – anonymous; Dispelling the vapor around cloud computing (2010),
   http://www.ibm.com/support/techdocs/atsmastr.nsf/WebIndex/WP101684
5. Transaction Processing Performance Council – Anonymous; TPC Pricing Specification Version 1.6.0 (2010),
   http://www.tpc.org/pricing/spec/Price_V1.6.0.pdf
6. Transaction Processing Performance Council – Anonymous; TPC Benchmark C Specification Version 5.11.0 (2010),
   http://www.tpc.org/tpcc/spec/tpcc_current.pdf
7. Transaction Processing Performance Council – Anonymous; TPC Benchmark E Specification Version 1.12.0 (2010),
   http://www.tpc.org/tpce/spec/v1.12.0/TPCE-v1.12.0.pdf
8. Transaction Processing Performance Council – Anonymous; TPC Benchmark H Specification Version 2.14.2 (2011),
   http://www.tpc.org/tpch/spec/tpch2.14.2.pdf
9. Transaction Processing Performance Council – Anonymous; TPC Energy Specification Version 1.2.0 (2010), http://www.tpc.org/tpc_energy/spec/TPC-Energy_Specification_1.2.0.pdf
10. Huppler, K.: Price and the TPC. In: Nambiar, R., Poess, M. (eds.) TPCTC 2010. LNCS, vol. 6417, pp. 73–84. Springer, Heidelberg (2011)

Extending TPC-E to Measure
Availability in Database Systems

Yantao Li and Charles Levine

One Microsoft Way, Redmond, WA 98052 USA
{yantaoli,clevine}@microsoft.com

Abstract. High-availability is a critical feature to database customers; having a way to measure and characterize availability is important for guiding system development and evaluating different HA technologies. This paper describes extensions to the TPC-E benchmark for availability measurement, including HA scenario simulation, fault injection, and availability metric reporting. The implementation details and exemplary test results on SQL Server 2008 Database Mirroring are also described.

Keywords: High-availability measurement, database planned/unplanned downtime, fault simulation, failover/failback, time-to-recover, TPC-E, benchmark.

1   Introduction

High-availability (HA) is required for mission-critical applications to ensure business continuity in spite of various failures. There are many approaches in use today to achieve HA, spanning hardware and software, including database solutions that can mask hardware and software faults so that service downtime is minimized.

Microsoft SQL Server has several offerings that improve database availability [1], including Failover Clustering, Database Mirroring [2], Log Shipping, and Replication. HA continues to be a significant investment area for SQL Server going forward.

Being able to measure HA performance is critical to drive the engineering work required to improve HA capabilities. Availability is usually expressed as a percentage of uptime over a period of time, for example, 99.999% availability means ~5 minutes downtime per year. This is mainly based on observation of a live system over an extended period of time. To proactively understand the HA capability of a system, we need to define a representative workload and measurable metrics.

Availability is the product of both the time between failures and the time to recover after a failure occurs. Currently, there's no industry standard benchmark for characterizing either aspect in database systems. As TPC has defined representative benchmarks for performance and scalability, we can leverage those workloads and extend them to measure and characterize the recovery time aspects of database systems. Characterizing the time between failures is beyond the scope of this paper.

TPC-E [3] is an OLTP benchmark that simulates a brokerage firm workload, where customers generate transactions related to trades, account inquiries, and market research. Although the underlying business model is a brokerage firm, the benchmark is designed

R. Nambiar and M. Poess (Eds.): TPCTC 2011, LNCS 7144, pp. 111–122, 2012.

to be broadly representative of modern OLTP systems. In TPC-E there's a requirement of measuring and reporting 'business recovery time', which refers to the time needed for the database to recover from a single point of failure (loss of processing, storage, or external power). However, the business recovery process has a very limited scope focusing on basic durability tests. To measure availability, we need to extend TPC-E by adding more granular metrics and introducing more fault scenarios.

This paper describes an approach for measuring and characterizing high availability for database systems based on TPC-E. We have applied this approach to Microsoft SQL Server to track availability improvements for engineering and development.

The rest of the paper is organized as follows. Section 2 briefly summarizes related work. Section 3 presents HA scenarios and metrics. Section 4 describes the implementation details. Section 5 shows the test results on Microsoft SQL Server 2008 Database Mirroring, followed by conclusion and future work.

2   Related Work

Gray and Siewiorek [4] described key concepts and techniques to build high availability computer systems, explained the relationship between mean-time-to-failure and mean-time-to-repair, and assessed high availability system trends.

IFIP Working Group 10.4 [5] was established to identify and integrate methods and techniques for dependable computing, such as understanding various faults, methods for error detection, validation and design for testability and verifiability, etc. The notion 'dependability' includes system attributes such as reliability, availability, safety and security. Many workshops and conferences have been held to advance research in this area. Kanoun and Spainhower published a book [6] that gathered together dependability benchmarks developed by industry and academia (IFIP Special Interest Group on Dependability Benchmarking) and explained principles and concepts of dependability benchmarking.

The DBench-OLTP [7] project defines a general dependability benchmark model for OLTP systems using TPC-C. Vieira and Madeira describe various fault types to cover a broad range of scenarios impacting dependability. (In contrast, we focus only on recovery performance after a fault occurs, without regard for the source or cause of the fault.) Almeida etc. [8] proposed a framework to advance TPC benchmarks with dependability aspects.

3   Methodology

The TPC-E benchmark defines a workload portraying a brokerage firm, including database schema, transactions, implementation rules, and throughput and response time metrics. To measure and characterize availability aspects of a database system, we need to extend the workload by defining representative fault scenarios and availability metrics that can occur in the system.

The focus of this paper is to measure how fast an HA database system can recover the service after a fault occurs. Additionally, we quantify the performance overhead for HA compared to the non-HA system during normal operations. We have used this

this methodology to drive improvements in SQL Server availability. Although the methodology is not specific to the TPC-E workload or Microsoft SQL Server, we are not attempting to define a 'general-purpose' HA benchmark in this paper.

3.1   Terminologies and Scenarios

For the discussion in this paper, we assume an HA database system consists of four key components:

- Principal Server: The database instance that serves clients requests. In case of system faults, one of the Standby Servers becomes new Principal.
- Standby Server(s): A system can have one or more standby database instances, which can provide service when the Principal Server fails. For a 'hot' Standby Server, the database state is continuously replicated from the Principal Server. For a 'cold' Standby Server, generally a complete database recovery process is required for it to become the new Principal Server. In Microsoft SQL Server, Database Mirroring uses the hot standby approach and Failover Clustering uses the cold standby approach.
- Management component: The software module that monitors the system and decides which server is Principal.
- Connectivity component: The software module that directs database connections to current Principal Server.

Depending on the degree of availability an application needs, an HA database system may need redundancy in multiple layers, such as power supply, storage (e.g., disk RAID levels), NICs and network switches, number of standby database instances, and duplicated system in remote data center (for geographic disaster recovery).

In this paper we focus on how the RDBMS handles various faults. The TPC-E workload is extended to cover the following downtime scenarios:

- Planned downtime: A period of scheduled downtime for system maintenance, characterized by an orderly transition of service from Principal to Standby Server. The causes of scheduled downtime include OS & SQL patches, service pack, hardware maintenance, online servicing, etc.
- Unplanned downtime: A period of unscheduled downtime, often due to various faults, such as hardware faults, software bugs and human errors, causing an abrupt transition of service from Principal to Standby Server.

Failover refers to the transition of service from Principal to Standby Server. Ideally, the database system can automatically failover without administrative intervention for unplanned downtime. The administrator typically initiates a 'manual' failover process for planned downtime. Failback refers to transfer of service back to the original Principal Server (after planned/unplanned downtime). The operation is often similar to manual failover except that Principal/Standby Servers are flipped.

Figure 1 shows the key components in the test environment. Note that the System-Under-Test (SUT) definition in the TPC-E benchmark is extended to include the Connectivity component, which can physically run on either the TPC-E Driver machine (for example, SQL Server Native Client for Database Mirroring) or a server machine (for example, Virtual Network Name for Failover Clustering).

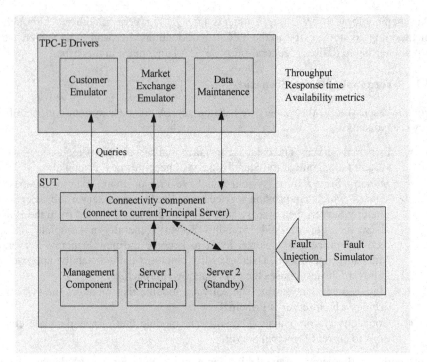

Fig. 1. Extending TPC-E for Availability Measurement

To simulate planned downtime, we can call failover APIs provided by the RDBMS while running the TPC-E workload. For unplanned downtime, we need to simulate various disruptive events that can occur in the system. Table 1 shows some fault examples.

Table 1. Fault Simulation

Category	Scenarios	Simulation on SQL Server
Planned downtime	• Patches, maintenance	• Call SQL Server APIs to initiate manual failover
Unplanned downtime	• Power outage • Disk corruption, network outage • System crash	• Force shutdown of machine • Bring disk/network offline • Abruptly stop SQL Server process

In our model we assume that the system follows the 'fail-fast' principle described by Gray and Siewiorek [4]. Provided that faults in hardware and software cause immediate failures, it's not necessary to test across an exhaustive set of failure modes. Thus we do not attempt to enumerate a 'complete' list of faults. The fail-fast attribute should be verified independently from the performance testing.

3.2   Metrics

The availability metrics need to reflect customer scenarios and cost of an HA system, which includes three main aspects:

- Capital cost: The cost of additional hardware and software needed for an HA system compared to an otherwise equivalent non-HA system.
- Performance impact: The impact to performance of HA capabilities during normal operations compared to the non-HA system.
- Recovery time: The time to restore the database service after a fault occurs.

Characterizing capital cost is beyond the scope of this paper, but we believe that the pricing model defined in the TPC-E specification can be used as is to compute system prices for both HA and non-HA configurations.

To understand the performance impact during normal operation, we measure TPC-E throughput in steady state on an HA system and compare that against a standalone system to characterize the difference.

The definition of time-to-recover may include (1) the server is up, (2) all data is accessible, and (3) the system is back to steady-state, i.e., it can deliver a certain percentage of the peak throughput within the response time constraint. In this paper our definition of time-to-recover is (3), which can be broken down into two phases:

- Service downtime: After a fault occurs, how long it takes for the system to come back and be ready to process new requests.
- Time-to-steady-state: How fast the system ramps up to deliver steady-state throughput.

Figure 2 is a conceptual throughput graph illustrating our metrics, including throughput impact, service downtime and time-to-steady-state.

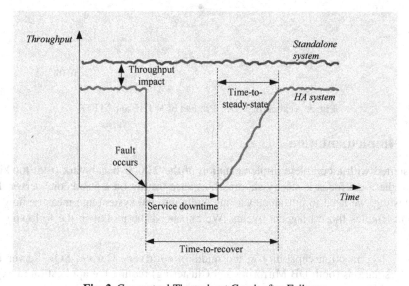

Fig. 2. Conceptual Throughput Graph after Failover

To derive system availability over an extended period of time (e.g. five nines over a year), we need to know both mean-time-between-failures (MTBF) and mean-time-to-recover (MTTR), where availability is quantified as MTBF/(MTBF+MTTR). MTBF and MTTR are orthogonal metrics. Figure 3 shows that availability is the product of both MTBF and MTTR. As illustrated in the graph by points A to D, availability can be improved by driving MTTR lower independent of any improvement in MTBF.

For example, if a failure occurs on average every ten days and recovery takes on average 0.1 days (2.4 hours), the overall availability is 0.99 ("two nines"). This is point B on the graph. Improving the average recovery time by a factor of 10 to 0.01 days (14.4 minutes) results in availability of 0.999 ("three nines"). This is point C on the graph. Similarly, a 10x improvement in MTBF with no change in recovery time produces the same net improvement to availability (points B to E in the graph).

For the RDBMS, the focus is to reduce recovery time. To understand MTBF generally requires certain estimates or modeling exercises (e.g., the probability of power outage in one area in one year), which is beyond the scope of this paper.

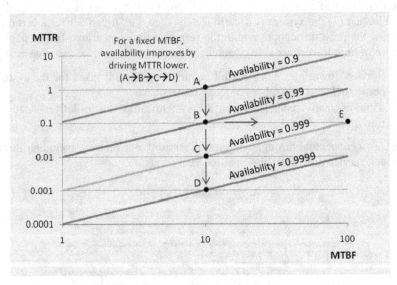

Fig. 3. Availability is the Product of MTBF and MTTR

4   Implementation

We started with a complete implementation of the TPC-E benchmark (the 'toolkit'), where the main focus is steady-state performance testing on a standalone server. For HA testing, we need to introduce various faults into the system and measure how the system handles those transient events. We enhanced the toolkit in the following aspects:

- Reconnection capability in the middle tier/drivers. Current SQL Server HA solutions (both DB Mirroring and Clustering) require the application to explicitly reconnect after a failover.

- HA metric reporting, including throughput impact, service downtime, and time-to-steady-state.
- Framework for planned/unplanned downtime simulation.

The toolkit provides a framework and shared components for HA performance measurement. On top of that various plug-ins are developed for different HA technologies in SQL Server.

4.1   System Workflow

Measuring throughput impact is straightforward. We first run the TPC-E workload on a standalone server for a certain duration of time, for example 2 hours, which gives the baseline performance; and then run the workload on an HA system to characterize the impact to throughput.

To characterize planned and unplanned downtime, we need to run both the TPC-E workload and the Fault Simulator simultaneously. Here is the description of the workflow:

- Run the TPC-E workload for 2 hours.
- Run the Fault Simulator in a separate process:
  1. Wait for a certain duration, such as 30 minutes, until the workload is in steady-state.
  2. Failover: Inject fault to initiate the failover. This results in transition of service from Principal to Standby Server.
  3. Wait 10 minutes (simulating downtime of the original Principal Server), during which the new Principal Server is processing TPC-E queries.
  4. Restart the original Principal Server.
  5. Wait 30 minutes.
  6. Failback: Orderly transition of service back to original Principal.

Note:

- *The time durations above, such as 2 hours, 10 minutes, 30 minutes, are all tunable parameters.*
- *The interval between failover & failback (30 minutes) is chosen based on empirical data; the minimal interval depends on how fast the original Principal Server can catch up (otherwise we can't failback).*
- *The Fault Simulator is an extensible framework that can simulate various faults by developing corresponding plug-ins. The plug-in is HA solution specific. For example, on SQL Server Database Mirroring:*
  - *Manual failover script (simulating planned downtime):*
    ALTER DATABASE FAILOVER
  - *Automatic failover script (unplanned downtime):*
    TASKKILL MSSQLSERVER.EXE

Figure 4 illustrates server role changes in the failover/failback process.

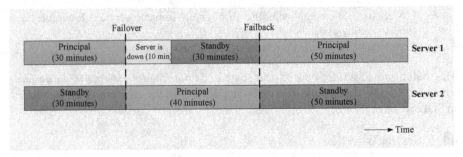

Fig. 4. Server State Changes in the Test Run

4.2   Compute Time-To-Steady-State

As noted in Section 3.2 time-to-recover includes both service downtime and time-to-steady-state. Service downtime is the duration from the client losing connection until the first successful transaction after reconnection. For time-to-steady-state, it is an interesting problem to mathematically define when the system has reached 'steady state'. The TPC-E benchmark [3] constrains allowable throughput variations in steady-state that are measured in sliding windows of 10 and 60 minutes (Clause 6.6.3). For an HA system, where time-to-steady-state can be well under one minute, a more granular model is needed. In this paper we use the following method to compute this metric:

- For a test run we can compute the throughput for each one-second interval. That is, for each second S, we have throughput T_S.

- For any duration of N seconds starting at S, we can calculate the mean value and standard deviation of the interval [S,N]:
  Mean value: $M_{S,N} = (T_S + ... + T_{S+N-1}) / N$

  Standard deviation: $D_{S,N} = \sqrt{\sum_{i=0}^{N-1} (T_{S+i} - M_{S,N})^2 / (N-1)}$

- For a normal test run (no faults in the tests) we compute M_{normal} and D_{normal} of the entire steady state as defined in the TPC-E specification.

- For planned and unplanned scenarios, for each second S after the system is up following a fault we compute the mean value and standard deviation of the 60-second interval from S to $S + 59$, $M_{S,60}$ and $D_{S,60}$.

  The system is considered to be in steady state starting at the first point S such that:

  $$D_{S,60} / M_{S,60} < \alpha * (D_{normal} / M_{normal})$$

  where α is a constant determined from empirical results; 1.8 in our tests

Note:

- *The rationale is to decide whether a certain moment is the 'start of steady-state' by looking at the throughput variation in the immediate following period of time.*
- *The 'window size' is a tunable parameter. By default we use 60 seconds, yet other window sizes might be used depending on the specific test scenarios.*
- *The 'time bucket' for computing throughput is 1 second by default. The time bucket size determines the maximum precision of the metrics, i.e., the metrics can be no more precise than the size of the time bucket.*
- *Determining whether the throughput slowly changes over a long period of time is an interesting problem. (For example throughput slowly declines within 12 hours). The method described above doesn't solve that problem.*

Figure 5 illustrates time to reach the steady-state after a failover. The throughput graph is from one test run (post failover). Note that the spike in throughput is due to the Limit Orders in TPC-E that are fulfilled after a certain time, as the Market Exchange Emulator continues to run while the database service is down (i.e., there is a backlog of work).

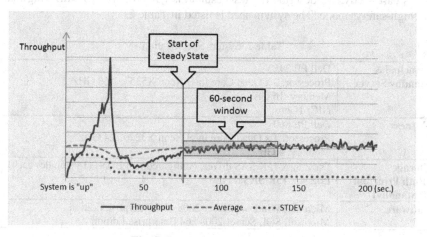

Fig. 5. Steady State after Failover

4.3   Reproducibility

Failover and failback are inherently transient events; achieving highly reproducible test results is challenging. For example, certain operations (e.g. checkpoints, as discussed below) follow a cyclical rhythm. It is critical to do fault injection at the same point in the cycle to get reproducible results. Important parameters that affect availability metrics include (1) number of concurrent users, (2) duration between shutting down the Principal Server until bringing it back, which affects time to catch-up, and (3) the rate at which users reconnect and submit transactions, which affects time-to-steady-state.

We also make sure there's no IO bottleneck in the tests by adequately sizing the storage subsystem. Otherwise the system might have different requirements on workload/SQL Server settings for good reproducibility.

One important setting for SQL Server is the checkpoint interval, which impacts database recovery time, throughput, and the system utilization. On a cold Standby Server, such as SQL Server Failover Clustering, it also has a big impact on service downtime. The Fault Simulator captures database checkpoint begin/complete events, and injects faults midway through a checkpoint in steady-state.

5   Experiment Results

The toolkit has been used for SQL Server internal performance engineering. This section summarizes exemplary test results on SQL Server 2008 DB Mirroring [2].

Note: The results shown here are provided as examples of applying the methodology. They should not be interpreted as definitive measurements of failover performance of SQL Server in production environments. *Your mileage may vary.*

5.1   Configuration

In this case study, we describe the test results on synchronous DB Mirroring that is the 'high-safety' mode. The system spec is listed in Table 2.

Table 2. System Specification

Principal & Standby Server	Dell PE 2950 Processor: 2 x Quad Core Intel Xeon X5355, 2.66 GHz Memory: 16 GB NIC: 1Gbps
Witness	Dell PE 860 Processor: 1 x Quad Core Intel Xeon X3220, 2.4 GHz Memory: 4 GB
Storage (Both Principal & Standby)	Data: 52 x 15K SAS drives; configured to 4 LUNs (14 spindles each) Log: 4 x 15K SAS drives
Software	Microsoft Windows Server 2008 x64 Enterprise Edition Microsoft SQL Server 2008 x64 Enterprise Edition

Table 3 summarizes TPC-E configuration. Note that in these experiments we don't strictly follow the scaling requirement specified in TPC-E benchmark spec; instead we drive CPU utilization to 100% to test the worst case.

5.2   Throughput Impact

As mentioned earlier our throughput comparison is based on a steady-state TPC-E run, which is ~30 minutes after starting the workload. Table 4 shows the comparison between Database Mirroring and Standalone system. Both Standalone and DB Mirroring were run on the same hardware with the same SQL Server settings.

Table 3. TPC-E Configuration

TPC-E Database Size	30,000 customers
Users	120 concurrent users: Drive to maximum load (CPU is 100% busy). Zero think time.
Start Rate (Users/Minute)	300
Connect Rate (Users/Minute)	300
Transaction Mix	Standard Benchmark Mix
SQL Server Memory	14,000 MB
Database Size	240 GB raw data size. Allocated about 395 GB in data files for growth

'Log Send Queue' and 'Redo Queue' are two performance counters in Database Mirroring, which can be viewed in the Performance Monitor tool in Microsoft Windows server operating system. Log Send Queue is the total number of kilobytes of log that have not yet been sent to the Standby server. Redo Queue is the total number of kilobytes of log that currently remain to be applied to the Standby database. If these queues become large, it means that the Standby is not keeping up with the Primary Server.

Table 4. DB Mirroring and Standalone Comparison

	DB Mirroring Normalized as % of Standalone	
	Principal	Standby
Throughput	98.6%	NA
CPU	100%	7%
DB Mirroring: Log Send Queue (KB)	0.1	NA
DB Mirroring: Redo Queue (KB)	NA	11

There are no IO bottlenecks (disk / network) in these runs. As illustrated in Table 4, the impact to throughput from Database Mirroring is quite small (~1.4%). CPU utilization on the Standby Server is 7%; and both Log Send Queue and Redo Queue are very small. Those counters illustrates that Database Mirroring performs well under heavy load.

5.3   Failover Performance

Table 5 summarizes the failover performance in unplanned downtime scenario for the test configuration that we measured. The database service is back to steady-state in about 40 seconds.

Table 5. TPC-E Failover Performance

Stage		Metric (in seconds)
Start the workload	Time-to-steady-state	21
Failover	Service downtime	17
	Time-to-steady-state	24
	Total time-to-recover	**41**

For time-to-steady-state, a good reference is how fast TPC-E can ramp up in the 'normal' situation. As noted in Table 5, when the system is under heavy load, it takes only slightly longer duration to reach steady state after failover compared to the start of workload.

The methodology was applied to Microsoft SQL Server for tracking availability improvements. Good reproducibility of the availability metrics has been achieved. For multiple runs on one SQL Server build, the throughput run-to-run variation is generally within 1% and the time-to-recover variation is generally within 5 seconds, both within the bounds needed to be effective for performance engineering.

6   Conclusion and Future Work

A methodology for measuring availability in database systems is developed based on TPC-E. SQL Server 2008 Database Mirroring is characterized as a case study. The methodology has been used for SQL Server internal performance engineering.

Future work includes developing more complex fault scenarios such as data is partially available, introducing HA metrics into other workloads, exploring modeling MTBF, etc. Further, the methodology could be used as a starting point to define an industry standard for availability measurement.

Acknowledgements. The authors would like to thank the following people for the discussions and suggestions: Sadashivan Krishnamurthy, David Powell, John Ludeman, Steve Lindell, Vineet Rao, Neeraj Joshi, Kaloian Manassiev, Ruchit Solanki, Song Li, Greg Yvkoff, David Lomet and Vivek Narasayya. Apurva Sahasrabudhe implemented the fault injection framework and availability metric reporting.

References

1. Microsoft SQL Server High Availability Solutions Overview, http://msdn.microsoft.com/en-us/library/ms190202(v=SQL.100).aspx
2. Microsoft SQL Server 2008 Database Mirroring Overview, http://msdn.microsoft.com/en-us/library/bb934127(v=SQL.100).aspx
3. TPC-E Benchmark, http://www.tpc.org/tpce/
4. Gray, J., Siewiorek, D.: High-Availability Computer Systems. Computer 24(9), 39–48 (1991)
5. IFIP WG 10.4 on Dependable Computing and Fault Tolerance, http://www.dependability.org/wg10.4/
6. Kanoun, K., Spainhower, L. (eds.): Dependability Benchmarking for Computer Systems. Wiley-IEEE Computer Society Press (2008)
7. Vieira, M., Madeira, H.: A dependability Benchmark for OLTP Application Environments. In: VLDB 2003, pp. 742–753 (2003)
8. Almeida, R., Poess, M., Nambiar, R., Patil, I., Vieira, M.: How to Advance TPC Benchmarks with Dependability Aspects. In: Nambiar, R., Poess, M. (eds.) TPCTC 2010. LNCS, vol. 6417, pp. 57–72. Springer, Heidelberg (2011)

SI-CV: Snapshot Isolation with Co-located Versions

Robert Gottstein, Ilia Petrov, and Alejandro Buchmann

Databases and Distributed Systems Group, TU-Darmstadt, Germany
{gottstein,petrov,buchman}@dvs.tu-darmstadt.de

Abstract. Snapshot Isolation is an established concurrency control algorithm, where each transaction executes against its own version/snapshot of the database. Version management may produce unnecessary random writes. Compared to magnetic disks Flash storage offers fundamentally different IO characteristics, e.g. excellent random read, low random write performance and strong read/write asymmetry. Therefore the performance of snapshot isolation can be improved by minimizing the random writes. We propose a variant of snapshot isolation (called SI-CV) that collocates tuple versions created by a transaction in adjacent blocks and therefore minimizes random writes at the cost of random reads. Its performance, relative to the original algorithm, in overloaded systems under heavy transactional loads in TPC-C scenarios on Flash SSD storage increases significantly. At high loads that bring the original system into overload, the transactional throughput of SI-CV increases further, while maintaining response times that are multiple factors lower.

Keywords: Snapshot Isolation, Flash, SSD, Solid State Drive, TPC-C, Multi Version Concurrency Control, MVCC, SI-CV, Collocation, Transaction Processing, Response Time.

1   Introduction

Database systems, their architecture and algorithms are built around the IO properties of the storage. In contrast to Hard Disk Drives (HDD), Flash Solid State Disks (SSD) exhibit fundamentally different characteristics: high random and sequential throughput, low latency and power consumption [4]. SSD throughput is asymmetric in contrast to magnetic storage, i.e. reads are significantly faster than writes. Random writes exhibit low performance, which also degrades over time. Therefore, to achieve balanced performance, random writes should be avoided at the cost of random reads.

Snapshot Isolation (SI) is a Multi-Version Concurrency Control (MVCC) algorithm, in which every transaction operates against its own workspace/snapshot of the database. Under SI read operations do not block writes and vice versa, which is a good match for the Flash SSD properties. SI provides significant performance improvements compared to two-phase locking schedulers. Whenever a transaction modifies a tuple in its workspace a new version of that tuple is created and linked to the chain of older versions. Such operations result in undesired random writes. On algorithmic level no provisioning is made for this case. On system level SI relies solely on the buffer manager to intercept random writes.

R. Nambiar and M. Poess (Eds.): TPCTC 2011, LNCS 7144, pp. 123–136, 2012.

We extended the classical SI algorithm to collocate/group tuple versions created by a transaction in the same or in adjacent database pages, employing a mechanism of page pre-allocation. We call the algorithm Snapshot Isolation with Co-located Versions (SI-CV).

The contributions of the paper are: (i) we implemented SI-CV in PostgreSQL (ii) SI-CV was tested in an OLTP environment with DBT2[6] (an open source version of TPC-C [8]) (iii) SI-CV performs up to 30% better than the original algorithm on flash SSDs and equally good on HDD; (iv) SI-CV performance is better under heavy loads; (v) SI-CV is space efficient, regardless of its pre-allocation mechanism.

The rest of the paper is organized as follows: in the following section we briefly review the related work; the properties of Flash SSDs are discussed in Section 3; then we introduce the original SI algorithm and SI-CV. Finally, section 6 describes the experimental results and analyses.

2   Related Work

The general SI-algorithm is introduced and discussed in [1]. The specifics of the PostgreSQL SI implementation are described in detail in [2,3]. As reported in [1] SI fails to enforce serializability. Recently a serializable version of SI was proposed [7] that is based on read/write dependency testing in serialization graphs. Serializable SI assumes that the storage provides enough random read throughput needed to determine the visible version of a tuple valid for a timestamp, making it ideal for Flash storage. [9] recently made an alternative proposal for SI serializability. In addition serializable SI has been implemented in the new (but still unstable) version of PostgreSQL and will appear as a standard feature in the upcoming release.

SI-CV presents a way to specially collocate data (versions) for each transaction leveraging the properties of the SSDs. There are several proposed approaches for flash storage managers, the majority of which explore the idea of append based storage [12] for SSDs [11, 10]. SI-CV differs in that it collocates per transaction but does not eliminate the concept of write in-place by converting all writes into appends.

Although it is our long term goal to integrate log-based storage mechanisms this is not part of this work.

In addition, there exist several proposals for page layouts [13] such as PAX [14] that aim at sorting row data in a column-based order with page sub-structures. Such approaches are developed within the context of Data Warehousing and show superior performance for read-mostly data. [15] explores how query processing algorithms and data structures such as FlashJoin [15] or FlashScan can benefit from such page organizations and the characteristics of Flash SSDs.

Furthermore, there have been numerous proposals of improving the logging and recovery mechanisms with respect to new types of memories (Flash SSDs, NVMemories). In-Page Logging [16] (IPL) is one such mechanism, that allows significant performance improvements by write reduction as well as page and log record collocation.

We expect that techniques such as Group Commit have a profound effect on version collocation approaches in MVCC environments. We have not explored those due to their effect on database crash recovery; however it is part of our future work. In [17] we explore the influence of database page size on the database performance on Flash storage.

In a series of papers, e.g. [2] Kemme et al. investigate database replication approaches coupled to SI. SI has been implemented in Oracle, PostgreSQL, Microsoft SQL Server 2005. In some systems as a separate isolation level, in others to handle serializable isolation.

To the best of our knowledge no version handling approaches for SI exist. This aspect has been left out of consideration by the most algorithms as well.

3   Enterprise Flash SSDs

The performance exhibited by Flash SSDs is significantly better than that of HDDs. Flash SSDs, are not merely a faster alternative to HDDs; just replacing them does not yield optimal performance. Below we discuss their characteristics.

(a) asymmetric read/write performance – the read performance is significantly better than the write performance – up to an order of magnitude (Fig. 1, Fig. 2). This is a result of the internal organization of the NAND memory, which comprises two types of structures: pages and blocks. A page (typically 4 KB) is a read and write unit. Pages are grouped into blocks of 32/128 pages (128/512KB). NAND memories support three operations: read, write, erase. Reads and writes are performed on a page-level, while erases are performed on a block level. Before performing a write, the whole block containing the page must be erased, which is a time-consuming operation. The respective raw latencies are: read-55µs; write 500µs; erase 900µs. In addition, writes should be evenly spread across the whole volume. Hence no write in-place as on HDDs, instead copy-and-write.

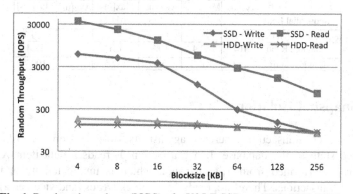

Fig. 1. Random throughput (IOPS) of a X25-E SSD vs. HDD 7200 RPM

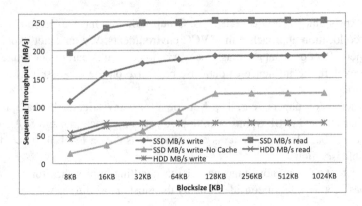

Fig. 2. Sequential throughput (MB/s) of an X25-E SSD vs. HDD 7200 RPM

(b) excellent random read throughput (IOPS) – especially for small block sizes. Small random reads are up to hundred times faster than on an HDD (Fig. 1). The good small block performance (4KB, 8KB) affects the present assumptions of generally larger database page sizes.

(c) low random write throughput – small random writes are five to ten times slower than reads (Fig. 1). Nonetheless, the random write throughput is an order of magnitude better than that of an HDD. Random writes are an issue not only in terms of performance but also yield long-term performance degradation due to Flash-internal fragmentation effects.

(d) good sequential read/write transfer (Fig. 1). Sequential operations are also asymmetric. However, due to read ahead, write back and good caching the asymmetry is below 25%.

Table 1. AVG/MAX latency of an X25-E SSD and 7200 RPM HDD

| | Write Cache (WC)-ON | | | | Write Cache-OFF | |
| | SSD | | HDD | | SSD | |
Blocksize 4 KB	Avg[µs]	Max[ms]	Avg[ms]	Max[ms]	Avg[µs]	Max[ms]
Sequential Read	53	12.3	0.133	109.2	–	12.3
Sequential Write	59	94.8	0.168	36.9	455	100.3
Random Read	167	12.4	10.8	121	–	12.4
Random Write	113	100.7	5.6	127.5	435	100.7

4   Snapshot Isolation

In SI [1] each transaction operates against its own version (snapshot) of the committed state of the database. If a transaction T_i reads a data item X, the read operation is performed from T_i's snapshot, which is unaffected by updates from concurrent transactions. Therefore, reads never block writes (and vice versa) and there is no need for read-locks. Modifications (inserts, updates, deletes - T_i's write set) are also performed on T_i's snapshot and upon successful commit become visible to appropriate transactions. During commit the transaction manager checks whether T_i's modifications overlap with the modifications of concurrent transactions. If write sets do not overlap T_i commits, otherwise it aborts. These commit-time checks are represented by two alternative rules: first-committer-wins[1] or first-updater-wins[1,3]. While the former is enforced in deferred manner at commit time, the latter results in immediate checks before each write. The first-updater-wins relies on write locks (see also Listing 1) and is implemented in PostgreSQL.

Apart from the general SI algorithm we also summarize its PostgreSQL implementation [1,2,3] (Listing 1). On begin of every new transaction it is assigned a unique transaction ID (TID) equivalent to a timestamp. Tuples in PostgreSQL are the unit of versioning. Every version V_i of a tuple X is annotated with two TIDs: t_xmin and t_xmax. t_xmin is TID of the transaction that created V_i. t_xmax is the TID of the transaction that created a new version V_j of X, a successor of V_i. In principle V_j invalidates V_i. If t_xmax is NULL, V_i is the most recent version. All versions are organised as a linked list in memory. Complementary to the tuple versions PostgreSQL maintains a *SnapshotData* structure for every running transaction T_i. Among other fields it contains: (i) $xmax$ – the TID of the next transaction ($T_{(i+1)}$ at time T_i started) and serves as a visibility threshold for transactions whose changes are not visible to T_i; (ii) $xmin$ – determines transactions whose updates are visible to T_i and depicts the TID of the lowest still running transaction (transactions with $TID<xmin$ are considered finished); (iii) xip – holds a TID list of all transactions concurrent to T_i. Finally PostgreSQL uses a main memory structure called PG_CLOG (previously pg_log), based on the database log, which allows for fast transaction status checks (aborted, committed, in progress).

Consider Listing 1: whenever transaction T_i reads a tuple X (line 2), SI first checks if X is in the writeset of T_i to determine whether it has to read its own or the last stable version of X (line 2-4). Its own version can be read directly, because it cannot be modified by another transaction. Otherwise SI has to determine the version of X visible to T_i. Tuple visibility can be expressed with two conditions (line 19 and 20). The first one requires the X to be created by a transaction that successfully committed before T_i started. The second one (line 20) forbids X to be modified (and committed) by a concurrent transaction T_j.

Before T_i writes X, SI first performs a version check to determine if the version was updated by a concurrent transaction. On a negative check T_i has to abort (line 6). On a positive check it requests a write-lock on X. If X is locked by a concurrent transaction T_k, T_i waits until the lock is granted. Otherwise, it acquires a write lock on X, the stable version $X.V_s$ is read and a new version $X.V_i$ is created. Ti sets the creation timestamp $X.V_i.t\_xmin$ and the invalidation timestamp $X.V_s.t\_xmax$ to its own timestamp tsi (lines 9,10).

On a commit or abort all acquired locks are released, waiting transactions are woken up and *PG_CLOG* is updated.

Listing 1. Snapshot Isolation

```
1.  Start Transaction Ti → tsi = timestamp( Ti );
2.  ON Ti.read( X ): // Transaction Ti reads tuple X
3.     IF(X IN { writeSet(Ti) }) X.Vi = readOwnVersion(X,Ti)
4.     ELSE      X.Vi  = readStableVersion( X, Ti )
5.  ON Ti.write( X ):   // Transaction Ti modifies tuple X
6.     IF( VersionCheck( X ) = FAILED) → Ti.rollback()
7.     Ti.lockX = requestXlock( X )
8.     IF(Ti.lockX==GRANTED){ //PerformUpdate→InstallUpdate
9.        X.Vs = readStableVersion(X,Ti); X.Vi =new Version(X);
10.       X.Vs.t_xmax=tsi;   X.Vi.t_min=tsi; X.Vi.t_max=NULL;
11.     } ELSE //another transaction acquired lock on X
12.    ENQUEUE(Ti.lockX) → … wait_for_lock … ON lock granted
13.    GOTO line 6; // restart write validation
       //avoid concurrent changes
14.    ON Ti.commit() or Ti.rollback() →
15.      Release All acquired locks, Wake Up Waiting
             Transactions, Update Log
16.    End Transaction Ti;
17.    readStableVersion(Tuple X,Transaction Ti){
18.    Find X.Va, created by transaction Tj such that:
19.    //Find X.Va created by the latest Tj that committed
       //before Ti started:
       X.Va.t_xmin | X.Va.t_xmin < Ti.SnapshotData.xmax AND
                     PG_CLOG( X.Va.t_xmin ) == committed
20.//Find X.Va that is untouched or was updated by Tj that
       //either aborted or
       //was in progress when Ti attempted to write:
       X.Va.t_xmax | X.Va.t_xmax==NULL OR
                 PG_CLOG( X.Va.t_xmax ) == aborted OR
                    X.Va.t_xmax IN {Ti.SnapshotData.xip}
21.    IF Checks FAIL return NULL ELSE return X.Va
22.  }
23.  VersionCheck( Tuple X ) {
24.    X.Vi = readStableVersion( X )
25.    IF(X.Vi==NULL) return FAILED
       //X updated by concurrent Tj
26.  }
```

Snapshot Isolation never deletes an old version, however a tuple version may still become effectively invisible to any running transaction, because of the rules in line 19 and 20. Such obsolete versions consume precious space and can be safely removed. PostgreSQL runs a Vacuum process, which removes obsolete versions and coalesces free space. A simple version of Vacuum marks obsolete versions as deleted thus freeing space, while the exhaustive Vacuum version removes such versions and coalesces the freed space. Unfortunately, it requires an exclusive table lock and generates heavy I/O.

5   Snapshot Isolation with Co-located Versions

As Listing 1 (lines 9,10) clearly shows, the present algorithm does not group the tuple versions created by transactions. It results into multiple updates (t_xmax of the old version and the newly created versions), which may lead to random writes. Our idea is to collocate all versions created by one transaction and group them into adjacent blocks. This not only minimizes the random writes, possibly converting them into sequential writes, but also uses potentially more random reads. Therefore SI-CV is a good match for SSD properties.

SI-CV (Fig. 3) introduces a new structure Barray in the database(shared) buffer of PostgreSQL. The Barray maps a transaction to a block-number. In SI-CV each transaction receives a pre-allocated block for inserts/updates of tuple versions, which is determined on the first write request. Read only or bulk-insert transactions have no entries in the Barray. With bulk inserts the storage manager writes sequentially, making it unnecessary to provision for that case. Upon the creation of the first new version of a tuple X by a transaction T_i an entry in Barray is created with an artificial block number. To determine a physical block SI-CV has to decide whether to use the free space map (FSM) or not. The FSM is a buffer manager structure that keeps track of block numbers that still have space left. If the FSM is used, an existing block with sufficient space for the new version is selected, which currently must not be in Barray. This is how we forbid multiple transactions to be mapped on the same block. However, one transaction may reserve multiple blocks in Barray. In absence of free space the FSM is not used, the relation is extended with a new block, which forms a new entry in the Barray structure together with the transaction ID. Upon transaction termination the entry in the Barray is deleted and made visible to the FSM. After the commit of a transaction, the buffer only contains committed data (versions).

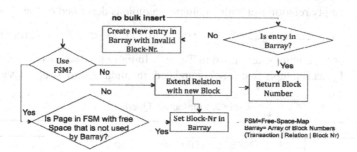

Fig. 3. SI-CV block diagram

We illustrate how SI-CV works based on a simple example (Fig. 4). Two transactions T_i and T_j modify the tuples K, R, X and Y in the relation Rel, in the following way: Start(T_i), Start(T_j), W_i[X], W_j[K], W_j[R], W_i[Y], Commit(T_i), W_j[K], W_j[R], Commit(T_j). According to SI-CV the Barray buffer manager structure will assign blocks uniquely to each transaction. These blocks will contain all versions created by the respective transaction (Fig. 4): transaction T_i with TID123 is mapped to Block1, while transaction T_j with TID124 is mapped to Block2. Upon T_i's commit Block1 is written, upon T_j's commit Block2 is written. However, if T_j aborts Block2 is not written, because not valid data is contained.

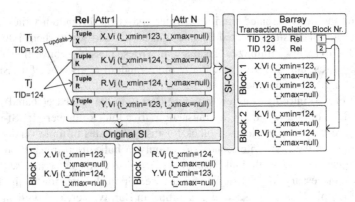

Fig. 4. SI-CV base example

The original SI will pick any block with enough free space to host the new version, regardless of whether it hosts versions of other transactions. This undoubtedly yields random writes. In Fig. 5 block O1 and O2 contain versions from both transactions, which predisposes them to be written multiple times. Upon T_i's commit both blocks are written, since tuples X and Y are distributed on both blocks. T_j updates tuples R and K which share the same blocks as X and Y; T_j commits and both blocks are re-written. However, if T_j aborts both blocks have to be re-written nonetheless since they contain valid data inserted by T_i.

The following example illustrates the concept of versioning in PostgreSQL. Assume the empty relation Rel with 3 columns, a tuple is described by the structure:

```
(t_xmin,t_xmax,col1<Int>,col2<String>,col3<String>)
```

There are four transactions, as shown in Table 2. Initially transactions T_i and T_j insert new tuples; T_h reads a tuple that is being updated/ invalidated and T_k updates a tuple.

Table 2. Transaction Queries

Transaction	TID	Query
T_i	123	INSERT INTO Rel (col1, col2, col3) VALUES (4, Lufthansa, London), (5, Lufthansa, Seattle);
T_j	124	INSERT INTO Rel (col1, col2, col3) VALUES(6, Lufthansa, Frankfurt);
T_h	129	SELECT * FROM Rel WHERE col3=Frankfurt;
T_k	131	UPDATE col2=Condor WHERE col3=Frankfurt;

The concurrent execution of all transactions results in the history:
Start(T_i),Start(T_j),W_i[W],W_j[Y],W_i[X],Commit[T_i],
Commit[T_j],Start[T_h],Start[T_k],R_k[W],R_k[X],R_k[Y],W_k[Y],
Commit[T_k],R_h[Y],Commit[R_h].

After commit of T_i and T_j the relation contains the tuples:

```
W.Vi=(123,null;col1=4,col2=Lufthansa,col3=London)
X.Vi=(123,null;col1=5,col2=Lufthansa,col3=Seattle)
Y.Vj=(124,null;col1=6,col2=Lufthansa, col3=Frankfurt)
```

After $W_k[Y]$ the relation contains a new tuple-version of Y and its invalidated predecessor (tuples W and X stay the same) the new tuple is already inserted logically into the relation.

```
Y.Vj=(124,131;col1=6,col2=Lufthansa,col3=Frankfurt)
Y.Vk=(131,null;col1=6,col2=Condor,col3=Frankfurt)
```

As soon as T_j has finished, the block which was used by it (respectively the entry in Barray) is free to be claimed by T_k. Fig. 5 illustrates the state after the commit of T_k, under SI-CV Block 2 is first used by T_j and then by T_k while original SI uses whichever block was available for insertion (with preference to the last one used for an insertion). According to the algorithm displayed in Listing 1 transaction T_h reads the tuple $Y.V_j$ while the changes of T_k ($Y.V_k$) are not visible to it. Immediately after the last transaction with TID smaller than 131 has finished, tuple Y.Vj becomes invisible to all running transactions.

SI-CV writes Block 1 once after the commit of Ti while original SI has to write Block O1 twice: the first time after the commit of T_i (respectively T_j) and the second time after commit of T_k that invalidated $Y.V_j$.

This clarifies the principles of SI-CV. A block belongs to a transaction as long as it is not committed. After it has finished, a block may be claimed by any other transaction that inserts tuples into that relation, as long as the block still has enough space left to hold the tuples. This scheme is applied to avoid excessive space consumption.

Based on these examples SI-CV not only minimizes on random writes and has better abort behavior, but should also perform better with higher number of transactions. We investigate this claim in the following section.

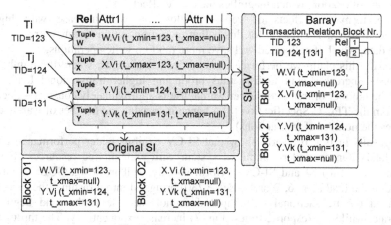

Fig. 5. SI-CV example with update

6   Evaluation

We implemented SI-CV using the PostgreSQL 8.4.2 codebase. The implementation spans several sub-modules of the storage manager, in particular the buffer and page mangers.

We tested SI-CV against the original SI algorithm on a machine with Intel Core 2 Duo 3GHz CPU and 512 MB RAM, running a 64-bit Ubuntu Server. In addition, we used an Intel X25-E/64GB enterprise SSD and an Hitachi HDS72161 7200RPM SATA2 HDD. The properties of both drives are described in Section 3. We enabled the write cache on SSD and HDD as well. The IO scheduling policy was set to "noop" on SSD and "deadline" on HDD. Virtual memory swapping was disabled. PostgreSQL is configured with a 24 MB shared buffer and activated simple vacuums (Section 4). The nominal DB size is 31GB. As benchmark we used DBT2[6], which is instrumented with 20 database connections and 20 terminals per warehouse. Every test run has a two hour duration, excluding the additional ramp-up time (which is proportional to the number of warehouses used).

Table 3. Maximum DBT2 Transaction Throughput [NoTPM] with the respective number of warehouses

Original SI [NoTPM]		SI-CV [NoTPM]			
SSD (270 Wh.)	HDD (80 Wh.)	SSD (270 Wh.)		HDD (80 Wh.)	
2500	210	3588	+30.3%	219	+3.8%

The DBT2 test results showing the maximum transaction throughput for SSDs and HDDs are displayed in Table 3. These show a performance increase of 30% with SI-CV on SSDs. SI-CV on HDDs performs slightly better with an improvement of 3.8%. The clear performance advantage of SI-CV on SSDs physically results from the reduction of random writes, at the cost of more random reads. As discussed in Section 3, both random operations have the same cost on a HDD, whereas random reads are much cheaper than random writes on a SSD. Hence the different rate of improvement (Table 3). In addition, a growing number of concurrent transactions, offers more room for version collocation, which magnifies the above effect.

The performance effects of version collocation will increase with higher transactional loads. The reason for this is that more transactions create more versions of tuple data, which if collocated will save more random write operations.

To verify this claim we performed a series of experiments, where the number of warehouses increases continuously thus producing higher transactional loads. (In TPC-C the number of transactions per warehouse is approximately constant – Section 5.2.3 from the TPC-C Specification [8] – hence increasing the number of warehouses increases the number of transactions).

The results in Fig. 6 clearly show that SI-CV exhibits better performance under higher loads. On an under-committed system with enough free resources (Fig. 6, Warehouses ≤ 180) SI and SI-CV perform equally well in PostgreSQL. A further increase of the load (Fig. 6, Warehouses ≥ 230) brings SI into thrashing; the system is overloaded the transactional throughput does not increase further and begins to deteriorate, while the response times (Fig. 7) increase exponentially. The throughput of SI-CV grows steadily for the same range of loads.

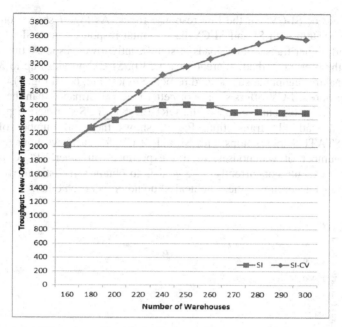

Fig. 6. Transaction Throughput (New Order Transactions per Minute) SI-CV vs. SI on SSD

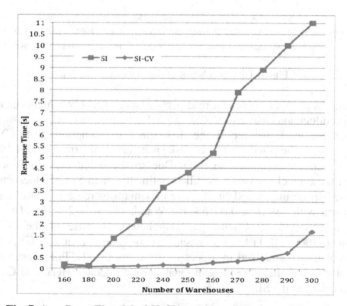

Fig. 7. Avg. Resp. Time [s] of SI-CV and SI on SSD (lower is better)

SI-CV achieves up to 30% higher transactional throughput, before going into thrashing. Such performance behavior is especially favorable to whenever peak loads need to be processed or load spikes occur in real systems. Another interesting characteristic of SI-CV are the low response times. As Fig. 7 shows, on an under-committed system both SI and SI-CV have similar response times. SI-CV, however, can support higher transactional loads at significantly lower response times. For peak loads (in the present testbed; Warehouses ≥ 230), SI-CV provides up to 30% higher transactional throughput at sub-second response times (Fig. 6 and Fig. 7).

Furthermore, SI-CV offers similar or better read performance than the original SI. To verify this statement we report the ORDER_STATUS transaction performance, which is a read-only transaction. Fig. 8 shows the total number of executed ORDER_STATUS transactions with SI and SI-CV for each two hour test run with different number of warehouses. In this experiment all other TPC-C transactions (read-write) execute concurrently. The goal is to obtain a realistic mixture of reads and writes that according to the canonical SI do not affect each other.

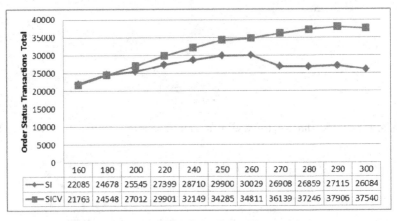

	160	180	200	220	240	250	260	270	280	290	300
SI	22085	24678	25545	27399	28710	29900	30029	26908	26859	27115	26084
SICV	21763	24548	27012	29901	32149	34285	34811	36139	37246	37906	37540

Fig. 8. Total number of Order Status Transactions

The numbers in Fig. 8 show that read performance of SI-CV remains unaffected by the version collocation changes.

Last but not least, we report the disk space consumption of SI-CV, for the following reason. The price per GB of disk space on an enterprise 15K RPM HDD is ~7x lower than on an enterprise SSD. Due to the block pre-allocation per new transaction these blocks may not be filled optimally: each SI-CV block may contain more unused space than an SI block. The maximum increase in space consumption was measured with less than 0.0016% per Warehouse after 2 hours of testing using 280 Warehouses and 20 Clients per Warehouse. Because of the difference in throughput (~1000 NOTPMs) between the original SI and SICV, this space measurement was normalized in aspect to the count of NOTPMs. Insertion of bulk loads is not affected; therefore no additional space utilization. Hence, SI-CV is almost as space efficient as the SI.

7   Conclusions

We developed an extension of Snapshot Isolation (SI), called Snapshot Isolation with Co-located Versions (SI-CV). It places versions of tuples created or modified by a transaction in pre-allocated blocks. Thus it reduces the amount of random writes, which leverages better the properties of Flash SSDs. SI-CV is implemented in PostgreSQL. TPC-C tests show that: (a) SI-CV performs better especially under heavy load conditions where the system is very I/O-bound. Under such conditions we achieved up to 30% better performance with SI-CV.

(b) The relative performance of SI-CV (to SI) increases with higher number of transactions.

(c) The transaction response time with SI-CV on an over-committed system remains significantly lower than that of SI. Under heavy load conditions SI-CV operates with sub-second response times.

(d) SI-CV utilizes a block pre-allocation strategy per transaction. We prove experimentally that it is almost as space efficient as SI. The space consumption difference is marginal and justifies the performance advantages of SI-CV.

(e) Finally, the read performance of SI-CV in comparison to SI is equally good or better.

Acknowledgments. The authors wish to thank Todor Ivanov for his kind assistance with setting up the experimental environment. This work was supported by the DFG project "Flashy-DB".

References

1. Berenson, H., Bernstein, P., Gray, J., Melton, J., O'Neil, E., O'Neil, P.: A critique of ANSI SQL isolation levels. In: Proc. the ACM SIGMOD 1995, San Jose, California, United States, May 22-25 (1995)
2. Wu, S., Kemme, B.: Postgres-R(SI): Combining Replica Control with Concurrency Control based on Snapshot Isolation. In: Proc. of the IEEE ICDE, Tokyo, Japan (2005)
3. Korth, H., Silberschatz, A.: Database System Concepts. McGraw-Hill Publishing Company (2001)
4. Chen, F., Koufaty, D.A., Zhang, X.: Understanding intrinsic characteristics and system implications of flash memory based solid state drives. In: Proc. of SIGMETRICS 2009 (2009)
5. Agrawal, N., Prabhakaran, V., Wobber, T., Davis, J.D., Manasse, M., Panigrahy, R.: Design tradeoffs for SSD performance. In: USENIX 2008, Boston, Massachusetts (June 2008)
6. Database Test Suite. DBT2, http://osdldbt.sourceforge.net/
7. Cahill, M.J., Röhm, U., Fekete, A.D.: Serializable isolation for snapshot databases. In: Proc. SIGMOD 2008, Vancouver, CA (2008)
8. TPC Benchmark C. Standard Specification. Revision 5.11 (February 2010), http://www.tpc.org/tpcc/spec/tpcc_current.pdf
9. Revilak, S., O'Neil, P., O'Neil, E.: Precisely Serializable Snapshot Isolation (PSSI). In: 2011 IEEE 27th International Conference on Data Engineering, ICDE, April 11-16 (2011)
10. Bernstein, P., Rein, C., Das, S.: Hyder – A Transactional Record Manager for Shared Flash. In: CIDR (2011)

11. Stoica, R., Athanassoulis, M., Johnson, R., Ailamaki, A.: Evaluating and repairing write performance on flash devices. In: Proceedings of the Fifth International Workshop on Data Management on New Hardware, DaMoN 2009 (2009)
12. Rosenblum, M., Ousterhout, J.: The design and implementation of a log-structured file system. ACM Trans. Comput. Syst. 10(1), 26–52 (1992)
13. Ailamaki, A., DeWitt, D., Hill, M.: Data page layouts for relational databases on deep memory hierarchies. The VLDB Journal 11(3), 198–215 (2002)
14. Ailamaki, A., DeWitt, D.J., Hill, M.D., Skounakis, M.: Weaving relations for cache performance. In: VLDB, pp. 169–180 (2001)
15. Tsirogiannis, D., Harizopoulos, S., Shah, M., Wiener, J., Graefe, G.: Query processing techniques for solid state drives. In: Proceedings of the 35th SIGMOD International Conference on Management of Data, SIGMOD 2009 (2009)
16. Lee, S.-W., Moon, B.: Design of flash-based DBMS: an in-page logging approach. In: Proceedings of the 2007 ACM International Conference on Management of Data, SIGMOD 2007 (2007)
17. Petrov, I., Gottstein, R., Ivanov, T., Bausch, D., Buchmann, A.: Page Size Selection for OLTP Databases on SSD RAID Storage. Journal of Information and Data Management 2(1) (2011)

Introducing Skew into the TPC-H Benchmark

Alain Crolotte and Ahmad Ghazal

Teradata Corporation, 100 N. Sepulveda Blvd.
El Segundo, Ca. 90245
{alain.crolotte,ahmad.ghazal}@teradata.com

Abstract. While uniform data distributions were a design choice for the TPC-D benchmark and its successor TPC-H, it has been universally recognized that data skew is prevalent in data warehousing. A modern benchmark should therefore provide a test bed to evaluate the ability of database engines to handle skew. This paper introduces a concrete and practical way to introduce skew in the TPC-H data model by modifying the customer and supplier tables to reflect non-uniform customer and supplier populations. The first proposal consists in defining customer and supplier populations by nation that are roughly proportional to the actual nation populations. In a second proposal, nations are divided into two groups, one with large and equal populations and the other with equal and small populations. We then experiment with the proposed skew models to show how the optimizer of a parallel system can recognize skew and potentially produce different plans depending on the presence of skew. A comparison is made between query performance with the proposed method vs. the original uniform TPC-H distributions. Finally, an approach is presented to introduce skew into TPC-H with the current query set that is compatible with the current benchmark specification rules and could be implemented today.

1 Introduction

The importance of data skew in database processing has been recognized for a very long time especially for parallel systems [1], [2]. In these systems, data skew could introduce load imbalances in the parallel join execution that could completely offset the performance advantages provided by parallelism. Solutions to the skew problem in parallel DBMS have been proposed via new algorithms mainly in the context of inner joins [3], [4], and more recently in the context of outer joins [5]. In order to handle skew effectively, a database machine must first recognize the skew and then the optimizer must make the correct planning choice. Skew testing is therefore an important area of benchmarking. While the TPC-H benchmark [6] has been widely successful as an industry standard benchmark and as a testing tool in research organizations and vendor shops, it does not include skew as all distributions in the benchmark are uniform. This paper addresses the introduction of skew in TPC-H.

R. Nambiar and M. Poess (Eds.): TPCTC 2011, LNCS 7144, pp. 137–145, 2012.

The paper is organized in three main sections. In section 2 we propose a very simple approach to introducing skew into TPC-H data. This can be accomplished today by modifying an existing TPC-H database using a random number generator and insert/select. The skewed data produced as a result will provide a test bed for skewed joins and skewed where clauses. The first approach described in section 2 and referred to as alternative 1 corresponds to actual nation populations in year 2000. The next alternative, also described in section 2, that corresponds to fictitious but skewed nation populations will be referred to as alternative 2. In alternative 2 the nations are arbitrarily split into two groups with high and low population counts respectively. In alternative 2 as in alternative 1 the nation to region association stays the same in TPC-H and the resulting region populations happen to be different from each other.

In section 3 we use the skewed data obtained by using the approach defined in section 2 to show how skew can be a challenge for query optimizers in parallel systems using the example of the Teradata database. Finally, in section 4 we propose a complete solution for introducing skew in the TPC-H benchmark. This solution, referred to as alternative 3 involves again fictitious and skewed nation populations with nations split into two groups with high and low population counts. The split is however performed in such a way that the region populations remain the same. As a result, skew alternative 3 can be implemented using the existing TPC-H queries with minimal disruption.

2   Introducing Skew in TPC-H Data

In the TPC-H benchmark all distributions are uniform as it is a requirement clearly spelled out in the benchmark specification [6]. In particular, there are five regions and five nations per region and the number of customers and suppliers per nation is constant. For instance, at scale factor 1000, there are approximately six million customers and four hundred thousand supplier per nation. So we could very easily introduce skew by making the number of customers and suppliers per nation variable so that we would have some nations with a lot of customers and suppliers and other regions with few customers and suppliers. By skewing these tables and nothing else we introduce skew in a manner that is the simplest possible and involves a very limited amount of change.

The first idea that comes to mind is to make the numbers of customers and suppliers associated with a particular nation proportional to the actual population of this nation. We have implemented this alternative using a census of population data for the year 2000 and the built-in Teradata SQL random number generator to obtain customer and supplier populations proportional to the corresponding nation populations at scale factor 1000. This entailed creating a copy of the customer and supplier tables and inserting all the original values from customer and supplier respectively except the nation key which is determined on the basis of which interval the value drawn by the random generator falls into, the intervals being determined by the nation populations. This very simple procedure can be used *mutatis mutandis* by anyone interested in the introduction of skew into TPC-H data. Because a built-in number generator is used, the resulting populations may differ somewhat from one database to another which is fine at this stage of proof of concept. When applied to a TPC-H database at scale factor 1000 the procedure described above produced the populations shown in Table 1 below.

Table 1. Customer and Supplier populations – alternative 1

nation-key	nation name	actual 2000 population	original #customers	#customers skewed	original #suppliers	#suppliers skewed
0	ALGERIA	32854000	5996505	1245313	399554	82867
1	ARGENTINA	38747000	5997462	1467640	399809	97991
2	BRAZIL	170000000	6001105	6434837	399867	429159
3	CANADA	31689000	5999735	1198883	401453	80387
4	EGYPT	74033000	6000340	2802655	400511	187411
5	ETHIOPIA	77431000	6000869	2932444	399905	195397
6	FRANCE	58921000	5996991	2230801	399798	148608
7	GERMANY	82000000	5997384	3106050	399948	207371
8	INDIA	1000000000	6001843	37861280	399240	2524131
9	INDONESIA	206264595	6001218	7803651	400048	519512
10	IRAN	69515000	6001889	2633616	400286	175430
11	IRAQ	28807000	6000601	1090553	399914	72641
12	JAPAN	127000000	5998850	4809793	399558	320661
13	JORDAN	5703000	6000889	215919	399629	14447
14	KENYA	34256000	5997420	1299102	399302	86798
15	MOROCCO	31478000	6003115	1193196	400295	79308
16	MOZAMBIQUE	19792000	5998481	747864	399604	50207
17	PERU	27968000	5997549	1058228	400593	70426
18	CHINA	1242612226	6001991	47039217	400303	3134599
19	ROMANIA	21711000	6002183	821699	400240	54773
20	SAUDI ARABIA	24573000	5998452	929786	400246	62114
21	VIETNAM	70000000	6003717	2648881	400471	175911
22	RUSSIA	147000000	6000916	5566052	399995	370747
23	UNITED KINGDOM	58459000	6000497	2211755	399662	147395
24	UNITED STATES	281421906	5999998	10650785	399769	711709
	TOTAL	3962235727	150000000	150000000	10000000	10000000

The advantage of the above procedure is that it produces data skew that is realistic since the populations are proportional to actual nation populations in 2000 which are observed numbers. So any tests conducted on this skewed data would have the potential of reflecting "real-life" situations. Its disadvantage in the context of TPC-H queries is that all queries involving the skewed customer and supplier tables would result in a different amount of work since all nations have now different number of rows in customer and supplier. This could be a problem if we wanted to define a number of equivalent queries with a nation drawn at random as it is the case in TPC-H. In order to remedy the situation, we have devised another way to introduce skew in customer and supplier. Again, the change involves only these tables and nothing else.

The main ingredient in skew is that performance will change when a nation with small population is chosen as opposed to a nation with a large population. So let us decide that there will be two kinds of nations, the first 13 with a small population, and the last 12 with a large population. Let us also decide that a highly populated nation is ten times the size of a nation with a small population. With these constraints at scale factor 1000 a small population will be 1,127,820 customers and 75,188 suppliers and large populations will ten times as much. Applying the same procedure with insert/select and the Teradata SQL random number generator to this case we obtain the customer and supplier populations portrayed in Table 2 below.

Table 2. Customer and Supplier populations – alternative 2

nation-key	nation name	original #customers	#customers skewed	original #suppliers	#suppliers skewed
0	ALGERIA	5996505	1127162	399554	75093
1	ARGENTINA	5997462	1129929	399809	75398
2	BRAZIL	6001105	1127874	399867	74755
3	CANADA	5999735	1127238	401453	75516
4	EGYPT	6000340	1127577	400511	75046
5	ETHIOPIA	6000869	1127826	399905	74787
6	FRANCE	5996991	1129149	399798	75531
7	GERMANY	5997384	1128233	399948	75052
8	INDIA	6001843	1126280	399240	75022
9	INDONESIA	6001218	1127706	400048	74966
10	IRAN	6001889	1127191	400286	75317
11	IRAQ	6000601	1125231	399914	74940
12	JAPAN	5998850	1127436	399558	75545
13	JORDAN	6000889	11275061	399629	750316
14	KENYA	5997420	11280163	399302	752856
15	MOROCCO	6003115	11277956	400295	750342
16	MOZAMBIQUE	5998481	11277392	399604	751458
17	PERU	5997549	11278474	400593	752394
18	CHINA	6001991	11275245	400303	751565
19	ROMANIA	6002183	11279797	400240	750950
20	SAUDI ARABIA	5998452	11280197	400246	752172
21	VIETNAM	6003717	11278040	400471	752970
22	RUSSIA	6000916	11275496	399995	753193
23	UNITED KINGDOM	6000497	11283291	399662	753027
24	UNITED STATES	5999998	11280056	399769	751789
	TOTAL	150000000	150000000	10000000	10000000

The advantage of this approach is that any nation in the first set of 13 or in the second set of 12 represents the same population size and therefore the same amount of work which could be of interest in developing queries with various nation names that involve the same amount of work. However, with this alternative, the population sizes will be different for all regions which is realistic. We now proceed to the next section where we show how the skew that we defined can pose challenges to optimizers in parallel systems.

3   Query Optimization with Skew

In this section we address the problem of query optimization when a where clause is applied on a skewed column. If the condition is applied with a value involving a large number of rows as opposed to a value involving a small number of rows we expect to have worse performance with the larger number of rows. This is especially true when the same plan is applied to both values. There can be cases however where a better plan can be found for the large value. We illustrate this issue here in the context of the Teradata database. The experiments were conducted on a small Teradata appliance, the same that was used to generate the skewed data.

In general, query optimizers need to be aware of skew and produce appropriate execution plans that may be different than those produced for uniform distributions. That intelligence can be implemented through rules or changes to the cost model. Normally as it is the case in Teradata, the cost model has detailed knowledge of the data distribution used to estimate the selectivity of predicates on skewed columns. If the skew columns are parts of joins, the unit of parallelism that has the most amount of data is used as a basis for costing.

In other words, the cost model behaves as if all the units of parallelism (called AMPs) have the same amount of rows as the one with the highest amount of rows. The query below, which is based on the TPC-H model with a skewed customer table as described in alternative 1, illustrates the impact of skew on query optimization. The query computes the total price of orders placed during 1997 by customers who live in certain nations.

```
SELECT c_mktsegment , SUM(o_totalprice) AS tot_price
FROM orders, customer
WHERE c_custkey = o_custkey
AND o_orderdate BETWEEN DATE '1997-12-31' - INTERVAL '1' YEAR
AND DATE '1997-12-31'
AND c_nationkey IN (<parm1>,<parm2>,<parm3>)
GROUP BY c_mktsegment;
```

The execution plan of the above query involves a join between orders and customer followed by an aggregate step. Assuming orders is hashed by o_orderkey and customer by c_custkey respectively, one of the tables need to be reshuffled to perform the join. Either the filtered rows of customer are duplicated on all the AMPs or the entire orders table is hash redistributed by o_custkey to al the AMPs. Teradata makes the decision between these two methods (and the join method as well) based on a cost function which is influenced by the number of rows in the three nations selected.

We ran the above query for a set of nations with smaller populations corresponding to nation keys 19, 16, and 13 (query Q1a). We also ran the same query for nations with larger populations corresponding to nation keys 2,8 and 9 (query Q1b). In Q1a, only 1% of all customers live in the selected nations and the Teradata optimizer chose to duplicate the filtered customer rows (see explain in Table 3 below). For Q1b however (see explain in Table 4), 35% of customers are selected and the cost of redistributing orders became cheaper. Redistributing orders is therefore selected for execution of query Q1b. In the case where uniform distributions are present which is the case for the original TPC-H data, both Q1a and Q1b select 12% of the customers and the optimal plan for both redistributes the orders table.

142   A. Crolotte and A. Ghazal

Table 3. Explain for Q1a

4) We execute the following steps in parallel.
   1) We do an all-AMPs RETRIEVE step from TPCD1000G.customer_skew
   by way of an all-rows scan with a condition of (
   "(TPCD1000G.customer_skew.C_NATIONKEY = 16) OR
   ((TPCD1000G.customer_skew.C_NATIONKEY = 13) OR
   (TPCD1000G.customer_skew.C_NATIONKEY = 19))") into **Spool 4**
   (all_amps) fanned out into 19 hash join partitions, which is
   duplicated on all AMPs. The size of Spool 4 is estimated
   with high confidence to be 128,554,704 rows (2,828,203,488
   bytes). The estimated time for this step is 24.83 seconds.
   2) We do an all-AMPs RETRIEVE step from 2 partitions of
   TPCD1000G.ordertbl with a condition of (
   "(TPCD1000G.ordertbl.O_ORDERDATE >= DATE '1996-12-31') AND
   (TPCD1000G.ordertbl.O_ORDERDATE <= DATE '1997-12-31')") into
   Spool 5 (all_amps) fanned out into 19 hash join partitions,
   which is built locally on the AMPs. The size of Spool 5 is
   estimated with high confidence to be 227,348,762 rows (
   5,683,719,050 bytes). The estimated time for this step is
   55.38 seconds.
5) We do an all-AMPs JOIN step from Spool 4 (Last Use) by way of an
  all-rows scan, which is joined to Spool 5 (Last Use) by way of an
  all-rows scan. Spool 4 and Spool 5 are joined using a hash join
  of 19 partitions, with a join condition of ("C_CUSTKEY = O_CUSTKEY").
  The result goes into Spool 3 (all_amps), which is built locally on
  the AMPs. The size of Spool 3 is estimated with low confidence to
  be 4,059,272 rows (113,659,616 bytes). The estimated time for
  this step is 10.05 seconds.

Table 4. Explain for Q1b

4) We execute the following steps in parallel.
   1) We do an all-AMPs RETRIEVE step from TPCD1000G.customer by
   way of an all-rows scan with a condition of (
   "(TPCD1000G.customer.C_NATIONKEY = 16) OR
   ((TPCD1000G.customer.C_NATIONKEY = 13) OR
   (TPCD1000G.customer.C_NATIONKEY = 19))") into Spool 4
   (all_amps) fanned out into 3 hash join partitions, which is
   built locally on the AMPs. The size of Spool 4 is estimated
   with high confidence to be 18,001,554 rows (396,034,188
   bytes). The estimated time for this step is 19.99 seconds.
   2) We do an all-AMPs RETRIEVE step from 2 partitions of
   TPCD1000G.ordertbl with a condition of (
   "(TPCD1000G.ordertbl.O_ORDERDATE >= DATE '1996-12-31') AND
   (TPCD1000G.ordertbl.O_ORDERDATE <= DATE '1997-12-31')") into
   Spool 5 (all_amps) fanned out into 3 hash join partitions,
   which is **redistributed by the hash code** of (
   TPCD1000G.ordertbl.O_CUSTKEY) to all AMPs. The size of Spool
   5 is estimated with high confidence to be 227,348,762 rows (
   5,683,719,050 bytes). The estimated time for this step is 1
   minute and 10 seconds.
5) We do an all-AMPs JOIN step from Spool 4 (Last Use) by way of an
  all-rows scan, which is joined to Spool 5 (Last Use) by way of an
  all-rows scan. Spool 4 and Spool 5 are joined using a hash join
  of 3 partitions, with a join condition of ("C_CUSTKEY = O_CUSTKEY").
  The result goes into Spool 3 (all_amps), which is built locally on
  the AMPs. The size of Spool 3 is estimated with low confidence to
  be 40,926,311 rows (1,145,936,708 bytes). The estimated time for
  this step is 8.48 seconds.

4   A Complete Skew Solution for TPC-H

In this section we address the very specific problem of introducing skew in TPC-H with the minimum amount of disruption to the current query set. We already know that the first alternative in which all nations had different populations could not be utilized because we need to respect the TPC-H protocol whereby several queries performing the same amount of work for a set of nations must be available. Using the second alternative is better because an original TPC-H query can be duplicated so that two versions of the same query can be used, one version with a small population and one with a large population. We will have 13 possible variations of the first version and 12 variations of the second version all involving the same amount of work within one version. Looking at the existing TPC-H queries involving the skewed tables customer or supplier or both it turns out that these tables can be accessed either via a nation name or a region name as shown in table 5 below.

Table 5. TPC-H queries involved in skew

Queries Involving the Skewed Tables			
CUSTOMER		SUPPLIER	
via nation	via region	via nation	via region
7, 8, 20, 21	5, 8	11, 7	2, 5

With alternative 2 the regions have different customer and supplier populations which presents a problem because queries 2, 5 and 8 now involve a different amount of work depending on what region is drawn by qgen. Queries 7, 11, 20 and 21 could easily be handled by duplication as proposed above. This shows the need for a third skew alternative that will create two sets of nations with respectively low and high populations and leave regions at the same size. This can be accomplished by dividing up the nations in two groups as in alternative 2 but this time we will apply a consistent strategy to all regions. Since there are 5 nations per region we define 3 nations with low population and 2 with high population everything else staying the same including the region to nation assignment. Using the same rule as before whereby the population of a large region is ten times the population of a small region we obtain the populations for the customer and supplier tables by nation portrayed in Table 6.

The customer and supplier populations by nation are in two groups and the regions are of the same size as in the current version of the benchmark. As a result, we do not have to worry about changing queries 2 and 5 which access the database on a region basis. For query 8 which has an explicit reference to both nation and region we will need only address the reference to nation. Even though skew will alter the performance of these queries compared to today because the joins are skewed but they are skewed in the same way and therefore involve the same amount of work regardless of the region selected. We now need to address the required changes to queries 7, 8, 10, 20 and 21.

Table 6. Customer and Supplier populations – alternative 3

regionkey	nationkey	nation name	# customers skewed	#suppliers skewed
0	0	ALGERIA	1303884	86904
0	5	ETHIOPIA	1306366	86958
0	14	KENYA	1303909	86896
0	15	MOROCCO	13038119	868515
0	16	MOZAMBIQUE	13041356	870138
1	1	ARGENTINA	1304942	86637
1	2	BRAZIL	1304372	87171
1	3	CANADA	1305311	86946
1	17	PERU	13043601	867792
1	24	UNITED STATES	13043469	868983
2	8	INDIA	1305191	87360
2	9	INDONESIA	1307374	86982
2	12	JAPAN	1304620	86859
2	18	CHINA	13037483	870543
2	21	VIETNAM	13045923	867881
3	6	FRANCE	1302458	86759
3	7	GERMANY	1304490	86768
3	19	ROMANIA	1304150	87165
3	22	RUSSIA	13045606	869921
3	23	UNITED KINGDOM	13043181	870220
4	4	EGYPT	1305456	87531
4	10	IRAN	1303462	87204
4	11	IRAQ	1304282	86814
4	13	JORDAN	13045058	871250
4	20	SAUDI ARABIA	13045937	869803
		total	150000000	10000000

Since query 7 involves two nations we could chose an approach whereby nation1 is chosen from the low population pool while nation2 is chosen from the high population pool. This would not require duplicating the query since all combinations would involve the same amount of work. The second approach would consist of duplicating query 7 and chose in version 1 of the query both nations from a low pool and in version 2 of the query both nations from the high pool. The first approach would dilute the effect of skew but still provide a large number of nation combinations while the second approach increases the effect of skew but results in a smaller number of nation combinations. For each query q where q is 8, 10, 20 and 21 (and perhaps 7 if so wanted) we will define two queries q.1 and q.2. While the nation name can be any of the nation names with a low population (15 possible values) in q.1, the nation name will be any of the nation names with a high population in q.2. This will increase the number of queries to at least 26 and skew will be present in TPC-H in a simple fashion although, from a benchmark specification perspective, the effort could be significant in terms of the utilities dbgen and qgen.

5   Conclusion

We have presented several approaches all very easy to implement that introduce skew into TPC-H. The first approach is of interest for companies or research institutions as it is realistic since resulting supplier and customer populations per nation are proportional to actual nation populations. The second alternative divides nations into two groups. In one group all nations are of equal size but small while in the other group all nations are also of equal size but large and regions are of different sizes. The third alternative, like the second, divides the nations into two groups, one with large and equal populations and the second with small but equal populations but leaves the regions equal in size (from a customer and supplier standpoint). Using the third alternative we have shown how it is possible to define a new TPC-H benchmark involving skew and the same query set with minimal disruption. Using a simple query we have also shown how skew can be a challenge for parallel database system optimizers.

References

[1] Lakshmi, S.M., Yu, P.S.: Effect of Skew on Join Performance in Parallel Architectures. In: International Symposium on Databases in Parallel and Distributed Systems (1988)
[2] Walton, C.B., Dale, A.G., Jenevein, R.M.: A Taxonomy and Performance Model of Data Skew Effects in Parallel Joins. In: Proceedings of VLDB, pp. 537–548 (1991)
[3] Wolf, J.L., Dias, D.M., Yu, P.S., Turek, J.: An Effective Algorithm for Parallelizing Hash Joins in the Presence of Data Skew. In: Proceedings of ICDE 1991 (1991)
[4] DeWitt, D.J., Naughton, J.F., Schneider, D.A., Seshadri, S.: Practical Skew Handling in Parallel Joins. In: Proceedings of VLDB 1992, pp. 27–40 (1992)
[5] Xu, Y., Kostamaa, P.: Efficient Outer Join Data Skew Handling in Parallel DBMS. In: Proceedings of VLDB, pp. 1390–1396 (2009)
[6] TPC Benchmark H (Decision Support) Standard Specification Revision 2.14.0, http://www.tpc.org

Time and Cost-Efficient Modeling and Generation of Large-Scale TPCC/TPCE/TPCH Workloads

Christina Delimitrou[1], Sriram Sankar[2], Badriddine Khessib[2],
Kushagra Vaid[2], and Christos Kozyrakis[1]

[1] Electrical Engineering Department, Stanford University, Stanford, CA, USA, 94305
{cdel,kozyraki}@stanford.edu
[2] Global Foundation Services, Microsoft, Redmond, WA, USA, 98052.
{srsankar,bkhessib,kvaid}@microsoft.com

Abstract. Large-scale TPC workloads are critical for the evaluation of datacenter-scale storage systems. However, these workloads have not been previously characterized, in-depth, and modeled in a DC environment. In this work, we categorize the TPC workloads into storage threads that have unique features and characterize the storage activity of TPCC, TPCE and TPCH based on I/O traces from real server installations. We also propose a framework for modeling and generation of large-scale TPC workloads, which allows us to conduct a wide spectrum of storage experiments without requiring knowledge on the structure of the application or the overhead of fully deploying it in different storage configurations. Using our framework, we eliminate the time for TPC setup and reduce the time for experiments by two orders of magnitude, due to the compression in storage activity enforced by the model. We demonstrate the accuracy of the model and the applicability of our method to significant datacenter storage challenges, including identification of early disk errors, and SSD caching.

Keywords: Workload, Modeling, Storage Traces, TPC benchmarks, Characterization, Storage Configuration, Datacenter.

1   Introduction

As cloud data-stores have emerged over the past decade, user data has started being increasingly stored in large-capacity and high-performance systems, which account for a significant portion of the total cost of ownership (TCO) of a datacenter (DC) [4]. Specifically for large-scale databases, data retrieval is often the bottleneck for application performance [1, 4], promoting efficient storage provisioning to a first-order design constraint. This makes the study of the TPC benchmarks (TPCC, TPCE and TPCH), which have traditionally been of fundamental importance for the configuration and evaluation of DC-scale systems, even more important. TPCC and TPCE especially, being clearly I/O-bound, are tailored for use in storage system studies, while TPCH also experiences significant challenges towards its optimal configuration. However, one of the main roadblocks when trying to evaluate storage

R. Nambiar and M. Poess (Eds.): TPCTC 2011, LNCS 7144, pp. 146–162, 2012.

system options using large instances of TPC is the *cost* in *time,* and *demand* for *expertise* for setting up and managing the workload itself. Applications like TPCC, TPCE and TPCH introduce high complexity in order to be correctly configured and setup to scale to hundreds of thousands of servers, while they demand in-depth knowledge of the structure and functionality of the workloads from the DC operators.

One of the main challenges when using large-scale applications to evaluate storage is the difficulty in replaying the entire application in all possible system configurations. The effort itself can be highly inefficient in both time and cost. Furthermore, applications like TPCC and TPCE differ from conventional desktop applications in that they cannot be approximated by single-machine benchmarking, therefore highly scalable experiments are required.

Despite the merit in understanding the characteristics of the workload in order to effectively provision its storage system, no in-depth, per-thread characterization of the I/O behavior of TPC applications exists. Previous work on workload generation [6, 10, 11, 13] lacks the ability to capture aspects of the workload like spatial and temporal locality which are critical for the accurate representation of the application's storage activity, while experiments are limited to small scales. This underlines the importance of investing in frameworks that enable extensive workload analysis, characterization and modeling, while permitting easy and fast setup for TPC applications, without requiring significant knowledge on the application's intricate details and functionality, therefore can be performed directly by storage experts.

In this work, we propose a framework that enables *fast* and *accurate* configuration and storage experiments for TPCC/E/H using a workload model and a tool that generates storage activity that is similar in I/O characteristics and performance metrics to that of the original application. This framework decouples performing large-scale storage experiments from the requirement to being an expert in the TPC workloads. This infrastructure includes probabilistic, state diagram-based models [1] that capture information of configurable granularity on the workload's access patterns. The models are developed from production traces of large instances of TPCC, TPCE and TPCH. We identify the optimal level of detail required for the model to accurately describe the storage activity of each application and design a tool that recognizes them and recreates access patterns with I/O features that resemble those of the original workloads. We have performed extensive validation on the accuracy of the infrastructure, in terms of the generated storage behavior and have verified the consistency and conciseness of the results [3]. Based on these models and the original traces we perform an in-depth, per-thread characterization of the storage activity of the TPC benchmarks and provide insights on their behavior.

The proposed framework can be used for research on large-scale storage systems. Specifically in this work we present two possible use cases, namely: identification of early errors in large-scale storage systems, and evaluation of incorporating SSD caching in the back-end servers to improve performance. The results demonstrate the accuracy of the modeling process, and the time and cost-efficiency in performing large-scale experiments for TPC benchmarks.

Succinctly, the main contributions of this work are:

- We perform an extensive, per-thread characterization of the access pattern and characteristics in the storage activity of the TPCC, TPCE and TPCH workloads and provide insights on the correlation between storage activity and specific query type.
- We provide a framework for accurate modeling, of configurable detail, of the storage activity for TPCC, TPCE and TPCH and verify the resemblance between original and synthetic application in I/O features and performance metrics.
- We greatly simplify the setup and configuration procedure for evaluating storage using large-scale TPC benchmarks, and remove the requirement for expertise in the application's structure, components and functionality, therefore enabling storage experts to independently perform storage configuration experiments.
- We greatly reduce the time required to perform large-scale storage experiments (e.g. SSD caching, from days in the original TPC setup, to minutes, when using the model i.e. a 150x time reduction), by compressing the storage behavior and removing the need to deploy the entire application in different storage configurations.
- We demonstrate the scalability of our methodology to a large number of servers, as well as the ability to perform accurate scaled-down experiments using fewer instances of the model.
- We show the applicability of this methodology to a wide spectrum of use cases, ranging from identifying early problems with storage (infant mortality), to storage configuration optimizations (e.g. use of SSDs, hybrid HDD/SSD systems).

This methodology enables studies previously impossible without a full TPC setup and without application deployment for every modification in the storage system. Thus it greatly reduces the overhead and complexity of performing large-scale studies, while offering the ability to setup the workloads to storage experts as well.

The rest of this paper is structured as follows. Section 2 discusses the motivation for this work. Section 3 presents related work on TPC characterization and storage modeling and generation. Section 4 provides a description of the model and an overview of the tool's implementation as well as an in-depth, per-thread characterization of the three applications. Section 5 discusses the validation of the methodology against the original TPC workloads, and a comparison of our toolset with a popularly used workload generator. Section 6 discusses the applicability of the tool in evaluating the important DC storage challenge of storage endurance and SSD caching. Finally, Section 7 presents topics for future work and concludes the paper.

2   Motivation

Datacenter applications are hard to model due to their varying user demand and large scale. Large enterprises typically use industry-standard TPC benchmarks for configuring their database systems prior to actual deployment. However, TPC benchmarks are extremely difficult to setup, sometimes taking multiple weeks to get a working configuration. In this work, we strive to reduce this setup time and the current need to have TPC as a full application deployment. In earlier large-scale TPC setups, there used to be disks with intermittent read failures or bad sectors that would create latency profiles with few outliers that were very difficult to identify. In present day setups, SSDs (Solid State Drives) encounter intermittent write performance issues that are difficult to detect in a full application deployment. For all these cases, we need improved storage testing ability. The objective of our modeling and I/O generation work is to provide such a facility.

In addition to reducing setup times and facilitating fast storage testing, we also use our framework to test new DC technologies, including tiered storage approaches. One recent development is the use of SSDs in traditional hard disk drive (HDD) space.

Since SSDs are significantly costlier per GB than HDDs, we need to configure the use of these devices such that the eventual cost-performance of the system is optimal. Such studies also require running the entire application setup, which takes a lot of time to test multiple configurations. Our framework is designed to address multiple test configurations in an efficient manner using intensity knobs.

3   Related Work

Performing scalable experiments using the TPC workloads is of great interest to hardware architects, especially when the target system is a large-scale DC. Specifically, because of their I/O-dominated behavior, TPCC and TPCE are of primary importance when configuring and evaluating the storage system of large DCs.

Significant prior work [7] has studied how to efficiently provision this part of the system, however, using the TPC workloads in this scope, introduces a large overhead, in terms of setup and maintenance for the application. An ideal way to overcome this is by using a model that captures the storage behavior of TPC benchmarks and a tool that recreates representative access patterns that resemble the original workload. Such a framework would provide insight on the storage behavior, and greatly reduce the time required for the setup and configuration of large-scale databases, as well as the time for storage configuration experiments.

Despite the obvious merit in developing such an infrastructure, most prior work on large-scale storage configuration is empirical, primarily relying on extracting the workload characteristics based on traces [8].

Kavalanekar et al. in [2] and [8] use a trace-based approach to characterize large online services for storage configuration and performance modeling respectively. Traces offer useful insight on the characteristics of large-scale workloads, but their usefulness is limited by the system upon which they have been collected. Generating TPC workloads with high fidelity can offer far richer information towards understanding their behavior and making experimenting with them easier and faster. It also enables addressing instrumental challenges in storage system design (error detection, SSD caching, data migration) when optimizing for performance, efficiency and/or cost.

Prior work on workload generators includes SQLIO [10], Vdbench [11], and IOMeter [6] which remains the most well-known open-source tool for workload generation. The main disadvantage of these tools is that, as in the case of IOMeter, they lack the ability to represent the spatial and temporal locality in the I/O accesses, which for applications like TPC is critical in distinguishing between hot and cold tables in the database. This makes these tools impractical, if not impossible, to be used for locality-aware studies, which are critical for many storage optimizations.

In this work we present a new framework for TPC workloads, which allows accurate modeling and generation of their I/O access patterns and greatly simplifies the setup of the infrastructure and the execution of large-scale experiments.

4   Modeling and Generating TPCC/E/H

Our framework consists of two main components. First, we train the model that captures the storage activity of the TPC workloads. Second, we have implemented a tool that recognizes these models and creates storage access patterns with similar characteristics as in the original applications.

4.1   Storage Workload Model

Our model is based on the Markov chain representation discussed in [1]. According to the model, states correspond to ranges of Logical Block Numbers (LBNs) on disk, and transitions, represent the probability of consecutive I/Os moving between states. The transitions are characterized by the following I/O features: *block size*, *type of request* (read, write), *randomness*, and *inter-arrival time* between subsequent requests. We present here the basic features of the state diagram. More details on the model can be found in [3]. The main insight behind the structure of the model is that spatial locality of I/Os can be represented by the clustering of requests in each state, and temporal locality by the transitions between states. The probability of each transition is calculated as the percentage of the requests that correspond to it. Figure 1(a) shows a simple state diagram with four states.

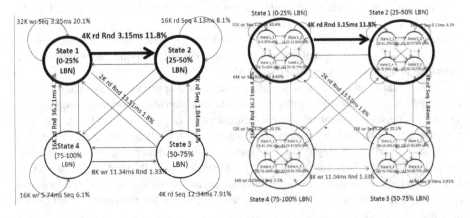

Fig. 1. State Diagram Model: (a) One level, (b) Two levels

In order to include more detailed information on the I/O access pattern we have extended this model to a hierarchical representation with each state expanding to become a new state diagram. This way, with a simple sensitivity study we can identify the optimal amount of information required by each application to make the model accurate. Figure 1(b) shows an example of such a model using two levels. Increasing the number of states per level to reduce the number of levels is possible but augments the complexity of the model, as the transition count increases substantially.

4.2   Generation Tool

The second part of the infrastructure consists of a tool that recognizes the storage workload model and creates a benchmark with activity similar to that of the original TPC application. For this purpose we have used and extended DiskSpd [5], a workload generator that works as a command line tool, initiating read/write requests in burst mode to disks and/or files. In order to account for the information captured in the model, we have implemented a set of additional features in DiskSpd, which briefly are:

- Initiating I/O requests with specified inter-arrival times, either static or time-varying to capture fluctuation in the intensity of storage activity.
- Maintaining transition probabilities between threads and guaranteeing that the generated workload is a compressed and accurate version of the original one.
- Varying the intensity of the generated workload using a knob that scales the inter-arrival times between subsequent I/O requests. This enables evaluation of alternative storage system configurations, e.g. SSD-based systems.

In Section 5 we present the comparison of the original TPC applications against the synthetic workloads to show the accuracy of the modeling and generation process.

4.3   Characterization of TPCC/TPCE/TPCH

We used the previously discussed models to characterize large-scale instances of TPCC, TPCE and TPCH workloads from real production DC systems. In order to reduce the dimensionality of the problem, we separate the application traces per thread and create a separate model for each thread. We observe the access patterns in the benchmark, along with the spatial and temporal locality characteristics captured by the model. We also evaluate the performance metrics (IOPS and average request latency) based on the information collected from the traces.

Table 1 shows this characterization for the three workloads in a per-thread manner. This separation is performed perceptively at the moment; however, as part of future work, we plan to develop automatic ways to recognize and categorize storage activity in thread types. Each row in Table 1 corresponds to a different thread type in the application. We categorize the threads based on their functionality (i.e. a Log or a Data Thread), activity (low or high I/O request rate) and fluctuation (constant activity or experiencing activity spikes) characteristics.

The categorization in thread types is:

- *Log Thread with high activity and low fluctuation (#0)*
- *Log Thread with low activity and high fluctuation (#1)*
- *Data Thread (SQL Queries) with high activity and low fluctuation (#2)*
- *Data Thread (SQL Queries) with high activity and high fluctuation (#3)*
- *Data Thread (SQL Queries) with medium activity and low fluctuation (#4)*
- *Data Thread (SQL Queries) with low activity and high fluctuation (#5)*
- *Data Thread (SQL Queries) with low activity and low fluctuation (#6)*
- *Data Thread (SQL Queries) with very low activity and fluctuation (#7)*

Specifically TPCC and TPCE have the following thread types:

Log #0, Log #1, Data #2, Data #3 and **Data #6**

While for TPCH the thread types are:

Log #0, Data #2, Data #3, Data #4, Data #5, Data #6 and **Data #7**

Those are the only combinations of activity-fluctuation pairs observed for the specific applications. For each type of thread we show the characteristics of the I/O requests (rd:wr ratio, percentage of sequential I/Os, average inter-arrival time between requests and average request size), as well as the spatial locality of accesses as captured by the model. Each state corresponds to a portion of the disk space in LBNs, e.g. St1 corresponds to the first 25% of logical block addresses. The thread weight column shows the percentage of requests that correspond to the specific thread. Finally, we show the average performance metrics (throughput and latency) for each thread type. The number of threads that belongs to each thread type for each application is shown in Table 2.

Table 1. Per thread I/O characteristics and performance metrics for TPCC/TPCE/TPCH

	Thread type	Fluctuation (11min)		Rd:Wr Ratio	Seq. % I/Os	Avg Int. Time(ms)	Avg Request Size (KB)	Spatial Locality				Thread Weight	Avg. IOPS	Avg Lat. (ms)
								St1	St2	St3	St4			
TPCC	**Total**			2.2:1	2.8	0.43	9.48	85.8	1.4	12	0.4	1.00	47,082	4.13
			R	2.2	0.08	0.08	4.13	88.5	1.5	9.8	0.3	0.68	35,720	6.47
			W	1	6.49	4.13	12.31	79.1	1.2	19	0.6	0.32	11,362	0.47
	#0 (Log)			1:99	1.8	2.56	2.09	88.3	11	0.7	0	1.2E-4	5.87	8.91
			R	1	0.02	3036.1	0.5	0	0	100	0	1.2E-6	0.58	8.97
			W	99	1.8	2.55	2.09	88.9	11	0.2	0	1.2E-4	5.29	8.91
	#1 (Log)			1:99	0.95	66.30	3.94	66.7	31	2	1	0.001	49.26	2.45
			R	1	0.01	107.8	0.5	75	0	25	0	1E-5	0.49	6.13
			W	99	0.95	65.8	3.94	66.1	31	1.9	1	99E-5	48.77	2.30
	#2 (SQL Queries)			2:1	25.0	2.60	14.625	86.4	0	14	0	0.17	8,403	3.01
			R	2	28.5	2.57	20.625	87.2	0	13	0	0.119	5,602	4.89
			W	1	18.0	2.72	8.192	99.7	0	0	0.3	0.059	2,802	0.41
	#3 (SQL Queries)			98:2	2.0	1.00	20.873	78.5	0	21	0.7	0.242	11,394	6.01
			R	98	2.1	1.00	1.024	78.4	0	21	0.7	0.241	11,166	6.05
			W	2	0.3	10.96	65.526	99.4	0	0	0.6	0.001	228	0.56
	#6 (SQL Queries)			100:1	14.7	5.27	32.893	100	0	0	0	0.02	945.42	5.47
			R	100	14.7	5.27	32.893	100	0	0	0	0.02	945.42	5.47
			W	0	-	-	-	-	-	-	-	0	0	-

Table 1. *(continued)*

	Thread type	Fluctuation (11min)		Rd:Wr Ratio	% Seq. I/Os	Avg Int. Time(ms)	Avg Request Size (KB)	Spatial Locality				Thread Weight	Avg. IOPS	Avg Lat. (ms)
								St1	St2	St3	St4			
TPCE	**Total**			**10.5:1**	**8.15**	**0.78**	**8.41**	**89.8**	**8.4**	**1.7**	**0.3**	**1.00**	**24,694**	**5.55**
			R	10.5	6.04	0.59	8.02	92.5	5.4	2.1	0	0.913	22,546	6.01
			W	1	23.75	6.89	14.68	56.0	27	15	2.1	0.087	2,148	0.69
	#0 (Log)			**1:99**	**11.75**	**9.09**	**2.05**	**88.8**	**10**	**1.0**	**0.3**	**5E-4**	**12.37**	**0.48**
			R	1	0.01	909.14	0.5	76	16.3	7.4	0.3	5E-6	0.12	5.63
			W	99	11.75	9.08	2.05	88.9	11	0.1	0	5E-4	12.25	0.47
	#1 (Log)			**1:100**	**1.42**	**77.1**	**2.10**	**89.0**	**11**	**0**	**0**	**2.2E-5**	**0.54**	**0.56**
			R	0	-	-	-	-	-	-	-	0	0	-
			W	100	1.42	77.1	2.10	89.0	11	0	0	2.2E-5	0.54	0.56
	#2 (SQL Queries)			**7:1**	**20.6**	**7.25**	**6.1**	**92.4**	**7.4**	**0.2**	**0**	**0.077**	**1,897**	**4.63**
			R	7	15.3	3.81	3.8	96.0	4.0	0	0	0.067	1,659	5.35
			W	1	37.9	12.89	16.0	87.7	10	2.3	0	0.009	238	0.47
	#3 (SQL Queries)			**12.5:1**	**16.3**	**4.38**	**8.02**	**91.0**	**8**	**0.2**	**1**	**0.048**	**1,172**	**5.67**
			R	12.5	11.65	2.37	8.02	90.8	8	0.4	1	0.044	1,086	6.13
			W	1	50	12.68	8.01	92	0	0	8	0.004	86	0.89
	#6 (SQL Queries)			**70.4:1**	**15.5**	**15.32**	**8.00**	**91.2**	**6.2**	**2.4**	**0**	**0.035**	**859.3**	**5.35**
			R	70.4	15.6	12.46	8.00	90.6	7.2	2.4	0	0.034	847.3	5.41
			W	1	7.1	287.3	4.01	99	0	0	1	0.0005	12.0	0.65
TPCH	**Total**			**29.4:1**	**35.5**	**0.327**	**16.13**	**92.7**	**6.2**	**1.3**	**0**	**1.00**	**3,296**	**5.92**
			R	29.4	35.6	0.317	16.19	89.8	10	0.1	0	0.967	3,188	6.01
			W	1	11.7	1.32	1.32	97.8	0	2.2	0	0.328	108.4	0.47
	#0 (Log)			**1:100**	**0**	**173.8**	**4.1**	**100**	**0**	**0**	**0**	**4.8E-6**	**0.016**	**0.44**
			R	0	-	-	-	-	-	-	-	0	0	-
			W	100	0	173.8	4.1	100	0	0	0	4.8E-6	0.016	0.44
	#2 (SQL Queries)			**100:1**	**74.8**	**10.8**	**524.2**	**97.8**	**2.2**	**0**	**0**	**0.012**	**40.4**	**5.31**
			R	100	74.8	10.8	524.2	97.8	2.2	0	0	0.012	40.4	5.31
			W	0	-	-	-	-	-	-	-	0	0	-
	#3 (SQL Queries)			**100:1**	**72.1**	**16.8**	**524.8**	**91.8**	**8.9**	**0.3**	**0**	**0.005**	**18.6**	**4.42**
			R	100	72.1	16.8	524.8	91.8	8.9	0.3	0	0.005	18.6	4.42
			W	0	-	-	-	-	-	-	-	0	0	-
	#4 (SQL Queries)			**99:1**	**63.8**	**48.63**	**128.8**	**95.4**	**4.6**	**0**	**0**	**0.002**	**7.20**	**5.31**
			R	99	63.9	48.5	128.9	95.4	4.3	0	0	0.002	7.19	5.46
			W	1	2.8	202.9	2.14	80	20	0	0	2E-5	0.01	0.46
	#5 (SQL Queries)			**100:1**	**50.9**	**315.8**	**524.8**	**80**	**0**	**20**	**0**	**0.0011**	**3.75**	**5.53**
			R	100	50.9	315.8	524.8	80	0	20	0	0.0011	3.75	5.53
			W	0	-	-	-	-	-	-	-	0	0	-
	#6 (SQL Queries)			**81:19**	**66.8**	**234.9**	**65.5**	**91.8**	**0**	**8.2**	**0**	**6.0E-4**	**1.99**	**5.42**
			R	81	70.2	123.7	65.5	100	0	0	0	4.8E-4	1.61	5.59
			W	19	12.8	869.4	4.01	80	0	20	0	1.2E-4	0.37	0.69
	#7 (SQL Queries)			**100:1**	**25.6**	**134.0**	**65.5**	**100**	**0**	**0**	**0**	**1.4E-8**	**4.6E-5**	**5.53**
			R	100	25.6	134.0	65.5	100	0	0	0	1.4E-8	4.6E-5	5.53
			W	0	-	-	-	-	-	-	-	0	0	-

Table 2. Number of threads and thread weights, for each thread-type for TPCC, TPCE and TPCH

Workload	Thread type	Number of Threads	Thread Weight /Thread	Thread Weight /Thread Type
TPCC	Total	26	-	**1.00**
	#0 (Log)	4	1.2E-4	4.8E-4
	#1 (Log)	12	0.001	0.012
	#2 (Data)	1	0.17	0.17
	#3 (Data)	3	0.242	0.726
	#6 (Data)	6	0.02	0.12
TPCE	Total	35	-	**1.00**
	#0 (Log)	6	5E-4	0.003
	#1 (Log)	9	2.2E-5	1.9E-4
	#2 (Data)	4	0.077	0.308
	#3 (Data)	9	0.048	0.432
	#6 (Data)	7	0.035	0.245
TPCH	Total	175	-	**1.00**
	#0 (Log)	13	4.8E-6	6.3E-5
	#2 (Data)	58	0.012	0.696
	#3 (Data)	52	0.005	0.26
	#4 (Data)	13	0.002	0.026
	#5 (Data)	6	0.0011	0.006
	#6 (Data)	11	6E-4	0.007
	#7 (Data)	22	1.4E-8	3E-7

Examining all three TPC applications, we see that read requests dominate. For TPCC that feature is not as evident as for TPCE and TPCH where the rd:wr ratio is over an order of magnitude higher. In terms of I/O features per thread, we present the main insight for each of the three applications:

I.TPCC

TPCC threads are divided between Log and Data threads, with the first accounting for a very small percentage of the total storage activity, while Data requests dominate. In terms of sequential over random I/O characteristics per thread type, we observe that Data #2 (high activity, low fluctuation) has a significant percentage of Sequential I/Os, and experiences minimal fluctuation in its storage activity. On the other hand, random-dominated threads like Data #3 have high fluctuation in their throughput, which might be a result of accessing many different files, and performing more complex queries. Regarding spatial locality, most I/O requests are directed to the first 25% of the storage capacity, with a smaller percentage belonging to St3.

II.TPCE

While TPCC only had 26 threads, TPCE has a significantly larger number of threads in this instance (35). Most of these threads service SQL Queries in the Data partitions of the storage, while 15 threads service Log requests with considerably lower intensity. Log threads, as with TPCC, are write-dominated, and have low throughput requirements, while Data threads are read-dominated and account for the large majority of the workload's storage activity. The differences between the threads' activity are smoother for TPCE than for TPCC, partially due to their larger number, which contributes to better load balance in the system. The main difference between SQL threads, apart from their throughput requirements, is their rd:wr ratio, which is 7:1 for Data #2 and reaches 70.4:1 for Data #6 (low activity, low fluctuation). This difference is appointed to the different type of queries serviced by each type of thread, and is consistent across threads of the same type. TPCE has even higher spatial locality than TPCC, with I/O requests being more aggregated in space, especially when it comes to Data requests. Most of the I/O accesses belonging to higher states are initiated as part of Log threads. This has motivated the TPC community to start using SSDs in order to limit the overprovisioning with respect to spatial locality.

III.TPCH
TPCH has been previously studied [9, 13] in terms of the large number of different queries it is comprised of. Here, we can correlate those types of queries with the underlying storage activity they initiate. In terms of aggregate I/O metrics, TPCH is significantly read-dominated, more than TPCE, and definitely more than TPCC. It is also a lot less intense than the previous two workloads, with average IOPS accounting for 5% of the average throughput of TPCC, and 10% of TPCE. However, the aspect where TPCH deviates most evidently from the I/O-dominated workloads is the number of threads it has, which is 175, almost an order of magnitude more than in either TPCC or TPCE. The interesting characterization of TPCH comes from studying the different types of these threads. Based on the storage activity and files visited, and without knowledge on the semantics of the application, we can deduce the type of query from the 22 TPCH query types [9].

Table 3. Correlation between Storage Activity and Queries for TPCH

Workload	Thread type	Query Type
TPCH	Total	Q1-Q8, Q10-Q22
	#0 (Log)	-
	#2 (Data)	Q1, Q5, Q7-Q10, Q16, Q18
	#3 (Data)	Q1, Q5, Q7, Q9, Q13, Q16, Q17
	#4 (Data)	Q3, Q5- Q8, Q17, Q19, Q21
	#5 (Data)	Q1, Q7, Q13-Q15, Q19, Q20
	#6 (Data)	Q2, Q4, Q6, Q14, Q15, Q22
	#7 (Data)	Q2, Q4, Q6, Q11, Q12, Q22

This means that a workload model can represent one or multiple query types and that by assembling the correct mix of per-thread workload models one can create a benchmark with the corresponding combination of queries without the requirement to know the functionality and structure of the application. Table 3 shows this correspondence between thread types and TPCH query types [9].

5   Validation

For each thread type, we create a separate workload model and a synthetic workload that resembles its storage activity. We create a thread mix based on the ratios in Table 2 to recreate the aggregate activity of each TPC application. We then run the synthetic workload using our framework and compare it against the original TPC applications. For our experiments we use real DC traces from a large-scale deployment of the TPC benchmarks, running on MS SQL Server. The synthetic workloads are run on a TPC-provisioned server with two sockets, 8 cores, 16GB of memory and 28 disks (5.4TB total storage) organized in RAID1+0 configuration. The metrics of interest are I/O characteristics per thread, as well as performance metrics (throughput and latency).

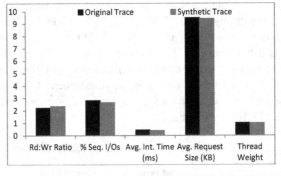

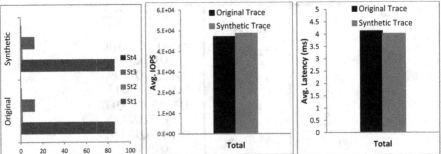

Fig. 2. Validation of *(a) I/O characteristics, (b) Spatial Locality* and *(c, d) Performance Metrics* between Original and Synthetic Trace for TPCC

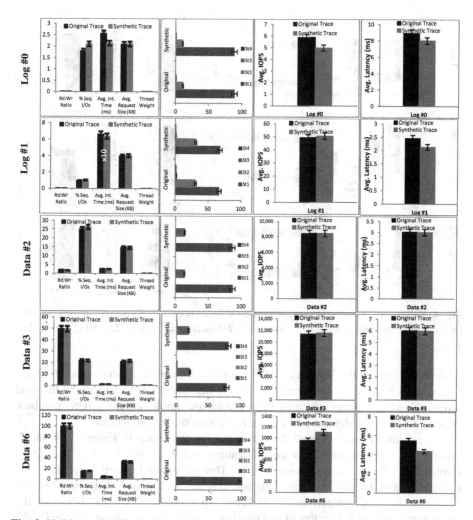

Fig. 3. Validation of *I/O characteristics*, *Spatial Locality* and *Performance Metrics* between Original and Synthetic Trace for: Log *#0* (1ˢᵗ row), *Log #1* (2ⁿᵈ row), *Data #2* (3ʳᵈ row), *Data #3* (4ᵗʰ row) and *Data #6* (5ᵗʰ row)

Figure 2(a) shows the validation of I/O features (Rd:Wr Ratio, % of Seq. I/Os, Avg. Inter-arrival Time, Avg. Request Size, Thread Weight), and Figure 2(b) the comparison in spatial locality between original and synthetic application for TPCC. The x-axis in Figure 2(a) shows the different I/O characteristics and the y-axis the value of the corresponding feature. The different bars in Figure 2(b) show the LBN ranges (i.e. each bar is 25% of the disk capacity). As we showed in Section 4.3 the vast majority of requests happen in State 1, while State 2 and State 3 have significantly lower percentages of I/O accesses. Figures 2(c) and 2(d) show the comparison for throughput and latency between original and synthetic application. For all metrics, the deviation is marginal (less than 5%), which shows that the model

158   C. Delimitrou et al.

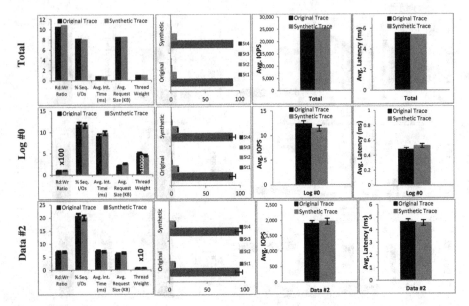

Fig. 4. Validation of *I/O characteristics*, *Spatial Locality* and *Performance Metrics* between Original and Synthetic Trace for: the *entire TPCE benchmark* (1st row), *Log #0* (2nd row), *Log #1* (3rd row)

accurately captures the behavior of the workload. Since the model is based on the logical level of the disk configuration, it is not dependent on the underlying physical layout. However, major changes in the database implementation (OS, database system) affect the model and will require re-training the state diagrams.

The per-thread results for all three applications are shown in Figures 3, 4 and 5. From left to right we show how the I/O features (Rd:Wr Ratio, %of Seq. I/Os, Avg. Inter-arrival Time, Avg. Request Size, Thread Weight), spatial locality and throughput and latency compare between original and synthetic application. For TPCC we show the comparison for all thread types and for TPCE and TPCH for the entire application, one Log thread and one Data thread. The results are similar for the other thread types as well. In all cases, the deviation is **less than 5%,** which demonstrates the accuracy of our modeling approach and generation process, even across threads with vastly different characteristics, like the low-activity, write-dominated Log threads and the high-activity, read-dominated Data threads. The error bars in each graph show the deviation between threads of the same type, in both original and synthetic applications.

For these experiments, we have used **2 levels** in the workload model. In order to decide on the optimal number of levels, we perform a sensitivity study; we increase the number of levels until performance stabilizes (less than 2% difference in throughput). This offers the highest amount of information with the least necessary complexity in the model. Additional level of detail is possible, and can reveal more fine-grained access patterns for the TPC workloads, but its study exceeds the scope of this work.

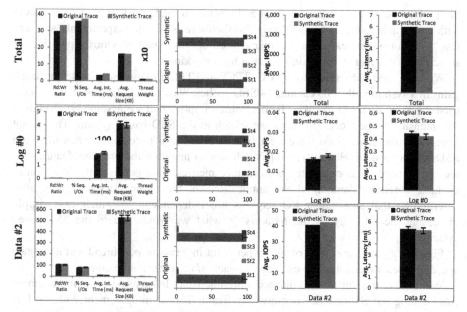

Fig. 5. Validation of *I/O characteristics*, *Spatial Locality* and *Performance Metrics* between Original and Synthetic Trace for: the *entire TPCH benchmark* (1st row), *Log #0* (2nd row), *Data #2* (3rd row)

6   Use Cases

6.1   Identifying Early Storage Problems

Providing a framework for characterization and replay of large-scale TPC workloads enables studies that can identify early problems with datacenter-scale storage systems. Infant mortality is a prominent issue in large-scale systems and results in significant cost in terms of infrastructure and effort to be detected and resolved. Running the models for TPCC/E/H, which offer a time-compressed version of the workload, can identify such problems very early on, thus saving significant portions of TCO and improving the reliability and availability of the system. It can also identify access patterns (i.e. thread types) that increase the risk of causing reliability problems.

Furthermore, the intensity knob included in the generation tool is helpful in that it can increase the I/O request rate and stress test the endurance of hard disks. More importantly it allows a fast identification of such errors, which eliminates faulty disks in the system and improves its longevity.

6.2   SSD Caching for TPC Workloads

Studying the spatial locality of the TPC workloads, per thread, has revealed that most accesses are limited to a small range on disk, while the vast majority of the storage capacity remains unutilized. This justifies the attention that SSD-based or HDD/SSD hybrid storage systems have recently attracted. Using our framework, we can *predict* the performance gains from using an SSD-based storage configuration or a system with SSD caches, for TPC workloads. Furthermore, since the experiments are very fast to perform, one can examine many more options, than previously possible, in search of an optimal storage configuration for a workload.

We have used our models for TPCC, TPCE and TPCH to evaluate the performance gains in a system with SSD caching (4 SSD caches, 8GB each [12]). For this, we have used the same disk I/O traces as before, which implies that we assume no change in the intensity of the workload when we switch to the SSD-based system. This is not necessarily the case, since we expect I/Os to arrive at a faster pace when there are SSDs in the system. However, we have chosen to maintain the previous features for the applications, to compare the performance metrics more consistently. We plan to evaluate a retuned version of the applications in the faster storage system, after determining that subsequent I/O requests are independent, in which case simply increasing the intensity of the requests, is what we would see in the SSD-based system.

Figure 6 shows the results of this experiment in terms of per thread and aggregate speedup when we enable SSD caching, for each of the three applications.

We observe that for threads that are more intense in I/O requests, the improvement from adding the SSD caches is more significant. This is in agreement with the fact that SSDs are more beneficial in very intense workloads, while disks are preferred for less frequent I/O requests. This also takes into account the fact that SSDs mainly benefit read-dominated thread types like *#2, #3* and *#7* for TPCH, while the write dominated Logs (*#0, #1*) and Data *#6* do not experience as high an improvement, with performance even worsening for Log #0 and #1 in TPCE. We expect that tuning the intensity of the workload to resemble the behavior in an SSD-based system, would accentuate even more the difference in performance benefit between ***intense, read-dominated*** and ***not intense, write-dominated*** thread types.

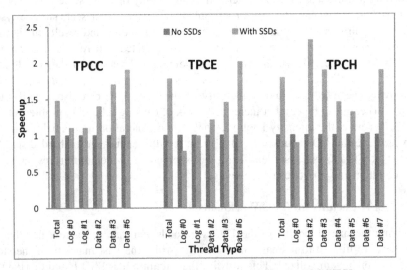

Fig. 6. Performance before and after the use of SSDs for TPCC/E/H

To show the need to capture spatial and temporal locality in the model we compare our results with those obtained by the most well-known open-source workload generator, IOMeter. IOMeter, does not have any notion of locality of I/O requests, in which case it is oblivious as to which blocks should be cached in SSDs. Therefore using it to study SSD caching should not demonstrate an improvement in performance. Indeed, as shown in Figure 7 there is a significant difference in the behavior of the two tools. DiskSpd knows which blocks experience temporal locality, therefore caches them in the SSDs, while IOMeter does not. The performance improvement is evident when using DiskSpd for the storage system evaluation, while IOMeter is not helpful in identifying the speedup from adding the SSDs to the system.

This experiment can also help with identifying the reasons behind the variability in write performance observed in systems with SSD storage. Adding SSDs in the system, has consistently made predicting write performance a lot more difficult than with HDDs, and as SSDs become more affordable, this problem is expected to aggravate. Characterizing the application, as performed in Section 4.3, can help with identifying the threads that are write-dominated and thus cause the performance variability, while running experiments using the workload generator can replicate and identify the reasons for this variability. It can also help with documenting the sensitivity of SSDs in write I/O intensity by increasing the rate at which write I/Os are issued and quantifying the impact on performance, and performance variability.

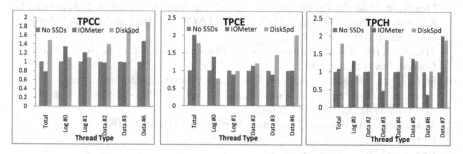

Fig. 7. Comparison between IOMeter and DiskSpd for TPCC/E/H when using SSD caching

7   Conclusions and Future Work

In this work we perform a detailed, per-thread characterization of the storage activity of the TPCC, TPCE and TPCH workloads, and provide insight on their behavior and access patterns. We propose a modeling and generation framework that greatly reduces the time to setup and perform storage experiments in large-scale instances of the TPC benchmarks. We demonstrate the accuracy of our methodology against the original applications, compare it to previous schemes, and present two possible use cases for the framework, early disk error detection and SSD caching. We believe that this framework offers a detailed understanding on the storage activity of TPCC/E/H, while decoupling performing datacenter storage studies from the overhead of setting up the application and the requirement to deploy it in all possible storage system configurations. We plan to demonstrate the applicability of our methodology by evaluating additional use cases for large-scale storage systems.

References

1. Sankar, S., Vaid, K.: Storage characterization for unstructured data in online services applications. In: Proceedings of the IEEE International Symposium on Workload Characterization, IISWC, Austin, TX (2009)
2. Kavalanekar, S., Worthington, B., Zha, Q., Sharda, V.: Characterization of storage workload traces from production Windows servers. In: Proceedings of IEEE International Symposium on Workload Characterization, IISWC 2008, Seattle, WA (September 2008)
3. Delimitrou, C., Sankar, S., Vaid, K., Kozyrakis, C.: Accurate Modeling and Generation of Storage I/O for Datacenter Workloads. In: Proceedings of the 2nd Workshop on Exascale Evaluation and Research Techniques, EXERT, Newport Beach, CA (March 2011)
4. Sankar, S., Vaid, K.: Addressing the stranded power problem in datacenters using storage workload characterization. In: Proceedings of the First WOSP/SIPEW International Conference on Performance Engineering, San Jose, CA (2010)
5. DiskSpd: File and Network I/O using Win32 and .NET API's on Windows XP, http://research.microsoft.com/en-us/um/siliconvalley/projects/sequentialio/
6. IOMeter, performance analysis tool, http://www.iometer.org/
7. Kozyrakis, C., Kansal, A., Sankar, S., Vaid, K.: Server Engineering Insights for Large-Scale Online Services. IEEE Micro 30(4) (July 2010)
8. Kavalanekar, S., Narayanan, D., Sankar, S., Thereska, E., Vaid, K., Worthington, B.: Measuring Database Performance in Online Services: A Trace-Based Approach. In: Nambiar, R., Poess, M. (eds.) TPCTC 2009. LNCS, vol. 5895, pp. 132–145. Springer, Heidelberg (2009)
9. TPC BENCHMARK-H (Decision Support). Standard Specification. Revision 2.14.0. TPC Council, San Francisco (2011)
10. SQLIO Disk Subsystem Benchmark Tool, http://www.microsoft.com/downloads/en/details.aspx?familyid=9a8b005b-84e4-4f24-8d65-cb53442d9e19&displaylang=en
11. Vandenbergh, H.: Vdbench: User Guide. Version: 5.00 (October 2008) http://garr.dl.sourceforge.net/project/vdbench/vdbench/Vdbench%205.00/vdbench.pdf
12. Adaptec MaxIQ. 32GB SSD Cache Performance Kit, http://www.adaptec.com/en-US/products/CloudComputing/MaxIQ/SSD-Cache-Performance/
13. Zhang, J., Sivasubramaniam, A., Franke, H., Gautham, N., Zhang, Y., Nagar, S.: Synthesizing Representative I/O Workloads for TPC-H. In: Proceedings of the International Symposium on High Performance Computer Architecture (HPCA), Madrid, Spain (February 2004)

When Free Is Not Really Free: What Does It Cost to Run a Database Workload in the Cloud?

Avrilia Floratou[1], Jignesh M. Patel[1], Willis Lang[1], and Alan Halverson[2]

[1] University of Wisconsin-Madison, U.S.A.
{floratou,jignesh,wlang}@cs.wisc.edu
[2] Microsoft Jim Gray Systems Lab, U.S.A.
alanhal@microsoft.com

Abstract. The current computing trend towards cloud-based Database-as-a-Service (DaaS) as an alternative to traditional on-site relational database management systems (RDBMSs) has largely been driven by the perceived simplicity and cost-effectiveness of migrating to a DaaS. However, customers that are attracted to these DaaS alternatives may find that the range of different services and pricing options available to them add an unexpected level of complexity to their decision making. Cloud service pricing models are typically 'pay-as-you-go' in which the customer is charged based on resource usage such as CPU and memory utilization. Thus, customers considering different DaaS options must take into account how the performance and efficiency of the DaaS will ultimately impact their monthly bill. In this paper, we show that the current DaaS model can produce unpleasant surprises – for example, the case study that we present in this paper illustrates a scenario in which a DaaS service powered by a DBMS that has a lower hourly rate actually costs more to the end user than a DaaS service that is powered by another DBMS that charges a higher hourly rate. Thus, what we need is a method for the end-user to get an accurate estimate of the true costs that will be incurred without worrying about the nuances of how the DaaS operates. One potential solution to this problem is for DaaS providers to offer a new service called Benchmark as a Service (BaaS) where in the user provides the parameters of their workload and SLA requirements, and get a price quote.

1 Introduction

One of the greatest hurdles associated with deploying traditional on-site relational database management systems (RDBMSs) is the overall complexity of choosing, configuring, and maintaining the RDBMS as well as the server it operates on. In choosing and configuring a particular RDBMS and server to deploy, the users must have a firm understanding of the characteristics of their particular workload. Some of the important characteristics include the size of the database, the nature of the queries (transactional or ad-hoc/analytic), and the desired metric of performance (latency or throughput). Along with the upfront decisions of a particular RDBMS and corresponding server, the user must consider the long-term licensing, maintenance, and administration costs of running

R. Nambiar and M. Poess (Eds.): TPCTC 2011, LNCS 7144, pp. 163–179, 2012.

the system. This complexity that is associated with managing onsite DBMSs is a key reason why cloud-based Database-as-a-Service (DaaS) is starting to gain in popularity as an alternative to on-site RDBMS systems, especially for small and mid-sized database users.

The widely perceived advantage of the DaaS paradigm is that the user has now transferred the complex and nuanced decisions, and the heavy costs of operating an on-site RDBMS to the DaaS provider. Specifically, by turning to a DaaS, the user stores the data in the DaaS, and uses the DaaS APIs to query their data, for a monthly subscriber fee. This monthly fee incorporates all the responsibilities (such as data availability) that the provider has taken on. This fee also includes an "on-demand" payment model for computing resources that are consumed (this later component includes the costs that are associated with the CPU cycles and the storage that is consumed). However, the DaaS providers recognize that the needs of the database users varies significantly, and that one fixed pricing model will alienate one or more segments of the customer market. Consequently, in order to appeal to the entire spectrum of potential users, the DaaS providers have begun to diversify their offerings with multiple pricing options, each promising different levels of computing power, storage capability, and measures of performance. However, from the users' perspective, there is now a bewildering set of choices. As with the process of choosing an on-site RDBMS, they must now fully understand the characteristics, such the raw DBMS performance and query workload characteristics, when choosing an appropriate DaaS product. In fact, with the addition of the pay-as-you-go model for the computing resources, they now have an additional factor to consider – namely, the impact of the computing resources usage on their bottom line.

Initially, it may seem that the DaaS products alleviate many of the pains that are associated with running an on-site RDBMS. However, as we show in this study, the truth is that the users are actually in a tough position – they must now make an upfront decision of choosing a DaaS offering, while the long-term performance and cost consequences of their decisions are harder to figure out.

A crucial point that we make in this paper is that currently the DaaS users do not have an effective method to compare the suitability of one DaaS option over another, and fully understand the actual "cost" of their service. In a traditional RDBMS setting, the database users know that they can always turn to well-established benchmarks (such as the TPC benchmarks), to estimate whether one solution is more suitable than another. However, while such benchmarks identify price and performance as key metrics, these metrics have not been defined for the complex variable pricing models of DaaS products. For instance, they do not consider storage costs of the database or the utilization hours as factors of the price/performance. Moreover, TPC benchmarks usually take into consideration the total cost of ownership as a primary metric. This is incompatible with the "pay-as-you-go" model of cloud computing since the cloud customers are not directly exposed to the hardware, software maintenance, and administration costs of the deployment.

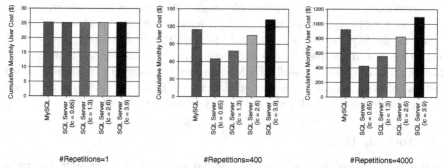

Fig. 1. Cumulative monthly user cost as a function of workload repetitions, DBMS type, and pricing model

To highlight the practical need for an easy to use and accurate pricing model, consider the popular Amazon Relational Database Service (RDS) [1]. While Amazon initially provided users with a database service backed by MySQL [11], recently they have unveiled an option to swap the back-end to an Oracle RDBMS instance [12]. Of course, these two options are not price equivalent, and currently the "Quadruple Extra Large DB" instance cost of the MySQL option is $2.60 per compute-hour, while the Oracle option is 31% more expensive at $3.40 per compute-hour. This price difference is largely due to the licensing cost ($0.80 per compute-hour) of the commercial Oracle system over the open-source MySQL system. While a cursory glance at these numbers would suggest that the cost-conscious user should buy the MySQL option, this choice ignores the fact that the often superior performance of a commercial DBMS may actually result in less computation time than the "free" MySQL option, and thus may actually be the cheaper option in some cases!

To better illustrate this point, consider running the following Wisconsin benchmark [7] query (Query 21):

```
INSERT INTO TMP
SELECT MIN (unique3) FROM TABLE1
GROUP BY onePercent
```

When we run this query on MySQL and a commercial DBMS (SQL Server) on the same physical machine (configuration details are described in Section 3), SQL Server runs this query in 185 seconds while MySQL takes 621 seconds to execute this query. How is the user's cost affected by this 3.3X performance gap when the user decides to run this workload on a DaaS?

Assuming a simple pricing model where the user pays a fixed cost of $1.30 per compute-hour for the specific DB Instance Class used, and a monthly storage fee of $25 for a database of 250GB, Figure 1 shows the cumulative monthly cost for the full deployment when these two RDBMSs are used, and when the workload consists of repetitions of the above query. For the SQL Server-based service, the user has to pay an extra hourly license fee/cost. Figure 1 examines four possible pricing models for the hourly license costs (`lc`) ranging from $0.65 to $3.90.

Interestingly, Figure 1 shows that although the user does not need to pay any license fee for MySQL, using this DBMS results in a higher total cost when the license fee for SQL Server is less than $3.90, and the user frequently issues such query requests. If the user load is high (e.g., around 4000 queries/month), then choosing the commercial-based RDBMS can save the user up to 54%. The reason for this behavior is that the higher efficiency of SQL Server results in decreased resource usage, and overall reduces the end-to-end cost for the user.

1.1 Towards BaaS

As the example above illustrates, the actual cost that a DaaS user will incur is hard to guess upfront. A simple approach to solve this pain point is to take the existing pricing model a step further. So in this scenario, the user provides the database and workload characteristics to the DaaS provider and in return the DaaS provider gives a price quote for running that workload. Along with the price quote the DaaS provider can attach a Service Level Agreement (SLA) that make guarantees on aspects such as performance variability and availability, and also lays out the penalty associated with SLA violations. (Alternatively, some parameters in the SLA could be provided upfront by the user, or the DaaS provider may come back with multiple price quotes at different SLA levels.)

Thus, what we need is for the DaaS providers to run another service – namely, "*Benchmark as a Service*" (BaaS) that makes it transparent to the user what it would cost to run their workload. Such a BaaS service could be free, and then would be crudely analogous to the utility model that is present in other parts of our lives – for example, internet service providers give an accurate price and specify the upper limit of the bandwidth. We acknowledge that a DaaS provider may have a more complicated problem at hand since the SLAs in a DaaS setting could be complex (hence, this is a promising direction for future work). But, from the perspective of the end-consumer of DaaS, a transparent pricing model could be very appealing, and perhaps a competitive advantage for the DaaS providers that choose to simplify their DaaS offering by coupling it with a BaaS service.

The BaaS approach also has a number of potential advantages for the DaaS provider as it provides a strong motivation to find the most optimal way of running the backend DBMS engine (rather than punting this decision to the end user), thereby reducing their operational cost (and perhaps improving their bottom line). Furthermore, the BaaS approach may provide more flexibility in managing the DaaS infrastructure – for example, a DaaS provider may not need to offer a range of DBMSs or data processing backends, and could simplify their infrastructure management by using only a single data processing engine. Finally, with a BaaS approach, the overall DaaS system potentially operates at a much higher operating efficiency (generally the queries across the system are likely to run far more efficiently then when the end user has to make nuanced decisions about configuring their DBMS and making bad choices), which in most cases is also likely to produce a more energy-efficient way of operating the DaaS, since in many cases the goal of energy efficiency lines ups with the goal of optimizing for traditional performance goals.

The remainder of this paper is organized as follows: Section 2 presents our cost model. Experimental results are presented in Section 3, while Section 4 discusses related work. Section 5 contains our concluding remarks and points to some directions for future work.

2   Cost Model

This section presents a simple cost model for using relational DBMSs in the cloud. The model considers the cost that is incurred by the end user in using a DaaS offering. We then use this model in our experiments (see Section 3) to explore the costs associated with using a DaaS product.

We patterned a simple pricing model crudely using Amazon's DaaS product as a reference. According to the Amazon's DaaS pricing model [1], the users pay only for the resources that they consume. Several parameters determine this cost. The first one, is an hourly fee that corresponds to the specific DB Instance Class chosen by the customer. The DB Instance is a database environment in the cloud with the compute and storage resources that the customer specifies. For example, currently in Amazon's RDS, 6 DB Instance Classes are provided. The "Small" DB Instance Class has 1.7GB of main memory and one 1.0-1.2 GHz CPU core (1 ECU), whereas the "Extra Large DB Instance" has 15GB of main memory and four 2.0-2.4 GHz CPU cores (8 ECUs). Generally, the hourly rates vary with the DB Instance Classes, since each class has different hardware characteristics. An extra hourly license cost/fee, is added for DB Instances backed by a commercial DBMS, which also varies according to the DB Instance Class chosen. The last parameter is a monthly storage fee per GB of the provisioned storage needed by the workload.

Consider a fixed database instance type chosen by the user with corresponding hourly cost dbc, an hourly license fee for the DBMS equal to lc, a monthly fee for the provisioned storage per GB equal to stc, and H hours of utilization per month of the DB instance. Given that the DB instance has associated capacity of DS GB, the monthly user cost (MUC) can be determined as:

$$MUC = H * (dbc + lc) + DS * stc \qquad (1)$$

To keep our model simple, we do not consider the monthly network related costs. We also do not consider the costs for the extra backup storage that may be needed. These rates affect the total cost in a way similar to the storage fee stc and can easily be added to the above equation. Moreover, our model assumes that only one database instance is used by the customer. Creating and validating a more complex model that considers a combination of different database instance classes and multiple database instances per class is part of future work.

3   Experimental Evaluation

In this section, we discuss our experimental results which include performance measurements of a database server running different workloads and using different storage organizations, using MySQL and SQL Server. Based on these

performance results and the pricing model presented in Section 2, we compare
the total cost that the user has to pay when using these two DBMSs in a DaaS.

The work by Schad et al. [13] presents experimental results showing that performance unpredictability is a major issue when running workloads in the cloud.
The variance observed can be attributed to several factors, including different
types of virtual systems provided by the service, different availability zones (distinct locations that are insulated from failures in other availability zones), and
time of the day/week when the workload was run. Similar observations are discussed in the work of Armbrust et al. [2]. All these parameters make it difficult
to estimate the impact on the cost and the performance of different database
systems serving applications in a cloud-based environment. In this study, in an
effort to eliminate these variances, we decided to measure the performance of
the different DBMSs on a stand-alone local server machine. We show that even
in this isolated environment, where variance due to the factors mentioned above
is eliminated, the impact of the workload type and the efficiency of the DBMS
on the monthly user's bill is not straightforward to estimate.

3.1   Server Configuration

Our test platform is a HP Proliant server with a dual quad-core hyperthreaded
Intel Xeon L5630 processors (@ 2.13GHz), 32 GB of memory, and 12 HP 146GB
10K RPM SAS drives.

The server is dual booted with 64-bit Ubuntu Server 9.10 and 64-bit Windows
Server 2008 R2 Enterprise Edition. The Linux version is used to run MySQL
(MySQL Community Server 5.5.9) and the Windows version to run SQL Server
2008 R2 (Data Center Edition). Each disk is partitioned roughly evenly between
the two operating systems. The first hard disk is used for the installation of the
operating systems and all the database binaries.

3.2   DBMS Configuration

In our experiments, the database buffer pool is set to 24GB for both DBMSs.
One disk is used to store the log files and the remaining 10 disks are reserved for
the data files and the temporary space that is needed during query execution.

For SQL Server, we created a "file group" of 20 data files across the 20 data
disk partitions (the 10 Windows partitions are further subdivided into two partitions). In this way, each of the 16 (hyperthreaded) cores can be assigned to
one disk partition to allow parallel query processing. MySQL currently does not
support such intra-query parallelism. For this reason, we created one data file
striped across the 10 data disks so that we can get a high aggregate disk bandwidth. For MySQL we used the InnoDB storage engine, which is the default
setting and the one used in Amazon's RDS.

3.3   The Wisconsin Benchmark

For our experiments we decided to use workloads based on the Wisconsin
benchmark [7]. Our decision was driven by the fact that it is a simple "mi-

cro" benchmark that is fairly easy to set up and does not have complicated rules about how to run and measure a benchmark. Furthermore, this benchmark contains a variety of queries including selections, joins, projections, aggregations and updates. These simple queries are building blocks for more complex workloads and provide good insights about the potential impact on more complex workload characteristics.

The benchmark uses three basic relations, two that have the same number of tuples (T) and one that contains $T/10$ tuples. Each relation consists of sixteen attributes, thirteen 4-byte signed integers and three 52-byte varchars. The most widely used attributes in the benchmark are unique1, unique2 and onePercent. The values of the unique1 attribute are uniformly distributed unique random numbers in the range 0 to $T - 1$. The values of unique2 are in sequential order from 0 to $T - 1$. The original benchmark paper [7] contains more information about each attribute and its values.

The benchmark explores two different kinds of storage organizations. The first one contains one heap file for each relation, and is called StorageOrg-H. This storage layout doesn't contain any primary key indices. In the second storage organization, called StorageOrg-I, each relation has a clustered index on the unique2 attribute, a unique non-clustered index on the unique1 attribute and a non-unique non-clustered index on the onePercent attribute.

3.4   Experimental Setting

For our experiments, we created six different types of workloads based on the Wisconsin benchmark. The first two workloads contain all the queries in the benchmark, and are called MixedWorkload1 and MixedWorkload2. The first workload, MixedWorkload1, uses heapfiles as the storage layout (StorageOrg-H), whereas the second workload, MixedWorkload2, uses the clustered and non-clustered indices defined by the benchmark (StorageOrg-I). We generated a DSS-like workload using a subset of the Wisconsin benchmark queries. From this set of queries, we created two DSS workloads, DSSWorkload1 and DSSWorkload2, corresponding to the two storage layouts (StorageOrg-H and StorageOrg-I respectively). Similarly, we generated two OLTP workloads consisting of OLTP-like queries. These two workloads are OLTPWorkload1 and OLTPWorkload2, and correspond to the storage layouts StorageOrg-H and StorageOrg-I respectively.

Note that some of the queries of the mixed workloads are not presented in the OLTP or in the DSS workloads. More specifically, the 10% selection queries (Q2, Q4, Q6) as well as the 1% selection to screen query (Q8) are only included in the mixed workloads. We did not include the 10% selections in the other workloads because we wanted to experiment with high-selective queries in the OLTP workloads, and we wanted the DSS workloads to mainly consist of join and aggregation queries. Query Q8 was omitted since most of its execution time with MySQL was spent in printing the output to the screen, and not actually evaluating the query result. In the original Wisconsin benchmark paper [7], some of the queries are executed only on either Storage-H or Storage-I. In this work, we decided to execute all the queries using both storage layouts. This decision was driven by the fact that for some queries the DBMSs don't pick the execution plan described in the benchmark. For example, Query 6 is supposed to use a non-clustered index, that's why it is tested only in `Storage-I`. However, in our experiments the actual plan picked by the optimizer of both DBMSs is a scan on the table. That's the reason why some of the queries are presented twice in some workloads (e.g., Q6 in `MixedWorkload1` and `MixedWorkload2`).

We created three data files using a Wisconsin benchmark generator. Each file corresponds to one relation of the benchmark. The two tables of the database contain 400M tuples, and the third one has 40M tuples. The size of the flat files for these tables is 80GB, 80GB, and 8GB respectively. Thus, the total raw database size is approximately 168GB. Between the executions of queries we purge the buffer pool (i.e., all reported numbers are "cold"). We also update the statistics for all the tables that are used in a query before its execution starts. The time to clean the buffer pool and update the statistics is not included in the experiment's total execution time. The temporary (TMP) tables that are used to store the results of each query are dropped after the query is executed and recreated when needed. Each query was run 3 times and the average value is reported. We did not see a lot of variance across runs of the same query. All the time values are reported in seconds. The data loading times were fairly similar across both DBMSs, and are not included in computing the total cost below.

We used the model presented in Section 2 to estimate the total cost incurred by the end DaaS subscriber/user. To compute the monthly user cost (MUC), we set the DB instance fee (`dbc`) to \$1.30 per hour. This `dbc` is equal to the rate of a high-memory double extra large DB Instance offered in Amazon RDS, which is the closest Amazon Instance configuration to our server. To get a better sense of how the total cost is affected by the license cost/fee (`lc`), we experimented with the following hourly license rates for the commercial DBMS: {\$0.65, \$1.30, \$2.60, \$3.90}. Since MySQL is open-source, its licensing fee is \$0. The monthly storage fee `stc` is set to \$0.10 per GB (similar to Amazon's RDS rate). We set the provisioned storage `DS` (data, log files and temporary space) for both DBMSs to 250GB.

To evaluate how the storage fee combined with the hourly fees affects the monthly user cost, we varied the number of repetitions of the workload, so that we can experiment with short and long-running workloads of the same type. We first report the cumulative user cost when the workload is executed only once (#repetitions=1). The next number of repetitions reported (#repetitions=N), corresponds to a total execution time close to a period of one month (computed based on the execution time of the workload on the slowest DBMS). This case represents the scenario were the end user application is driving the provisioned DBMS instance nearly to its peak capacity (for the slowest DBMS). Finally, we also present the comparative monthly costs when $N/10$ repetitions are performed. For example in Figure 1, $N = 4,000$, since the slowest DBMS (MySQL) can execute Query 21, approximately 4,000 times in a period of a month.

Table 1. Mixed Workload 1

Query	Query Description	SQL Server Time (secs)	MySQL Time (secs)
Q1	1% selection on **unique2**	224	665
Q2	10% selection on **unique2**	482	1185
Q5	1% selection on **unique1**	195	739
Q6	10% selection on **unique1**	332	1191
Q7	Single tuple selection to screen	191	555
Q8	1% selection to screen	236	1721
Q18	1% projection	129	1523
Q20	Min. aggregate	190	482
Q21	Min. aggregate with group by	185	621
Q22	Sum aggregate with group by	187	747
Q26	Insert 1 tuple	0.20	0.23
Q27	Delete 1 tuple	192	637
Q28	Update on unique2	192	595
Q32	Update on unique1	197	609
Total		**2932**	**11270**

Table 2. Mixed Workload 2

Query	Query Description	SQL Server Time (secs)	MySQL Time (secs)
Q3	1% selection on **unique2**	22	51
Q4	10% selection on **unique2**	203	551
Q6	10% selection on **unique1**	883	1146
Q7	Single tuple selection to screen	0.75	0.60
Q8	1% selection to screen	62	1245
Q12	JoinAselB	412	1071
Q13	JoinABPrime	408	1004
Q14	JoinCselAselB	583	1512
Q18	1% projection	864	1495
Q23	Minimum aggregate	0.21	0.83
Q29	Insert 1 tuple	0.99	0.57
Q30	Delete 1 tuple	0.65	0.66
Q31	Update on **unique2**	1.47	0.73
Q32	Update on **unique1**	0.75	0.71
Total		**3441**	**8079**

3.5 Mixed Workloads

The mixed workloads contain all the queries in the Wisconsin benchmark that finished within 3 hours with both DBMSs. Some queries (i.e., MySQL running joins in MixedWorkload1) were stopped after 14 hours of execution. Although the same queries were completed using SQL Server, we do not take into account these numbers. It is clear that having such queries in the workload will lead to poor performance and higher cost, and hence will favor the usage of the commercial DBMS. However, we believe it's interesting to see what happens with respect to performance and cost when all the queries of the workload are completed in both systems in a reasonable amount of time. Note that all the queries that MySQL could finish within 14 hours were also completed by SQL Server within 14 hours.

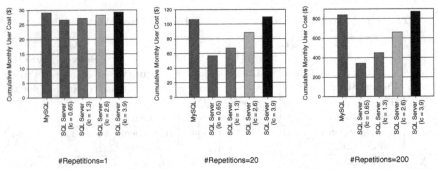

Fig. 2. Cumulative monthly user cost as a function of workload repetitions, DBMS type and pricing model (`MixedWorkload1`)

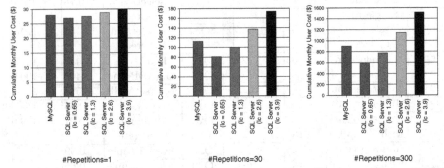

Fig. 3. Cumulative monthly user cost as a function of workload repetitions, DBMS type and pricing model (`MixedWorkload2`)

Tables 1 and 2 contain the execution times for both DBMSs using `MixedWorkload1` and `MixedWorkload2` respectively. The last rows of the tables contain the total execution time for each database system used. Figures 2 and 3 show the estimated monthly cost for the customer when MySQL or SQL Server is used.

As shown in Table 1, when the database consists only of heapfiles (`MixedWorkload1`), MySQL is approximately 3.84X (2.3 hours) slower than SQL Server. Notice that Table 1 does not show the original Wisconsin benchmark Queries 9-17 – these are join queries that did not complete with MySQL but completed using SQL Server in a reasonable amount of time (between 400-1000 seconds for each query).

Figure 2 shows how the total user cost is affected by the performance gap that exists between the two systems, when the repetitions of the workload as well as the hourly license fee for the commercial DBMS is varied. As shown in this figure, when the workload is executed only once, the difference in cost between SQL Server and MySQL is very small. In this case, the execution time is not long enough to make a significant impact, and thus the total cost is dominated by the monthly storage fee. The difference in the total cost between the two systems increases with the number of queries issued. As shown in the figure, the

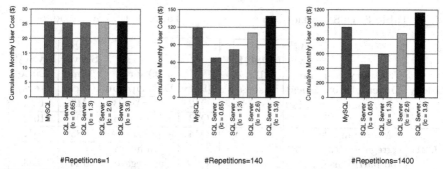

Fig. 4. Cumulative monthly user cost as a function of workload repetitions, DBMS type and pricing model (DSS Workload 1)

"free" open-source DBMS results in higher total cost when the license fee for the commercial DBMS is below $3.90. When the workload is executed 20 times the cost savings with SQL Server is 17%(lc = $2.60), 37% ($lc$ = $1.30) and 47% ($lc$ = $0.65). In the case of 200 repetitions (almost a month running time with MySQL), when the license fee is $2.60, using MySQL results in a 21% increase in the user's monthly bill. In the case of a license fee of $0.65, the increase is more significant(59%). Regarding, the performance of the MixedWorkload2, as shown in Table 2, when the clustered and non-clustered indices are used, MySQL is approximately 2.34X (1.28 hours) slower than SQL Server. In this case, the existence of the clustered index on the unique2 attribute significantly improved the execution of some joins (Q12, Q13, Q14) as well selections (Q3, Q4) and updates (Q29, Q31). The existence of the non-clustered index on the unique1 attribute improved the performance of the queries 30 and 32. However, it had an adverse impact on other queries (e.g Q5 in MySQL). This behavior can be attributed to the fact that the non-clustered index contains only two attributes: unique1 and the primary key unique2. However, the query result contains all the 16 attributes of the relation. Evaluating this query using the non-clustered index as an access method possibly results in high random I/O behavior. A clustered index scan would probably result in a more efficient query execution (as was the case for the similar Q6 in both MySQL and SQL Server).

Figure 3 presents the total user cost similarly to Figure 2 for MixedWorkload2. As before, the free MySQL systems often results in higher costs, though now the license fee for the commercial DBMS has to be lower (around or below $1.30) than it was in Figure 2 to win over MySQL.

3.6 DSS Workloads

In this section, we evaluate the performance of the two DBMSs when the workload contains only decision-support queries. Similar to Section 3.5, based on these results and the cost model developed in Section 2 we estimate the total user cost for both cases. The DSS workload includes all the join and aggregation queries of the Wisconsin benchmark. Again, we report execution times only for the queries that were completed in both systems.

Table 3. DSS Workload 1

Query	Query Description	SQL Server Time (secs)	MySQL Time (secs)
Q20	Minimum aggregate	190	482
Q21	Minimum aggregate with 100 partitions	185	621
Q22	Sum aggregate with 100 partitions	187	747
All		562	1850

Table 4. DSS Workload 2

Query	Query Description	SQL Server Time (secs)	MySQL Time (secs)
Q12	JoinAselB	412	1071
Q13	JoinABprime	408	1004
Q14	JoinCselAselB	583	1512
Q23	Minimum aggregate	0.21	0.83
All		1403	3588

Regarding DSSWorkload1, as it is shown in Table 3, when using heapfiles as a storage layout only the aggregation queries were completed in both systems. In this case, MySQL was approximately 3.29X slower than SQL Server.

Figure 3 presents the total cost for the user varying the same parameters as in Figures 2 and 3. As it is shown in this figure, a similar pattern to that of MixedWorkload1 is observed. The per hour cheap option (MySQL) does not always result in the lowest total cost. In fact, when the hourly license fee for SQL Server is less or equal to $2.60, choosing that over the free DBMS can result in cost savings of up to 53% (lc = $0.65, 1400 repetitions). On the other hand, using MySQL can result in cost savings of up to 17% when the license fee is equal to $3.90 and the workload is executed 1400 times.

Table 4 presents performance results for DSSWorkload2. The existence of the indices allows many joins to complete with MySQL, but negatively affected some aggregation queries. The reasons for this behavior are discussed in section 3.5. In this case, MySQL is 2.55X slower than SQL Server.

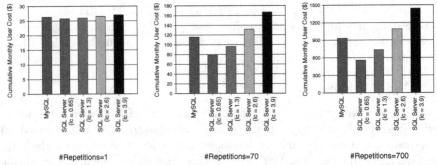

Fig. 5. Cumulative monthly user cost as a function of workload repetitions, DBMS type and pricing model (DSS Workload 2)

Table 5. OLTP Workload 1

Query	Query Description	SQL Server Time (secs)	MySQL Time (secs)
Q1	1% selection on unique2	224	665
Q5	1% selection on unique1	195	739
Q7	Single tuple selection to screen	191	555
Q26	Insert 1 tuple	0.2	0.23
Q27	Delete 1 tuple	192	637
Q28	Update on unique2	192	595
Q32	Update on unique1	197	609
All		1191	3800

Table 6. OLTP Workload 2

Query	Query Description	SQL Server Time (secs)	MySQL Time (secs)
Q3	1% selection on unique2	22	51
Q7	Single tuple selection to screen	0.75	0.60
Q29	Insert 1 tuple	0.99	0.57
Q30	Delete 1 tuple	0.65	0.66
Q31	Update on unique2	1.47	0.73
Q32	Update on unique1	0.75	0.71
All		26.61	54.27

The corresponding user cost is presented in Figure 5. Similarly to the previous results, the open-source DBMS is a more cost-effective choice when the license fee is greater or equal to $2.60. As before, the cost savings increases as the execution time increases, since in this case the monthly storage fee does not have a significant impact on the total cost.

3.7 OLTP Workloads

The OLTP workload consists of the queries of the Wisconsin benchmark that contain high-selective selections, insertions, deletions and updates. Similarly to the previous experiments, only the queries that were completed in both DBMSs are reported for each workload.

As shown in Table 5, when the database consists only of heapfiles, MySQL is 3.19X slower than SQL Server. The corresponding user's cost is presented in Figure 6. Similarly to the previous experiments, MySQL is the most cost-effective option when the hourly license fee is equal to $3.90. In all the other cases, the cost savings when using SQL Server can be as high as 51%.

When indices are used, MySQL is approximately 2X slower than SQL Server. Table 6 and Figure 7 present the performance results and the associated user cost.

3.8 Discussion

We have shown that the process of estimating the cost of a DaaS is not straight-foward, even in the simple case where the database system in not deployed in a virtualized environment and factors such as different availability zones, locations

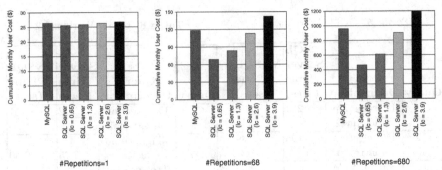

Fig. 6. Cumulative monthly user cost as a function of workload repetitions, DBMS type and pricing model (OLTP Workload 1)

or points of time are not taken into consideration. Parameters such as database efficiency, type of workload, and pricing model can all affect the resulting user cost. Consequently, often the option that initially seems cheap per hour, e.g., an open-source DBMS, can actually result in a higher monthly bill than that of a non-free, licensed DBMS.

4   Related Work

DBMS benchmarking is an age-old sport in the database community. The Wisconsin benchmark [7] was one of the first benchmarks developed for evaluating RDBMSs. Today, the series of the TPC benchmarks [16] are widely used for measuring the performance and the cost or relational database systems.

Following the advent of cloud computing, recent work has evaluated different cloud services on different types of workloads. More specifically, a recent paper [3] presents some initial ideas on what a general cloud benchmark should consider, focusing on the different kinds of cloud services and architectures and their corresponding pricing plans. One of the (many) considerations in this paper

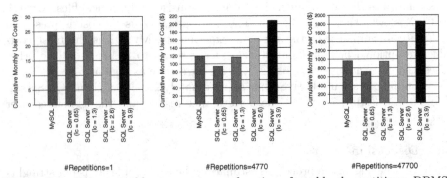

Fig. 7. Cumulative monthly user cost as a function of workload repetitions, DBMS type and pricing model (OLTP Workload 2)

is the end-user cost. A follow-up work [9] presents an evaluation of different cloud services when running enterprise web applications with OLTP workloads. Along the same lines, Berkeley's Cloudstone project [15] proposes a workload and metrics to study cloud infrastructures that deploy Web 2.0 applications. Comparing different cloud services has also been the focus of the recent work by Garfinkel [8], which evaluates three popular Amazon Computing Services (EC2, S3 and SQS). Another work [6] compares a traditional open-source RDMS and existing cloud computing technology (HBase). Cooper et al. [5] propose a benchmark to compare different popular datastores like Cassandra and PNUTS.

Virtualization techniques have been widely adopted in cloud-based environments. In a recent paper [10], the performance of relational database systems running on top of virtual machines has been studied. Bose et al. [4] present performance results from experiments running TPC database workloads on top of virtual machines, and make the case for a database benchmark on top of virtual machines. The follow-up work [14] presents a high-level overview of TPC-V, a benchmark designed for database workloads running in virtualized environments.

5 Concluding Remarks and Directions for Future Work

This paper has explored how two important dimensions in cloud environments, namely performance and cost, are influenced when different types of DBMSs are chosen by a DaaS user. More specifically, we have used a variety of simple workloads and storage organizations to evaluate two different relational DBMSs (one open-source and one commercial RDBMS). Our results show that given the range of the pricing models and the flexibility of the "on-demand" allocation of resources in cloud-based environments, it is hard for a user to figure out their actual monthly cost upfront. Interestingly, DaaS settings that at first sight seem cheaper per hour (since the backend is an open-source DBMS) and thus more-cost effective, can result in higher total costs in the long-run, since the backend DBMS may have poor performance characteristics on the users' workload. On the other hand, a DaaS setting backed by a high performance commercial DBMSs, while more expensive on a per hour basis, may be cheaper overall since its higher performance more than makes up for the hourly price differential. We note that these results should not be construed to mean that free open source DBMSs are always more expensive in the DaaS environment (or vice versa) – we have only tried two DBMSs in this paper, picking the most popular free open-source DBMS and a commercial DBMS. Rather, our work highlights that the real cost of running a workload in the DaaS is complicated, and may in some cases produce surprising results.

Thus, what we need is real transparency and clarity in pricing DaaS. An approach to this problem that we propose in this paper is "Benchmark as a Service" (BaaS), where by the DaaS provider can take the user workload as input (with SLA parameters) and provide an accurate price for that workload, or perhaps different prices at different SLA levels. This BaaS approach would move the DaaS offering closer to a true utility model (like gas and electricity, or internet service). But, we acknowledge that setting up a BaaS is challenging as there are important aspects that need to be considered. For example, how to specify the workload. A starting point for describing this workload could be for the user to provide the database schema, average tuple sizes for each table, and a query set. But, additional parameters may be required, such as estimated database growth rates, or acceptable ranges for SLA parameters (e.g., query/workload response time or throughput). For simplicity from the users' perspective it is desirable that the workload specifications should not be overly complicated, but from the DaaS provider's perspective more details are probably required. Finding a good and practical balance is one direction for future work. Other aspects of future work include designing methods for a DaaS provider to efficiently run a mix of workloads that started with a BaaS, and monitoring and reacting to changes in workloads that started with a price quote from the BaaS.

Acknowledgement. This research was supported in part by a grant from the Microsoft Jim Gray Systems Lab, Madison, WI, and by the National Science Foundation under grant IIS-0963993. Any opinions, findings, and conclusions or recommendations expressed in this material are those of the author(s) and do not necessarily reflect the views of the funding source or the organizations that employ the authors.

References

1. Amazon Relational Database Service, http://aws.amazon.com/rds/
2. Armbrust, M., Fox, A., Griffith, R., Joseph, A.D., Katz, R.H., Konwinski, A., Lee, G., Patterson, D.A., Rabkin, A., Zaharia, M.: Above the Clouds: A Berkeley View of Cloud Computing (2009)
3. Binnig, C., Kossmann, D., Kraska, T., Loesing, S.: How is the weather tomorrow?: towards a benchmark for the cloud. In: DBTest (2009)
4. Bose, S., Mishra, P., Sethuraman, P., Taheri, R.: Benchmarking Database Performance in a Virtual Environment. In: Nambiar, R., Poess, M. (eds.) TPCTC 2009. LNCS, vol. 5895, pp. 167–182. Springer, Heidelberg (2009)
5. Cooper, B.F., Silberstein, A., Tam, E., Ramakrishnan, R., Sears, R.: Benchmarking cloud serving systems with ycsb. In: SoCC, pp. 143–154 (2010)
6. Cryans, J.-D., April, A., Abran, A.: Criteria to Compare Cloud Computing with Current Database Technology. In: Dumke, R.R., Braungarten, R., Büren, G., Abran, A., Cuadrado-Gallego, J.J. (eds.) IWSM 2008. LNCS, vol. 5338, pp. 114–126. Springer, Heidelberg (2008)
7. DeWitt, D.J.: The wisconsin benchmark: Past, present, and future. In: Gray, J. (ed.) The Benchmark Handbook. Morgan Kaufmann (1993)
8. Garfinkel, S.L.: An evaluation of amazon's grid computing services: Ec2, s3 and sqs. Technical report (2007)
9. Kossmann, D., Kraska, T., Loesing, S.: An evaluation of alternative architectures for transaction processing in the cloud. In: SIGMOD Conference, pp. 579–590 (2010)
10. Minhas, U.F., Yadav, J., Aboulnaga, A., Salem, K.: Database systems on virtual machines: How much do you lose? In: ICDE Workshops, pp. 35–41 (2008)
11. MySQL, http://www.mysql.com/
12. Oracle Database, http://www.oracle.com/us/products/database/index.html

13. Schad, J., Dittrich, J., Quiané-Ruiz, J.-A.: Runtime measurements in the cloud: Observing, analyzing, and reducing variance. PVLDB 3(1), 460–471 (2010)
14. Sethuraman, P., Reza Taheri, H.: TPC-V: A Benchmark for Evaluating the Performance of Database Applications in Virtual Environments. In: Nambiar, R., Poess, M. (eds.) TPCTC 2010. LNCS, vol. 6417, pp. 121–135. Springer, Heidelberg (2011)
15. Sobel, W., Subramanyam, S., Sucharitakul, A., Nguyen, J., Wong, H., Klepchukov, A., Patil, S., Fox, O., Patterson, D.: Cloudstone: Multi-platform, multi-language benchmark and measurement tools for web 2.0 (2008)
16. TPC Benchmarks, http://www.tpc.org/information/benchmarks.asp

A Fine-Grained Performance-Based Decision Model for Virtualization Application Solution*

Jianhai Chen, Dawei Huang, Bei Wang, Deshi Ye, Qinming He,
and Wenzhi Chen

College of Computer Science, Zhejiang University,
Zheda Rd. 38, Hangdog 310027, China
{chenjh919,tossboyhdw,wangbei,yedeshi,hqm,chenwz}@zju.edu.cn

Abstract. Virtualization technology has been widely applied across a broad range of contemporary datacenters. While constructing a datacenter, architects have to choose a Virtualization Application Solution (VAS) to maximize performance as well as minimize cost. However, the performance of a VAS involves a great number of metric concerns, such as virtualization overhead, isolation, manageability, consolidation, and so on. Further, datacenter architects have their own preference of metrics correlate with datacenters' specific application scenarios. Nevertheless, previous research on virtualization performance either focus on a single performance concern or test several metrics respectively, rather than gives a holistic evaluation, which leads to the difficulties in VAS decision-making. In this paper, we propose a fine-grained performance-based decision model termed as VirtDM to aid architects to determine the best VAS for them via quantifying the overall performance of VAS according to datacenter architects' own preference. First, our model defines a measurable, in-depth, fine-grained, human friendly metric system with organized hierarchy to achieve accurate and precise quantitative results. Second, the model harnesses a number of classic Multiple Criteria Decision-Making (MCDM) methods, such as the Analytical Hierarchical Process (AHP), to relieve people's effort of deciding the weight of different metrics base on their own preference accordingly. Our case study addresses an decision process based on three real VAS candidates as an empirical example exploiting VirtDM and demonstrates the effectiveness of our VirtDM model.

Keywords: virtualization, performance evaluation, benchmark, datacenter, decision making, analytic hierarchical process.

1 Introduction

Virtualization technology has been widely applied across a wide-spread of contemporary datacenters due to its benefits of improved utilization, reduced-cost,

* This work is funded by the National 973 Basic Research Program of China under grant NO.2007CB310900 and National Natural Science Foundation of China under grant NO. 60970125.

R. Nambiar and M. Poess (Eds.): TPCTC 2011, LNCS 7144, pp. 180–195, 2012.

saved-energy, manageability and reliability. Gartner reported that the installed base of Virtual Machines (VMs) will grow 5 times from 2009 to 2012, and by 2012 half of the server installed base will be virtualized [1].

Moreover, contemporary datacenters and cloud infrastructures have grown to a grand scale. For example, Google had owned more than 450,000 servers early in 2006 [2]. On the other hand, various kinds of virtualization technologies has been designed and implemented, such as para-virtualization, hardware assistant virtualization, live migration strategies and so on, which offers abundant alternatives to deploy virtualization in a datacenter. As a result, datacenter architects face the crucial issue that how to choose a Virtualization Application Solution (VAS) so that it could maximize performance and best adapt to the demand of their datacenter. In other word, we have to find an evaluation method to compare different virtualization solutions of a datacenter.

Nevertheless, the performance of a VAS involves a great number of performance concerns, such as virtualization overhead, isolation, manageability, consolidation, and so on [3]. Furthermore, a datacenter has its own preference of metrics correlate with specific application scenarios.

Previous research on virtualization performance either focus on a single performance concern or test several metrics respectively. A great number of researches devoted to the characterization and analysis of server consolidation [4,5,6]. Matthews *et al.* investigated the evaluation on the performance isolation of virtual machine [7]. Several works summarized the primary performance perspectives of virtualization and discussed their metrics [8,9,10], while others studied their measurement and benchmarking method [11,12]. These studies didn't provide an overall evaluation method to adaptively compare different VASes, which leads to the difficulties of deciding a VAS best fit into a datacenter's requirement.

In this paper, we propose a fine-grained performance-based decision model for VAS, termed as VirtDM. It provides an overall quantification method to compare different VASes according to the architects' preference, to solve the VAS decision-making problem in a datacenter. VirtDM divides VAS decision-making problem into three sub-problems:

1. What metrics should be taken into account to measured a VAS?
2. How to quantify a datacenter architect's preference on these metrics?
3. How to achieve an overall decision from different metrics' results and architects' preference?

To solve problem 1, we define a fine-grained, hierarchical metrics system and provide their measurements or quantification methods. Certainly the metrics should be chosen so much human-friendly that can be easily used for decision. For problem 2, VirtDM allows people to input pairwise comparison ratios other than to directly give the weights, thus eases people's comparison effort as well as improves the accuracy and precision. For problem 3, we harness a number of classic Multiple Criteria Decision-Making (MCDM) methods, such as Analytical Hierarchical Process (AHP) [13]. VirtDM will normalize different metrics' results, calculate metrics' weights and finally provide an overall numeric result for each VAS. Then datacenter architects could decide the VAS best fit into their requests.

The contributions of our work are three-fold. First, we design an effective model VirtDM to assist the VAS decision making for a datacenter. We implement an algorithm for our model and validate our model by a case study. Second, we build a fine-grained hierarchical metrics system to evaluate different performance characteristics of VAS. We give their measurements or quantification methods. Third, we offer a convenient way to calculate metrics' weights using classic MCDM methods, and provides an overall VAS evaluation method adaptive to datacenter architects' preferences.

The rest of this paper is organized as follows. Section 2 presents the architecture of VirtDM. Section 3 describes metrics system for how to choose the metrics for our model. Section 4 explains the implementation of VirtDM, especially of the metrics' results normalization and metrics' weights identification. Section 5 demonstrates a case study, including both the experiments and the overall decision process. Finally, section 6 provides our conclusions & future work.

2   Architecture of VirtDM Model

In this section, we describe the architecture of VirtDM model.

The VirtDM model is designed to achieve the right decision from different VAS candidates for a datacenter. In VirtDM, we embraces different components which will contribute to the accuracy of final decision result. Fig. 1 shows the architecture of VirtDM. It consists of five abstract components: VAS Candidates, Metrics System, Preference, MCDM-Processor, Decision Result. Basing on the Metrics System and the Preference, the MCDM-Processor will carry out the decision making process over different VAS candidates, and finally yields the Decision Result.

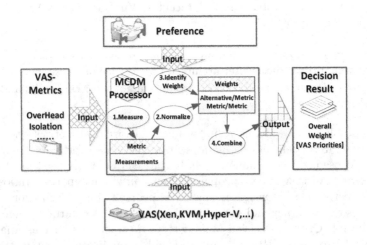

Fig. 1. The architecture of VirtDM

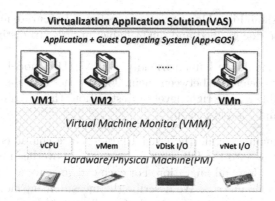

Fig. 2. The components of VAS

A VAS candidate refers to a specific software and hardware implementation of virtualization technologies. It involves Hardware, Virtual Machine monitor(VMM) and Virtual Machine(VM), as Fig 2 shows. The performance of a VAS depends on the software virtualization technologies regarding the VMM, e.g. as Xen, KVM, VMWare etc., and the hardware virtualization technologies like Intel-VT, AMD-SVM, Extended Page Tables, and so on.

Metrics System determinates which virtualization performances are concerned and how they are measured. In VirtDM, we construct a fine-grained, quantifiable, hierarchical and human friendly metrics system, covering essential performance characteristics of virtualization in a datacenter, and set up their measurement or quantification methods as accurate and precise as possible. We will discuss the details of our Metrics System in section 3.

The preference of decision-makers impacts how much final Decision Result fit into a datacenter's definite demand. Because different datacenters might have their individual application scenarios, which results in different preferences. For example, if a datacenter would perform large mount of I/O processing, the architects will care much more about the I/O overhead metric of a VAS.

Furthermore, the MCDM-processor is central in our VirtDM model. It constitutes the key decision making process logic. The procedure of VirtDM involves four primary tasks including measuring, normalization, the weights identification and the combination of decision results. We will talk about more details in section 4.

3   Metrics Choosing

We should choose right performance metrics so that our VirtDM model could produce more accurate and precise quantitative results. We break down this big picture into following criteria while choosing the metrics:

- The metrics should cover all of the essential performance characteristics embracing both advantage and disadvantage facets of virtualization in a datacenter.

- The metrics should be able to produce precise and accurate numeric results. They must be fine-grained and quantifiable, in order to distinguish VASes' performance.
- The metrics should be human friendly. Our VirtDM model involves architects to make preference between them. The metrics must be well-organized and comparable on the right level of abstraction, thus architects can easily understand and compare them.

In VirtDM, we mainly divide the crucial performance characteristics of datacenter virtualization into the following five categories: overhead, manageability, isolation, consolidation and migration. For each category, we will discuss its significance and specific metrics. We describe the measurement methods for some metrics, and the quantification methods for others which cannot be directly measured.

3.1   Virtualization Overhead

Virtualization overhead is usually one of the major roadblocks getting in the way of employing virtualization. Added layer of VMM introduces extra resources consumption and performance degradation of the Guest OS, due to its tasks of hardware resources managements and its interactions with the Guest OS.

We should define specific overhead metrics and their measurements. The VirtDM requires human's participation in weighting the importance of different metrics. In VirtDM, the overhead is measured by calculating the performance degradation of a workload running on a virtualization solution platform against a non-virtualization platform on the same physical host, to exclude the performance impact of other factors.

We test the overhead of a VAS through the following four essential workloads: 1) CPU task; 2) Memory task; 3) I/O task; 4) Context switch. We consult the micro-benchmarks of LMbench [14] to generate these workloads and acquire their throughput results. The workload of context switch is implemented by the fork() system call function. Each workload is implemented to last long enough for precision.

3.2   Manageability

Manageability leads to the operational efficiency and automation, e.g. rapid provisioning, automated workload management, workload live migration etc. In VirtDM, we define the following specific metrics to represent the manageability of a VAS:

1. **VM resource scalability**. It refers to how much virtual or physical resources could be allocated to a virtual machine, usually limited by VMM implementation, such as vSMP Scalability, pSMP Scalability [8].
2. **Migration function**. It refers to whether a VAS has the capacity of live migration or storage migration.
3. **Consolidation functional scalability**. It refers to how many VMs could be allocated to a physical machine, usually limited by VMM implementation.

4. **VM snapshot save/resume efficiency.**
5. **VM start/shutdown efficiency.**

We measure 4) and 5) using their response time. For 2) and 3) we consider that their functions are provided or not, but leave the evaluation of their efficiency in following subsections. Notice that 1), 2) and 3) are not measurable metrics. In Section 4.2, we will describe how to obtain the numeric values for these immeasurable metrics.

Here we just think about what functions are provided to facilitate manageability. We temporarily exclude the consideration of how well a VAS manages physical resources, since it would involve automatic management policies which is difficult to measure.

3.3 Isolation

Virtualization enhances the degree of isolation by restricting multiple software stacks in their own VMs. But security isolation and environment isolation problems will remain as long as the physical resources are shared among different VMs. Therefore, we dwell on the performance isolation. Performance isolation refers to how well a virtualization solution is able to limit the impact of a misbehaving VM on other well-behaving VMs.

We consult previous works on isolation benchmarking [7]. In VirtDM, we run different stress tests - CPU bomb, memory bomb, I/O bomb - to cause extreme resource consumption and refer their VMs as bad VMs. Then we measure the performance degradation of the normal workloads on a well-behaving VM, caused by the bad VM sharing the hardware resource of the same physical host.

3.4 Consolidation

Server consolidation is the most common practice of virtualization in datacenters. It refers to running multiple VMs concurrently on one physical host, to increase resource utilization and reduce cost such as power, space and cooling devices etc. [5].

We use SPECvirt_sc2010 [15] to measure the performance of server consolidation. SPECvirt_sc2010 scales the workloads on the System Under Test (SUT) until the SUT reaches its peak performance, when additional workload VMs either fails the QoS(Quality of Service) or fails to improve overall metric.

3.5 Migration

Migration allows a running VM to be moved from one physical machine to another without any disruption of service or perceived downtime. It provides an essence capacity required for dynamic load balancing, VM replacement, high availability of service during maintenance, and declined power consumption.

We use Virt-LM benchmark [16] to measure the performance of live migration, which provide the results of four metrics - downtime, total migration time, the amount of migrated data and migration overhead across a wide range of classic application workloads in a datacenter.

4   VirtDM Modeling

In this section, we specify our VirtDM to achieve an overall decision making method process and illustrate the relevant components. We will formulate the MCDM problem and detail its implementation. Before modeling, it is necessary to identify the candidate VASes with specific metrics, and give a clear definition for the MCDM problem of VirtDM.

Generally the goal of choosing VASes in datacenter is to satisfy the daily demand of the multiple application services such as web hosting, e-business sites, and enterprise systems etc. Datacenter architects will combine the existing physical machines and VMMs occasionally to full utilize the hardware/software resources with virtualization technology. The combinations compose a variety of VASes. Further, based on the performance measurements of multiple metrics these VASes will arise special performance features as a well proof of decision-making. Thus, the decision problem induces the considerations on the given VASes, the metrics, additionally, more importantly, as well as the human preference.

Besides, MCDM researchers have constructed a number of MCDM methods, such as AHP [13], LINMAP, TOPIS [17,18], etc. We primary consult the AHP technique which is one of the most efficient MCDM method to implement the MCDM-Processor of VirtDM. The VirtDM aims to find the optimal weight of attribute for a group of VAS alternatives, to determine a rational ranking order as well.

4.1   VirtDM Formulation

In this section we state the MCDM problem of VirtDM and present its formulation in order to express the decision-making process conveniently.

Problem 1. (**Generalization problem**). The MCDM problem of the VirtDM is provided with a hierarchy structure and must be decomposed into levels as shown in Fig. 3. It comprises L-levels ($L >= 3$): alternative(VAS candidate, one

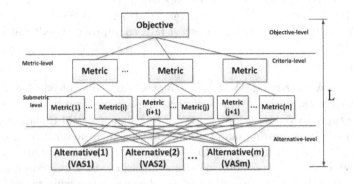

Fig. 3. The formulation of VirtDM with hierarchical structure

fixed level), criteria (one or more of metric levels, apparently equal to $L - 2$ levels) as well as objective (decision objective level, one fixed level).

Each level incorporates several elements. The elements of a given level can be comparable with the elements of the same level which elements are mutually exclusive. VirtDM presumes that the elements of a given level are affected by elements at the level directly above them besides the top level.

Problem 2. (**Special case**). Let $L = 4$ in problem 1, then we have a new hierarchy MCDM problem with four levels. In this way, in addition to the alternative-level and objective-level, the metric-level of general problem is divided into two levels: ML(metric-level) and SML(sub-metric level) as illustrated in Fig. 3. Each metric of the metric-level can be composed of several sub-metrics of the sub-metric level.

For simplification, we use problem 2 to implement the decision process of VirtDM. Some constraints are initialized in the following two definitions.

Definition 1. *(Size of the hierarchy structure). Assume problem 2 contain m alternatives(VASes), n sub-metrics and s metrics in the criteria level as well as 1 objective at the top level. Two adjacent levels are directly related.*

If the i_{th} given metric of the metric-level contains n_i sub-metrics, it will satisfy the equation: $\sum_{i=1}^{s} n_i = n$.

Definition 2. *(Decision Attribute Matrix). For each alternative, we can obtain a numerical value, called an attribute, for each metric of sub-metrics. Then, in problem 2 we have $m \times n$ attributes which comprise the decision basis of VirtDM. To store the decision attributes, we give a matrix:* $D = (d_{ij})_{m \times n}, (i = 1, ..., m, j = 1, ..., n)$, *where the element d_{ij} represents the jth sub-metric value of the ith VAS alternative. This matrix is called Decision attribute matrix (DAM).*

4.2   VirtDM Implementation

Besides problem formulation, to achieve the aim, the implementation of VirtDM is covering with several procedures as the follows.

1. Metrics Quantification. The metrics (elements) in **DAM** must be quantified before the weight identification. In problem 2 the metrics are categorized into two groups: quantitative and qualitative. Only the immeasurable metrics which are qualitative require to be expressed by numerical value. The qualitative metrics are commonly quantified by fuzzy language such as Bipolar scale method. The Bipolar scale has 10 cells with the common used scope of $1-9$. Here "Bipolar" means it can be used to quantify both Cost-type metrics and Benefit-type metrics. Regardless of what type of metrics, the maximum preference is identified as 9.0, while the minimum one identified as 1.0.

2. Metrics Normalization. We can begin the weight identification after all metrics in **DAM** D are quantified.

However, the metric numerical values typically exist three issues: the inconsistency dimension, the mixture of qualitative and quantitative metrics, as well as the difference of attribute orientation. Moreover, before the weight determination, the values should be normalized to be consistent attribute orientation and dimensionless. The metrics can be categorized into two types: benefit-criteria and cost-criteria which have different normalization ways.

The VirtDM incorporates three normalization means such as vector normalization method, linear scale transformation method and $(0 - 1)$ interval conversion method [19].

Besides, for the using of the AHP technique, we also use Formula(1), a simple additive weighting method to over again normalize the metric value:

$$r_{ij} = d_{ij} / \sum_{i=1}^{m} d_{ij}. \tag{1}$$

As mentioned in above Formulas, we obtain the matrix $R = (r_{ij})_{m \times n}$, a new normalized decision making matrix.

The purpose of our MCDM is to calculate an overall score for each alternative based on the metrics.

The basis process of weight identification is as follows. From the bottom alternative level to the top objective level one-by-one, VirtDM identifies the weights of the elements in a given level relative to the elements of the level directly above them. VirtDM applies MCDM with a weighted sum model (WSM) [19] as a uniform evaluation method. The ith alternative is given a score by Formula(2).

$$Score(A_i) = \sum_{j=1}^{n} r_{ij} * w_j. \tag{2}$$

3. Weight Identification. We use the pairwise comparison method to identify the weights of metric at each metric-level in associate with decision-maker's preference in problem 2. We consider the weights hierarchically. First the weights of metrics in metric-level need to be identified relative to one objective of the objective-level. Then, each metric of metric-level consists of several sub-metrics of sub-metric level. So N metrics of metric-level require N iterations identification to the weights of metrics of sub-metric level relative to the each metric of metric-level. Totally we will have $N + 1$ iterations weight identifications in problem 2.

We suppose the weights of metric in metric-level relative to objective of top level is denoted as W_2 and the weights of metric in sub-metric level relative to metric of metric-level with N metrics is expressed by $W_{3i}, i = 1...N$, where N denotes N metrics of metric-level and the dimensions of W_{3i} depends on the amount of sub-metrics.

Each iteration weight identification has the same process. We present an algorithm Alg_WIA for weight identification as shown in Algorithm 1.

Algorithm 1. Algorithm WIA : weight identification of pairwise comparison method

---

Require:
    The amount of metrics for pairwise comparison, N;
    The random index corresponding to N dimension, RI;
    The pairwise comparison matrix, $P = (x_{ij})_{N \times N}$;
Ensure:
    The weight vector of metrics, $W = (w_i)^T, i = 1..N$;
 1: Determining and input the elements of P according to decision maker's preference by Satty's scale method [13].
 2: Use geometric mean method as Formula (3): an approximate method to calculate the weight $W = (w_i)^T, i = 1..N$.

$$m_i = \prod_{j=1}^{N} x_{ij}, \qquad \overline{w_i} = \sqrt[n]{m_i}, \qquad w_i = \overline{w_i} / \sum_{i=1}^{n} \overline{w_i}. \qquad (3)$$

 3: Using Formula (4): an approximate method to calculate the maximum eigenvalue of P.

$$\lambda_{max} = \sum_{i=1}^{n} (\sum x_{ij} W)_i / n \cdot w_i. \qquad (4)$$

 4: Using Formula (5) to carry out CI and CR.

$$CI = (\lambda_{max} - n)/(n - 1), \qquad CR = CI/RI. \qquad (5)$$

 5: If $CR < 0.5$ then goto step (6) to output the result weight vector: W; else goto step (1);
 6: **return** W.

---

4. Weight Combination. Eventually, after all the weights identification in each level are completed, we can combine them into just one vector by multiplying all the weight vectors as the following Formula (6):

$$V = R * W3 * W2 * W1, \qquad (6)$$

where R is a normalized decision attribute matrix; V is an overall VAS priority vector, stands for the satisfaction degree of the decision making results.

5   Case Study

In this section, we demonstrate a case study applying VirtDM model to make decision the best VAS alternative among three ones, supposing a datacenter be deployed preferring I/O performance. Fig. 4 shows the hierarchy structure of our decision case and the chosen metrics are simplified ignoring human subjects for the goal is just to illustrate the whole process of how VirtDM works to validate its usefulness. On the other hand, this case could easily be extended to complex ones with more VAS candidates or more complicated metrics concerns.

5.1   Experimental Environment Setup

We experiment our VirtDM method on three VAS platforms, as following shows.

1. VAS-XEN-HV: The physical host is a Dell PowerEdge T710, with dual quad-core Intel Xeon processor E5620 at 2.4GHZ and 24GB of memory. The VMM is Xen-3.3.1 with Linux Kernel 2.6.18.8-xen. The VM is Linux 2.6.21 with 1GB memory and 1 vcpu binding to a particular physical CPU core.
2. VAS-XEN-PV: Using the same host and VMM as VAS-XEN-HV but with a para-virtualized VM.
3. VAS-KVM: Using the same host and VM as VAS-XEN-HV but with a different VMM — KVM.

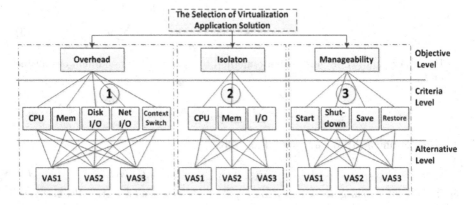

Fig. 4. The case of the hierarchy of the VAS decision making problem. $VAS1$ refers to VAS-XEN-HV, $VAS2$ denotes VAS-XEN-HV and $VAS3$ represents VAS-KVM.

5.2   Performance Measurement

To simplify the illustration of VirtDM process, ignoring human subjective or qualitative metrics, we choose three categories of measurable metrics — overhead, isolation, manageability — in our experiment. Of course our VirtDM model could be extended to other different metrics choices using the same course of our case study. Fig. 5 provides the metrics results of the three different VAS alternatives and Table 1 shows the performance measurements.

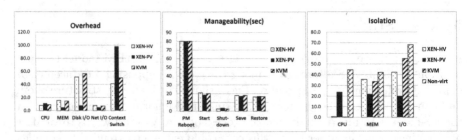

Fig. 5. The metrics results of three VASes

Table 1. Performance measurements from three VASes: XEN-HV, XEN-PV, KVM

	Overhead[%]				Isolation[%]			Manageability[sec]			
	CPU	Mem	Disk I/O	Net I/O	C.S.	CPU	Mem	I/O	start	shut.	save	rest.
XEN-HV	8.1	15.5	51.1	7.7	41	0.6	35.7	42.4	21	2.4	17.9	16.2
XEN-PV	11.13	4.8	7.9	4.8	98	23.8	21.8	20.1	18.5	3.5	17.2	16.9
KVM	9.13	14.5	56.3	7.0	50	0.4	33.5	55.0	20	2.5	18	16.5

Overhead. According to Section 3.1, we measure the virtualization overhead of four workloads: CPU task, memory task, I/O task and Context Switch task. The metric results are calculated by the performance degradation percentage of the workloads running on the VAS against running on the physical host. Lower is better. As Fig. 5 shows, all VAS alternatives achieved less overhead on CPU and Memory tasks, but greater overhead on I/O and Context Switch tasks, because I/O and context switch tasks would cause more interactions of VMM. However, VAS-XEN-PV gained much better performance on I/O overhead test, especially on disk I/O test, although it produces the worst performance about the context switch overhead. The reason is that para-virtualization mechanism using modified I/O driver which could significantly decrease the number of VMM context switches.

Isolation. According to Section 3.3, we measure the isolation with the normal VM's performance degradation cause by a "bad"VM which produces extreme resources consumption. We tested three kind of performance isolation using different kinds of "bad"VMs — the CPU stressed, the Memory stressed and the I/O stressed. Hence, lower is better. For comparison, we also test the performance isolation of non-virtualization case, in which the normal workload are impacted by a stressed workload within the same single OS.

As Fig. 5 demonstrates, CPU isolation is generally better than the other two. Further, VAS-XEN-HV and VAS-KVM had really poor memory isolation, while VAS-XEN-PV illustrated quite bad I/O isolation.

Manageability. In this experiment we merely test the duration of general VM operation – VM start, shutdown, save and restore. Lower is better. We also the duration of the physical machine's reboot to illustrate the virtualization efficiency. The three VASes attained very close results of each metrics as displayed in Fig. 5.

5.3 Overall Decision Process

In this section we show the steps of the decision process using our VirtDM model.

Example 1. As an example shown in Fig. 4, it provides a hierarchy MCDM including 4-levels. Besides bottom and top level, the criteria level is composed of two levels: 1) metric-level which involves three metrics: overhead, isolation and manageability metrics; 2) the sub-metrics of the sub-metric level. All sub-metrics are cost-type and have been measured before decision. The metrics of the metric-level derive from the synthesization of the sub-metrics in the level directly below them.

Step 1. Normalizing the attribute data to be dimensionless.
According to the common normalizing methods, we normalize the raw metrics results data shown in Table 1 to be dimensionless by using Formula (7) and the cost-criteria linear conversion method.

$$r_{ij} = \min_{1 \le i \le m} x_{ij}/x_{ij}. \tag{7}$$

Further, we again normalize the weights by simple weighted mean method to satisfy the sum of the weights of all VAS alternatives in the alternative-level added up to 1. For example, the following equation is right for each sub-metric: $w(VAS1)+w(VAS2)+w(VAS3) = 1$. The normalized result is shown in Table 2.

Table 2. The normalized data

	Overhead[%]					Isolation[%]			Manageability[sec.]			
	CPU	Mem	Disk I/O	Net I/O	C.S.	CPU	Mem	I/O	Start	Shut.	Save	Rest.
XEN-HV	0.38	0.19	0.12	0.27	0.45	0.38	0.27	0.26	0.31	0.38	0.33	0.34
XEN-PV	0.28	0.61	0.77	0.43	0.19	0.01	0.44	0.54	0.36	0.26	0.34	0.33
KVM	0.34	0.20	0.11	0.30	0.36	0.61	0.29	0.20	0.33	0.36	0.33	0.33

Step 2. Constructing the decision-making matrix.
For the convenient calculation, we extract the metrics from Table 2 to create three decision Matrices: O—Overhead decision matrix; I—Isolation decision matrix; M—Manageability decision matrix, where,

$$O = \begin{bmatrix} 0.38 & 0.19 & 0.12 & 0.27 & 0.45 \\ 0.28 & 0.61 & 0.77 & 0.43 & 0.19 \\ 0.34 & 0.20 & 0.11 & 0.30 & 0.36 \end{bmatrix}, I = \begin{bmatrix} 0.38 & 0.27 & 0.26 \\ 0.01 & 0.44 & 0.54 \\ 0.61 & 0.29 & 0.20 \end{bmatrix}, M = \begin{bmatrix} 0.31 & 0.38 & 0.33 & 0.34 \\ 0.36 & 0.26 & 0.34 & 0.33 \\ 0.33 & 0.36 & 0.33 & 0.33 \end{bmatrix}$$

Step 3. Identifying the weights for sub-metrics and metrics.
In this MCDM, without immeasurable metrics in the sub-metrics, the weights of the alternative-level relative to the metrics of the sub-metric level do not required to be determined by using preference in pair wise comparison method but immediately be identified from the measurements in the decision matrix. On the contrary, the identifications of weights using pair wise comparison method concentrate on the metrics of the sub-metric level relative to the metrics of metric-level. Each metric of the metric-level relative to the relevant sub-metrics need one iteration weight identification. It indicates that three metrics reflect three iterations. In addition, the weight of metrics of metric level relative to

the top level(objective level) needs one iteration. Hence, this MCDM exists four iterations using pair wise comparison method to determine weights.

This weight determination method associates decision-maker's preference with the pairwise comparison matrix. According to the requirement of the pairwise comparison method, we determine the weights with the help of eigenvector theory-based acceptance validation, and obtain the rational weight vectors, respectively.

We create four pairwise comparison matrices: PO, PI, PM and PP as follows:

$$PO = \begin{array}{c} \\ CPU \\ Mem \\ DiskI/O \\ NetI/O \\ Cont.S \end{array} \begin{array}{ccccc} CPU & Mem & DiskI/O & NetI/O & Cont.S \\ \left[\begin{array}{ccccc} 1 & 1 & 0.111 & 0.14 & 0.333 \\ 1 & 1 & 0.143 & 0.125 & 0.2 \\ 9 & 7 & 1 & 0.5 & 2 \\ 7 & 8 & 2 & 1 & 3 \\ 3 & 5 & 0.5 & 0.333 & 1 \end{array}\right] \end{array}, PI = \begin{array}{c} \\ CPU \\ Mem \\ I/O \end{array} \begin{array}{ccc} CPU & Mem & I/O \\ \left[\begin{array}{ccc} 1 & 3 & 5 \\ 0.33 & 1 & 3 \\ 0.2 & 0.33 & 1 \end{array}\right] \end{array},$$

$$PM = \begin{array}{c} \\ start \\ shut. \\ save \\ res. \end{array} \begin{array}{cccc} start & shut. & save & res. \\ \left[\begin{array}{cccc} 1 & 1 & 0.17 & 0.17 \\ 1 & 1 & 0.2 & 0.2 \\ 6 & 5 & 1 & 1 \\ 6 & 5 & 1 & 1 \end{array}\right] \end{array}, PP = \begin{array}{c} PCM1 \\ ove. \\ iso. \\ man. \end{array} \begin{array}{ccc} ove. & iso. & man. \\ \left[\begin{array}{ccc} 1 & 3 & 9 \\ 0.33 & 1 & 4 \\ 0.11 & 0.25 & 1 \end{array}\right] \end{array}$$

- (1) PO is used to identify the weights of sub-metrics: CPU, Disk I/O, Net I/O, Context Switch(Cont.S) relative to the metric overhead.
- (2) PI is used to identify the of sub-metrics: CPU, Memory, I/O relative to isolation metric.
- (3) PM is used to identify the weights of sub-metrics: start time, shutdown time(shut.), save time(save.), restore time(rest.) relative to manageability metric.
- (4) PP is used to identify the weights of metrics: overhead (ove.), isolation (iso.), and manageability (man.) in the metric-level relative to the objective top-level.

In this MCDM, we assume that datacenter administrators are to make decision of choosing a high performance VAS with better I/O performance. Therefore the metric disk I/O and Net I/O are given a high preference value in the matrices.

Based on each comparison matrix, we calculate all relevant weight vectors by eigenvector theory and calculate the approximate weights by geometry mean method. All the pairwise comparison matrices get through the consistency validation.

Finally, the relevant valid weights are expressed as follows:

(1)$Wo = (0.048, 0.044, 0.311, 0.435, 0.163)^T$ is the overhead weight vector,

(2)$Wi = (0.634, 0.260, 0.106)^T$ is the isolation weight vector,

(3)$Wm = (0.075, 0.081, 0.422, 0.422)^T$ is the manageability weight vector,

(4)$Wp = (0.681, 0.250, 0.069)^T$ is the synthetic weight vector.

Step 4. Combining the weights and result analysis.

We calculate the combined weights of overhead (W_1), isolation (W_2), as well as manageability (W_3) as follows.

$$(1) W_1 = O \cdot Wo = \begin{bmatrix} 0.38 & 0.19 & 0.12 & 0.27 & 0.45 \\ 0.28 & 0.61 & 0.77 & 0.43 & 0.19 \\ 0.34 & 0.20 & 0.11 & 0.30 & 0.30 \end{bmatrix} \cdot \begin{bmatrix} 0.048 \\ 0.044 \\ 0.311 \\ 0.435 \\ 0.163 \end{bmatrix} = (0.254, 0.499, 0.248)^T$$

$$(2) W_2 = I \cdot Wi = \begin{bmatrix} 0.38 & 0.27 & 0.26 \\ 0.01 & 0.44 & 0.54 \\ 0.61 & 0.29 & 0.20 \end{bmatrix} \cdot \begin{bmatrix} 0.634 \\ 0.260 \\ 0.106 \end{bmatrix} = (0.338, 0.178, 0.484)^T,$$

$$(3) W_3 = M \cdot Wm = \begin{bmatrix} 0.31 & 0.38 & 0.33 & 0.34 \\ 0.36 & 0.26 & 0.34 & 0.33 \\ 0.33 & 0.36 & 0.33 & 0.33 \end{bmatrix} \cdot \begin{bmatrix} 0.075 \\ 0.081 \\ 0.422 \\ 0.422 \end{bmatrix} = (0.337, 0.330, 0.333)^T.$$

The final result of the decision-making process is concluded by the following Formula:

$$V = (W_1, W_2, W_3) \cdot Wp = \begin{bmatrix} 0.254 & 0.499 & 0.248 \\ 0.338 & 0.178 & 0.484 \\ 0.337 & 0.330 & 0.0.333 \end{bmatrix} \cdot \begin{bmatrix} 0.681 \\ 0.250 \\ 0.069 \end{bmatrix} = (0.281, 0.407, 0.313)^T.$$

It concludes the combined vector V which represents the VAS priority. It indicates the rank order: $0.281 < 0.313 < 0.407$, which is corresponding to $VAS1 < VAS3 < VAS2$. Thus, the second VAS alternative, namely, XEN-PV, is the best choice for our given MCDM problem in the case.

6   Conclusions and Future Work

In this paper, we design and implement the VirtDM model to serve the VAS decision making in a datacenter. We define a fine-grained, in-depth, and human friendly metrics system to cover essential performance characteristics of a VAS. We employ classic MCDM methods to ease the quantification of people's preference. VirtDM will measure different metrics, normalize their results, calculate their weights fit into people's preference and finally give an overall decision from given VAS candidates.

However, many aspects of VirtDM are far from satisfying. For example, our metrics system is fair rough and omits some metrics difficult to measure, e.g. the efficiency of the automatic policies of consolidation or migration. Further, our model are primarily based on AHP method and other MCDM methods maybe more sophisticated and more appropriate. These deserve our further investigation and effort to improve.

References

1. Bittman, T., Webinar, G.: Server virtualization: From virtual machines to clouds (2010)

2. Blachman, N., Peek, J.: How google works. (GoogleGuide) (retrieved April 20, 2007)

3. Uhlig, R., Neiger, G., Rodgers, D., Santoni, A., Martins, F., Anderson, A., Bennett, S., Kagi, A., Leung, F., Smith, L.: Intel virtualization technology. Computer 38(5), 48–56 (2005)

4. Apparao, P., Iyer, R., Zhang, X., Newell, D., Adelmeyer, T.: Characterization & analysis of a server consolidation benchmark. In: Proceedings of the Fourth ACM SIGPLAN/SIGOPS International Conference on Virtual Execution Environments, pp. 21–30. ACM (2008)

5. Padala, P., Zhu, X., Wang, Z., Singhal, S., Shin, K.: Performance evaluation of virtualization technologies for server consolidation. HP Labs Tec. Report (2007)

6. Makhija, V., Herndon, B., Smith, P., Roderick, L., Zamost, E., Anderson, J.: Vm-mark: A scalable benchmark for virtualized systems. VMware Inc., CA, Tech. Rep. VMware-TR-2006-002 (September 2006)

7. Matthews, J., Hu, W., Hapuarachchi, M., Deshane, T., Dimatos, D., Hamilton, G., McCabe, M., Owens, J.: Quantifying the performance isolation properties of virtualization systems. In: Proceedings of the 2007 Workshop on Experimental Computer Science, p. 6-es. ACM (2007)

8. McDougall, R., Anderson, J.: Virtualization performance: perspectives and challenges ahead. ACM SIGOPS Operating Systems Review 44(4), 40–56 (2010)

9. Huber, N., von Quast, M., Brosig, F., Kounev, S.: Analysis of the Performance-Influencing Factors of Virtualization Platforms. In: Meersman, R., Dillon, T., Herrero, P. (eds.) OTM 2010. LNCS, vol. 6427, pp. 811–828. Springer, Heidelberg (2010)

10. Kundu, S., Rangaswami, R., Dutta, K., Zhao, M.: Application performance modeling in a virtualized environment. In: 2010 IEEE 16th International Symposium on High Performance Computer Architecture, HPCA, pp. 1–10. IEEE (2010)

11. Ye, K., Che, J., Jiang, X., Chen, J., Li, X.: vtestkit: A performance benchmarking framework for virtualization environments. In: The Fifth Annual China Grid Conference, pp. 130–136. IEEE (2010)

12. Moller, K.: Virtual machine benchmarking (2007)

13. Saaty, T.: Decision-making with the ahp: Why is the principal eigenvector necessary. European Journal of Operational Research 145(1), 85–91 (2003)

14. McVoy, L., Staelin, C.: lmbench: Portable tools for performance analysis. In: Proceedings of the 1996 Annual Conference on USENIX Annual Technical Conference, pp. 23–23. Usenix Association (1996)

15. specvirt_sc (2010), http://www.spec.org/virt_sc2010/

16. Huang, D., Ye, D., He, Q., Chen, J., Ye, K.: Virt-lm: a benchmark for live migration of virtual machine. In: Proceeding of the Second Joint WOSP/SIPEW International Conference on Performance Engineering, pp. 307–316. ACM (2011)

17. Wang, P., Chao, K., Lo, C.: On optimal decision for qos-aware composite service selection. Expert Systems with Applications 37(1), 440–449 (2010)

18. Tarighi, M., Motamedi, S., Sharifian, S.: A new model for virtual machine migration in virtualized cluster server based on fuzzy decision making. Arxiv preprint arXiv:1002.3329 (2010)

19. Hwang, C., Yoon, K.: Multiple attribute decision making: methods and applications: a state-of-the-art survey, vol. 13. Springer (1981)

A PDGF Implementation for TPC-H

Meikel Poess [1], Tilmann Rabl[2], Michael Frank[3], and Manuel Danisch[3]

[1] Oracle Corporation, 500 Oracle Pkwy, Redwood Shores, CA-94065
meikel.poess@oracle.com
[2] Middleware Systems Research Group, Department of Computer Science,
University of Toronto, 10 King's College Road, Toronto, Ontario, Canada, M5S 3G4
tilmann.rabl@utoronto.ca
[3] Fakultät für Informatik und Mathematik, Universität Passau, Innstraße 43, 94032 Passau
{frank,danisch}@fim.uni-passau.de

Abstract. With 182 benchmark results[1] from 20 hardware vendors, TPC-H has established itself as the industry standard benchmark to measure performance of decision support systems. The release of TPC-H twelve years ago by the Transaction Processing Performance Council's (TPC) was based on an earlier decision support benchmark, called TPC-D, which was released 1994. TPC-H inherited TPC-D's data and query generators, DBgen and Qgen. As systems evolved over time, maintenance of these tools has become a major burden for the TPC. DBgen and Qgen need to be ported on new hardware architectures and adapted as the system grew in size to multiple terabytes. In this paper we demonstrate how Parallel Data Generation Framework (PDGF), a generic data generator, developed at the University of Passau for massively parallel data generation, can be adapted for TPC-H.

Keywords: Performance Analysis, Benchmark Standards, TPC-H, Data Generation.

1 Introduction

Since its introduction in 1999 by the Transaction Processing Performance Council (TPC) 20 system vendors have published 182 benchmark results on hundreds of system configurations using the TPC-H benchmark specification. This establishes TPC-H as the de facto industry standard to measure performance of decision support systems. Closely tight to its specification are its data and query generators, DBgen and Qgen respectively, which are implemented in the programming language C. Their development, originally used in TPC's first decision support benchmarks (TPC-D), was completed in 1994. Since that time, the code has been ported to 20 separate platforms, spanning OS versions from UNIX to Windows, and from VMS, to MVS, to Linux.

Since the introduction of DBgen and Qgen in 1994 systems used in TPC benchmark publications have evolved greatly causing the maintenance of these tools to be a

---

[1] As of May 9th, 2011.

R. Nambiar and M. Poess (Eds.): TPCTC 2011, LNCS 7144, pp. 196–212, 2012.

major burden for the TPC. While systems that published TPC-D benchmarks only employed few single core processors on data warehouse of up to one Terabyte, systems running TPC-H today employ clusters of multi-core processor nodes, totaling hundreds of cores, on data warehouses of up to 30 Terabytes and multi Terabytes of main memory. Recently the frequency at which bugs are reported increased dramatically, which lead to a discussion of completely rewriting DBgen. However, this turned out to be cost prohibitive. As an alternative this paper investigates the feasibility of using the Parallel Data Generation Framework (PDGF), developed at the University of Passau, for TPC-H. Originally developed for massively parallel data generation of cloud scale databases, PDGF has many advantages over DBgen: It is written in the platform independent language Java, which makes portability needless. Studies have shown that it is able to generate terabytes of data quickly and reliably [2]. Its separation into a data generation engine and a file defining the metadata about the data to be generated makes it easily maintainable and, if necessary quickly extensible. Finally, since it is a generic data generation tool, it can also be adapted by other benchmarks in which case the TPC only needs to maintain one data generator.

The remainder of this paper is organized as follows. Section 2 gives a quick overview of the different data generation requirements of TPC-H. Section 3 introduces PDGF and develops the metadata file that allows PDGF to generate TPC-H data. It also explains some of the modifications that needed to be implemented in PDGF to allow for the different data types. In Section 4 a detailed analysis of the data generated by PDGF is presented. The paper concludes in Section 5. We have included the two metadata files (Appendix A) and all SQL compliance queries (Appendix B) as supporting material to this paper.

2   Overview Data Generation in TPC-H

TPC-H models the activity of any industry which manages, sells, and distributes products worldwide. It uses a 3rd normal form schema consisting of eight base tables, (see Figure 1). They are populated with synthetic data, scaled to a scale factor (SF) that determines the size of the raw data outside the database, e.g. SF=1000 means that the sum of all base tables equals 1 Terabyte. Sizes of all tables, except for nation and region scale linearly with SF (see [1,6] for more details on TPC-H).

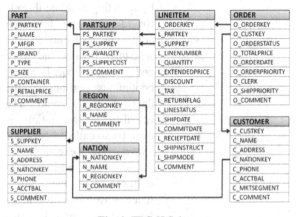

Fig. 1. TPC-H Schema

In order to guarantee that every database publication uses the same data in the base tables, the TPC-H specification defines the content of every column very precisely using the following primitives: Date, Phone Number, Random String, Random Value, Random v-String, Text Appended Digit and Text String. Table 1 shows how these data generation primitives are used in defining column content. For space reasons we only list a representative subset of all TPC-H columns. For a full list of column definition see Clause 4.2 in [6]. In TPC-H the term "random" means independently selected and uniformly distributed over the specified range of values.

Table 1. Example usage of data generation primitives in TPC-H

Column	Use of data generation primitive	Sample output
O_Orderdate	Date, uniformly distributed between 1992-01-01and 1998-08-02	1995-05-26
S_Phone	Phone Number	16-421-927-9442
L_Shipinstruct	Random String [instructions], where Instructions={DELIVER IN PERSON, COLLECT COD,NONE, TAKE BACK RETURN}	TAKE BACK RETURN
S_Nationkey	Random Value [0 .. 24]	23
S_Address	Random v-String[10,40]	vs50U4?e5i
S_Name	Text Appended with Digit ["Supplier", S_Suppkey]	Supplier5628
PS_Comment	Text String [49,198]	dependencies beyo

3   Implementing TPC-H in PDGF

PDGF is an extensible Parallel Data Generation Framework, developed at the University of Passau, to generate Exabytes of synthetic data by utilizing deterministic parallel pseudo random number generators. In its current form it is limited to generating data for relational database management systems (RDBMS). However, its design can be extended to allow for the generation of structurally different data, e.g. XML.

PDGF's architecture is designed for large data sets, maximum performance and easy extensibility. Figure 2 shows a sample setup with three nodes. The controller, executed in the center node, reads meta-data about the schema, its distributions, output format and system configuration from XML files and initiates the data generations by spanning multiple threads (by default one for each core) on each node. The scheduler divides the work and assigns equal sized, continuous portions of the data to each thread. The actual data generation is done by so called generators, which are executed in threads. To generate non-uniform data the system features various distributions that can be applied to the random numbers.

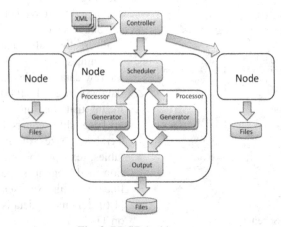

Fig. 2. PDGF Architecture

Its unique seeding approach allows PDGF to generate random values for each field deterministically. To generate a single value for a column (e.g. name), a hierarchy of random number generators is used: Table→Column→Row →NameGenerator. Even for large relational schemas the total number of seeds required can be cached in PDGF. This approach enables PDGF to generate all values for all columns of all tables independently and deterministically. Dependencies of columns, i.e. Intra-Row (e.g. ZIP→city), Intra-Table (e.g. surrogate key sequence) and Inter-Table (e.g. referential integrity) can be resolved without caching all values or re-reading previously generated data back in. For a discussion of the generation of data dependencies please refer to [3].

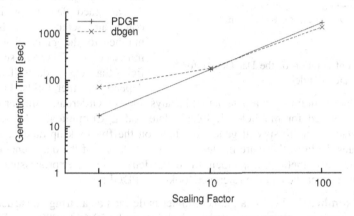

Fig. 3. Performance Comparison DBGen and PDGF

In [2] a comparison of the generation speed of DBgen vs. PDGF was presented, for reference we show these results here again in Figure 3. Although PDGF is a generic data generator, it has a comparable generation speed to DBgen as can be seen in the figure. PDGF includes a range of generators that allow the generation of all common relational data types, these include numeric values, random strings and datestamps. New generators can be added to PDGF as plug-ins. This is especially useful for benchmarks like TPC-H that have very special requirements for its data specification. For example, TPC-H has various interdependencies in the data definition and special data generation rules. Therefore, a plug-in for TPC-H was implemented that encapsulates all TPC-H specific generators. An actual extension to the PDGF core was a cache for the active row. Although in principle all values can be computed it is much more efficient to cache a single row than to compute all values several times for a single row. This is necessary for intra-row dependencies which can be found for example in Part, where P_Retailprice is calculated based on P_Partkey. Besides this extension only TPC-H specific generators had to be implemented. The following paragraphs give details on the implementation and how to configure PDGF to generate data for the generation primitives, presented in Section 2. The generation specification resembles the relational schema: it is an XML file that contains an element table for each table in the schema. Each of the table elements has multiple field subelements. These represent a column in the table. For each table element the PDGF will generate a single file in which each row consists a number of fields that is defined by the field subelements.

Appendix A contains a full list of the TPCH.pdgf file that generates the entire data set for TPC-H for a given SF.

Date (min,max). Since date is a fairly common data type in relational data, PDGF comes with a generic date generator, called DateGenerator. Figure 4 shows how DateGenerator can be configured to generate O_Orderdate, which are uniformly distributed between 1/1/1992 and 8/2/1998 (see StartDate and EndDate tags in the example). To do so, it converts the assigned date range in milliseconds and scales down the random number to the given date range in milliseconds. There are several other fields that require dates. They directly depend on other fields. For example

```
<field name="O_ORDERDATE">
  <type>java.sql.Types.DATE</type>
  <generator name="DateGenerator">
    <startDate>1992-01-01</startDate>
    <endDate>1998-08-02</endDate>
  </generator>
</field>
```

Fig. 4. Configuration of the DateGene-rator for O_Orderdate of Order

L_Shipdate is defined as a date 1 to 121 days after O_Orderdate. Similar dependencies are defined for the fields L_Receiptdate and L_Commitdate. These intra-row dependencies require special generators that, on the fly, look up dates and compute other dates. In Java, these are implemented as subclasses of the date generator adding simple date arithmetic to implement the dependency. For faster processing they make use of the row cache and the reference lookup in PDGF.

Phone Number. In TPC-H a phone number is defined as a string constructed of four random numbers that are separated by dashes, e.g. 1-650-633-8000. The PhoneNumberGenerator, is specifically designed for TPC-H. For each of the four segments of the phone number a separate random number is generated in the specified interval and the numbers are concatenated. Since there are no

```
<field name="S_PHONE">
  <type>java.sql.Types.VARCHAR</type>
  <size>15</size>
  <generator name="PhoneNumberGenerator" />
</field>
```

Fig. 5. Configuration of the PhoneNumberGene-rator for S_Phone of Supplier

further restrictions, the call to PhoneNumberGenerator has no arguments as can be seen for the configuration of S_Phone of the supplier table in Figure 5.

Random String. Random String values are generated by randomly picking one element from one or multiple lists. If a single list is used PDGF's DictListGenerator can be used. Figure 6 shows the configuration of the O_Orderpriority field, which can be one of {1-URGENT, 2-HIGH, 3-MEDIUM, 4-NOT SPECIFIED, 5-LOW}. In general it randomly chooses values from a dictionary with a uniform distribution. Other distributions can

```
<field name="O_ORDERPRIORITY">
  <type>java.sql.Types.VARCHAR</type>
  <size>15</size>
  <generator name="DictList">
    <file>dicts/priorities.dict</file>
  </generator>
</field>
```

Fig. 6. Configuration of the DictList generator for O_Orderpriority of Order

be specified explicitly. The dictionary is stored in a file, whose name can be specified with the file tag. Fields that require multiple lists can be generated with the same generator by creating a dictionary file that contains all combinations of the lists. This is a feasible solution since all TPC-H lists contain only few elements. The maximum number of entries is 150 (see P_Type of the Part table in [6]). For a faster generation PDGF caches dictionaries in memory.

Random Value: Random values can be generated using the IntGenerator. It is called with min and max values and an optional distribution function, such as normal, Gaussian or Zipf. TPC-H only requires uniform distributions. Figure 7 shows the configuration of the S_Nationkey. It is randomly picked between 0 and 24.

```
<field name="S_NATIONKEY">
  <type>java.sql.Types.INTEGER</type>
  <generator name="IntGenerator">
    <min>0</min>
    <max>24</max>
  </generator>
</field>
```

Fig. 7. Configuration of the random integer number generator of N_Nationkey of Nation

Random v-String: In TPC-H Random V-string primitive denotes a randomly generated string over an alphabet of 64 characters. The length of the string is uniformly distributed between a 10 and 40. Random v-String is implemented in PDGF with the RandomVString. It randomly chooses the length of the string between the given min and max values and then fills the string by randomly picking elements from an alphabet of 64 characters. In TPC-H Random v-Strings are used for address fields, such as S_Address. The specification for S_Address is depicted in Figure 8.

```
<field name="S_ADDRESS">
  <type>java.sql.Types.VARCHAR</type>
  <size>40</size>
  <generator name="RandomVSTring" />
</field>
```

Fig. 8. Configuration of the RandomVString generator

Text Appended Digit: In TPC-H the Text Append Digit primitive specifies a field that consists of a text followed by '#' and a random integer number. Most fields use this type in connection with intra-row dependencies. For example, the name of a customer C_Name consists of the text "Customer", a '#' sign and value of the field C_Custkey of the same row. The specification of C_Name can be seen in Figure 9; the digitSource element specifies that the value of C_Custkey will be used as the number in the generation of C_Name.

```
<field name="C_NAME">
  <type>java.sql.Types.VARCHAR</type>
  <size>25</size>
  <generator name="TextAppendedWithDigit">
    <text>Customer</text>
    <digitSource>C_CUSTKEY</digitSource>
  </generator> </field>
```

Fig. 9. Configuration of the TextAppendedWithDigit generator of S_Address of Supplier

Another special case is the generation of P_Brand, the brand of a part. It dependens on P_Mfgr, the manufacturer of a part. Both fields are text, appended with digits, but the random number of P_Brand is preceded by the random number of P_Mfgr of the same row. Since P_Mfgr is not a number, the generator cannot simply use the digitSource element. To reduce the computational overhead, this is implemented as a special case in the generator. The generator caches the last random number of P_Mfgr in order to reuse it in P_Brand.

Text String: The most difficult primitive in TPC-H is the Text String primitive. It is used in multiple comment fields such as C_Comment of Customer. The generated value is a random substring of a 300 MByte pseudo text file. The length of the string is randomly chosen between specified upper and lower bounds. The offset of the string is also randomly chosen. The 300 MByte file is populated with a grammar definition. The grammar emulates the composition of English texts. TPC-H also specifies a lists of verbs, nouns, adjectives and the like which are used as terminals for the grammar.

```
<field name="N_COMMENT">
  <type>java.sql.Types.VARCHAR</type>
  <size>117</size>
  <generator name="TextString">
    <min>29</min>
    <max>116</max>
  </generator>
</field>
```

Fig. 10. Configuration of the TextString generator of N_Comment of Nation

Although it would be possible to cache the pseudo text it can also be computed on the fly. The TextString generator loads word lists and generates sentences using the specified grammar. For performance reasons the text generator is implemented as a singleton object. The XML specification for the TextString generator can be seen in Figure 10. A special case of the TextString primitive is used in field S_Comment of Supplier. 0.05 percent of S_Comment entries are complaints and 0.05 percent of the entries are recommendations. These have to include the string "Customer" followed by a random number of characters, followed by either the string "Complaints" or the string "Recommends". In PDGF text for S_Comment is generated using the same pseudo text generator as above, additionally complaints and recommendations are inserted in the text with given probabilities.

Apart from these types and their specializations, several custom generators for single fields were implemented. These usually have dependencies that make a generic implementation inefficient. An example is L_Extendedprice; it is calculated as L_Quantity * P_Retailprice, where P_Partkey = L_Partkey in the according rows. Obviously, it is easier implement the logic in a generator instead of implementing a generic generator that allows these kinds of dependencies.

4   TPC-H.pdgf Verification

This section describes our approach to verify whether PDGF, using the attached TPC-H.pdgf file generates data that complies with the current TPC-H specification, Version 2.14.0. To demonstrate functional compliance with the current TPC-H specification, we need to analyze whether all columns of all tables contain data that is compliant with Clause 4.2.3 of the specification, which we reviewed in Section 2. First we verify the cardinalities in each table, followed by one section for each data primitives: Date, Phone Number, Random String, Random Value, Random v-String, Text Appended Digit, Text String and Unique Value. At the end of these sections, we list some columns that do not quite follow the generation primitives. They are in a section labeled special cases.

Most of the primitives refer to the term random. According to the TPC-H specification the term "random" means "independently selected and uniformly distributed over the specified range of values." That is, n unique values V of a column are uniformly distributed if $P(V = v) = \frac{1}{n}$. Since we use pseudo random number generators, perfectly uniform distributions are impossible to guarantee. Hence, we define a column C with n unique values V to be uniformly distributed if the coefficient of variation of its values is less than ε. Formally, given the mean of V as $\mu = \frac{1}{n}\sum_{i=1}^{n} v_i$ and its standard deviation $\sigma = \sqrt{\sum_{i=1}^{n}(v_i - \mu)^2}$, then the following must be true: $\frac{\sigma}{\mu} \leq \varepsilon$. ε is column specific. ε is not defined in the specification. However, we can obtain ε for each column by calculating the coefficient of variation on the data generated by DBgen. PDGF data is then compliant if it yields a similar ε.

Row Cardinalities: The cardinalities of most tables depend on the scale factor or their cardinality is fixed. These are: Orders (SF*1,500,000), Customer (SF * 150,000), Supplier (SF * 10,000), Part (SF * 200,000) and Partsupp (SF * 800,000). The cardinalities of nation (25) and region (5) are scale factor independent. Verification of their cardinalities can be done with the SQL query listed in Figure 11, where T is the table name and S is its scaling relative to the scale factor SF.

```
SELECT CASE WHEN cnt=SF*S
            THEN 'OK' END
FROM (SELECT count(*) cnt
       FROM T);
```

Fig. 11. Table car-dinality compliance query

Table 2. Cardinalities DBgen and PDGF

Table	Table cardinalities @ SF=100		
	Specification	DBgen	PDGF
Orders	150 Million	150 Million	150 Million
Customer	15 Million	15 Million	15 Million
Supplier	1 Million	1 Million	1 Million
Part	20 Million	20 Million	20 Million
Partsupp	80 Million	80 Million	80 Million
Nation	25	25	25
Region	5	5	5

The cardinalities of Lineitem, on the other hand, depend on the cardinalities of other orders. To each row in the Orders table correspond a random number of rows within [1 .. 7] in the Lineitem table. More generally, to each row in the parent table P correspond n rows in the dependent table D. For dependencies like this three characteristics need to be analyzed i) Join Frequency. Given that each row of the parent table can join between 1 and 7 times to the dependent table, we need to calculate the range of join frequencies of parent to dependent rows ii) Coefficient of the frequency distribution, i.e. the distribution of how often rows of the parent table join to the dependent table is uniform. iii) Row counts. The following two SQL statements show how the relationship between Lineitem and Orders can be verified in SQL. Running these SQL statements on 100 SF databases, populated with DBgen and PDGF shows that the range of the join frequency is one to seven with roughly 21 Million records each and a coefficient of variation of 0.000197 for DBgen and 0.000002 of PDGF. The row count differs slightly. Dbgen generates 600,037,902 rows, while PDGF generates 600,000,000.

```
SELECT bucket                              SELECT stddev(bucketsize)
      ,bucketsize                                /avg(bucketsize)
      ,SUM(bucketsize) OVER                 FROM(SELECT bucket
       (ORDER BY bucket ROWS                           ,COUNT(*) bucketsize
        BETWEEN UNBOUNDED PRECEDING         FROM (SELECT l_orderkey
    AND CURRENT ROW) TotalBucketsize                  ,COUNT(*) bucket
FROM(SELECT bucket                                 FROM lineitem
           ,COUNT(*) bucketsize                        ,orders
     FROM (SELECT l_orderkey                       WHERE l_orderkey
                 ,COUNT(*) bucket                        =o_orderkey
           FROM lineitem                          GROUP BY l_orderkey)
                ,orders                       GROUP BY bucket);
           WHERE l_orderkey=o_orderkey
           GROUP BY l_orderkey)
     GROUP BY bucket);
```

Date (min,max): The Date primitive generates a string of numeric characters separated by hyphens and comprised of a four digit year, two digit month and two digit day of the month, e.g. "1996-04-01". The TPC-H schema contains four date columns, L_Shipdate, O_Orderdate, L_Commitdate and L_Receiptdate. O_Orderdate is generated with a random date between Startdate and Enddate -151 days, while L_Shipdate, L_Commitdate and L_Receiptdate are generated by adding a random number as offset between to O_Orderdate, i.e. l_shipdate = o_orderdate + random value [1 .. 121], l_commitdate = o_orderdate + random value [30 .. 90], l_receiptdate = o_orderdate + random value [1 .. 30].

```
SELECT MIN(O_Orderdate)
      ,MAX(O_Orderdate)
      ,count(distinct O_Orderdate)
FROM Orders;

SELECT STDDEV(c)/AVG(c)
FROM (SELECT O_Orderdate,count(*) c
      FROM Orders
      GROUP BY O_Orderdate);
```

Fig. 12. Sample date column compliance query

To demonstrate compliance with the specification, we need to show three data characteristics for each date field i) the minimum and maximum dates are correct and iii) the date interval is dense, i.e. the number of distinct dates equals the number of dates between min and max and iii) the dates are uniformly distributed (see Figure 12).

Table 3. Comparison Date Distribution DBgen and PDGF

Column	CoV of dates		Date Range DBgen			Date Range PDGF		
	DBgen	PDGF	Min	Max	#distinct	Min	Max	#distinct
O_Orderdate	0.00388	0.00398	1992-01-01	1998-08-02	2406	1992-01-01	1998-08-02	2406
L_Shipdate	0.17970	0.17969	1992-01-02	1998-12-01	2526	1992-01-02	1998-12-01	2526
L_Commitdate	0.12762	0.12763	1992-01-31	1998-10-31	2466	1992-01-31	1998-10-31	2466
L_Receiptdate	0.20888	0.20887	1992-01-03	1998-12-31	2555	1992-01-03	1998-12-31	2555

Phone Number: The Phone Number primitive generates a string of numeric characters separated by hyphens and represented as follows: [1 .. 25]"-" [100 .. 999]"-" [100 .. 999]"-" [1000 .. 9999]. To demonstrate compliance with the specification, each of the four sections of the phone number needs to be investigated separately. For each we need to determine three characteristics i) the minimum and maximum values ii) the number of unique values and iii) whether the values are distributed uniformly. The phone number primitive applies to the fields S_Phone and C_Phone. The following four SQL statements, one for each section of the phone number field, show how the supplier phone number field S_Phone can be verified in SQL:

```
SELECT MIN(cc),MAX(cc),COUNT(*),STDDEV(cnt),STDDEV(cnt)/AVG(cnt)
FROM (SELECT SUBSTR(s_phone,1,2) cc,COUNT(*) CNT
      FROM supplier
      GROUP BY SUBSTR(s_phone,1,2));
SELECT MIN(cc),MAX(cc),COUNT(*),STDDEV(cnt),STDDEV(cnt)/AVG(cnt)
FROM (SELECT SUBSTR(s_phone,4,3) cc,COUNT(*) CNT
      FROM supplier
      GROUP BY SUBSTR(s_phone,4,3));
SELECT MIN(cc),MAX(cc),COUNT(*),STDDEV(cnt),STDDEV(cnt)/AVG(cnt)
FROM (SELECT SUBSTR(s_phone,8,3) cc,COUNT(*) CNT
      FROM supplier
      GROUP BY SUBSTR(s_phone,8,3));
SELECT MIN(cc),MAX(cc),COUNT(*),STDDEV(cnt),STDDEV(cnt)/AVG(cnt)
FROM (SELECT SUBSTR(s_phone,12,4) cc,COUNT(*) CNT
      FROM supplier
      GROUP BY SUBSTR(s_phone,12,4));
```

Fig. 13. SQL statements to verify compliance of S_Phone data

Table 4. Comparison Phone fields DBgen and PDGF

	DBgen				PDGF			
Phone# Section	MIN	MAX	Distinct	CoV	MIN	MAX	Distinct	CoV
Country Code	10	34	25	0.0042	10	34	25	0.0039
Area Code	100	999	900	0.0293	100	999	900	0.0288
Phone # Part 1	100	999	900	0.0308	100	999	900	0.0301
Phone # Part 2	1000	9999	9000	0.0952	1000	9999	9000	0.0950
Country Code	10	34	25	0.0011	10	34	25	0.0013
Area Code	100	999	900	0.0076	100	999	900	0.0078
Phone # Part 1	100	999	900	0.0077	100	999	900	0.0082
Phone # Part 2	1000	9999	9000	0.0245	1000	9999	9000	0.0246

Table 5. CoV of Random String values

Column	CoV		Idential
	DBgen	PDGF	List_name
P_Type	0.00280	0.00293	Yes
P_Container	0.00142	0.00131	Yes
C_Mktsegment	0.00062	0.00054	Yes
L_Shipinstruct	0.00008	0.00012	Yes
L_Shipmode	0.00011	0.00012	Yes
O_Orderpriority	0.00012	0.00009	Yes

Random String (list_name): The Random String primitive generates a string selected at random within a list of strings (list_name). Each string is selected with equal probability. It applies to columns P_Type, P_Container, C_Mktsegment, L_Shipinstruct, L_Shipmode and O_Orderpriority. For each of these fields we need to verify the following two data characteristics i) The distinct elements in the column correspond to the TPC-H specific

```
SELECT UNIQUE C_Mktsegment
FROM CUSTOMER;

SELECT STDDEV(cnt)/AVG(cnt)
FROM (SELECT C_Mktsegment mseg
            ,COUNT(*) cnt
      FROM customer
      GROUP BY C_Mktsegment);
```

Fig. 14. SQL to verify compliance of C_Mktsegment data

and ii) the distribution of the elements is random. Figure 14 shows an example how to verify i) and ii) for C_Mktsegment using SQL and Table 5 shows the results for running this type of SQL for all Random String columns. For a list of SQL statements for all other columns using the Random String primitive, please refer to Appendix B

Random Value (min,max): The Random Value primitive defines random values between min and max inclusively, with a mean of (min+max)/2. The columns using this primitive are P_Size, Ps_Availqty, Ps_Supplycost, C_Acctbal, L_Partkey, C_Nationkey L_Discount, L_Tax, L_Quantity, S_Nationkey and S_Acctbal. For each column we need to verify three characteristic i) min and max values ii) number of distinct values and iii) coefficient of variation of the value probabilities. The following two SQL statements verify S_Nationkey column, a foreign key to the Nation table in Supplier. For a list of SQL statements for all columns using the Random Value primitive, please refer to Appendix B.

```
SELECT MIN(S_Nationkey),MAX(S_Nationkey),COUNT(DISTINCT S_Nationkey)
FROM Supplier;
SELECT STDDEV(cnt)/AVG(cnt)
FROM (SELECT S_Nationkey,COUNT(*) FROM SUPPLIER GROUP BY S_Nationkey);
```

Fig. 15. SQL statements to verify compliance of S_Nationkey data

Table 6. CoV or Random Values

Column	DBgen				PDGF			
	MIN	MAX	Distinct	CoV	MIN	MAX	Distinct	CoV
P_Size	1	50	50	0.00151	1	50	50	0.00149
Ps_Availqty	1	9999	9999	0.01083	1	9999	9999	0.10003
Ps_Supplycost	1.00	1000.00	99901	0.03469	1.00	1000.00	99897	0.31573
C_Acctbal	-999.99	9999.99	1099998	0.26985	-999.99	9999.99	1099999	0.27089
L_Partkey	1	20e6	20e6	0.15503	1	20e6	20e6	0.18264
C_Nationkey	0	24	25	0.00105	0	24	25	0.00110
L_Discount	0	0.1	11	0.00011	0	0.1	11	0.00012
L_Tax	0	0.08	9	0.00007	0	0.08	9	0.00014
L_Quantity	1	50	50	0.00028	1	50	50	0.00032
S_Nationkey	0	24	25	0.0042	0	24	25	0.00519
S_Acctbal	-999.99	9999.98	656803	0.50379	-999.99	9999.98	656803	0.50393

Random v-String: A Random v-String primitive represents a string comprised of randomly generated alphanumeric characters within a character set of at least 64 symbols. The length of the string is a random value between values min and max inclusive. Columns using this data generation primitive are the address columns: C_Address, S_Address, C_Address. For each column we need to determine three data characteristics i) domain over which the strings are generated ii) are the strings picked randomly? iii) min, max length of each string and distribution of length across all fields. i) can be determined with SQL in Figure 16. ii) can be determined with the SQL in Figure 17 and iii) can be determined with the SQL in Figure 18.

```
SELECT SUM(LENGTH(S_Address)-LENGTH(REPLACE(S_Address,CHR(0),''))) S0
    ,SUM(LENGTH(S_Address)-LENGTH(REPLACE(S_Address,CHR(1),''))) S1,…
    ,SUM(LENGTH(S_Address)-LENGTH(REPLACE(S_Address,CHR(255),''))) S255
  FROM SUPPLIER;
```

Fig. 16. SQL statement to verify compliance of v-String data

```
SELECT STDDEV(Col)/AVG(Stddev)FROM(
SELECT SUM(LENGTH(s_address)-LENGTH(REPLACE(s_address,CHR(0),'')))COL0
FROM SUPPLIER UNION ALL
SELECT SUM(LENGTH(s_address)-LENGTH(REPLACE(s_address,CHR(1),'')))COL1
FROM SUPPLIER UNION ALL ,…,UNION ALL
SELECT SUM(LENGTH(s_address)-LENGTH(REPLACE(s_address,CHR(255),'')))COL
FROM SUPPLIER);
```

Fig. 17. SQL compliance query to determine random distribution of characters

```
Select min(length(s_address)
      ,max(length(s_address)
      ,stddev(length(s_address)/avg(length(s_address))
From supplier;
```

Fig. 18. SQL compliance query to determine minimal, maximal length and length distribution

Text Appended with Digit: The Text Appended with Digit primitive represents a string generated by concatenating a sub-string text with a number. Columns using this primitive are S_Name, C_Name, P_Mfgr, P_Brand and O_Clerk. Columns S_Name and C_Name append the content of another column (of the same row), while p_Mfgr, P_Brand and O_Clerk append a random number within *min* and *max*. To demonstrate compliance with the specification of columns appending the value of another column, we

Table 7. CoV of Text Appended with Digit values

Column	CoV		Specification		PDGF	
	DBgen	PDGF	min/max		min/max	
O_Clerk	0.02587	0.02587	1	100000	1	100000
P_Mfgr	0.00031	0.00033	1	5	1	5
P_Brand	0.00044	0.00043	1	5	1	5

need to demonstrate that the appended value is equal to the value of the other column. **Figure 19** shows a compliance query that counts the number of rows where the values are different. A result of 0 indicates compliance with the specification. To demonstrate compliance with the specification of columns adding a random number, we need to demonstrate three data characteristics i) the minimum and maximum values of the appended number correspond to the *min* and *max* values of the specification; ii) the number of distinct values and iii) the values are distributed randomly. Figure 20 shows a compliance query that computes the minimum and maximum values, the number of distinct values and the coefficient of variation of the distribution of the values between minimum and maximum. For a list of all columns using the Text Appended with Digit primitive, please refer to the appendix.

```
select sum(case when s_suppkey = col then 0 else 1 end)
from (select to_number(substr(s_NAME,10,length(s_NAME)-9)) col
             ,s_suppkey
      from supplier);
```

Fig. 19. Compliance query for Text with Append Digit primitive (column)

```
select min(col)
      ,max(col)
      ,count(*)
      stddev(cnt)/avg(cnt)
from (select to_number(substr(o_clerk,10,length(o_clerk)-9)) col
             ,count(*) cnt
      from orders
      group by to_number(substr(o_clerk,10,length(o_clerk)-9)));
```

Fig. 20. Compliance query for Text with Append Digit primitive (random number)

Unique Value (min,max): The Unique Value primitive generates unique values between 1 and x. Columns using this primitive are S_Suppkey [1 .. sf * 10,000], P_Partkey [1 .. sf * 200,000], C_Custkey [1 .. sf * 150,000],

```
SELECT MIN(S_Suppkey)
      ,MAX(S_Suppkey)
      ,COUNT(DISTINCT S_Suppkey)
      ,COUNT(S_Suppkey)
FROM Supplier;
```

Fig. 21. SQL to verify Unique Values

N_Nationkey [0 .. 24], R_Regionkey [0 .. 4] and O_Orderkey [1 .. sf * 1,500,000 * 4]. O_Orderkey has an additional requirement, as only the first 8 keys of each 32 are to be populated. For each column we have to verify four data characteristics i) minimum value ii) maximum values iii) number of distinct values and iv) number of rows. Data is generated correctly if the minimum and maximum values correspond to the specification and the number of distinct values equals the number of rows. The following table lists the result of the Query listed in Figure 21 for Dbgen and PDGF.

Table 8. Results of Unique Value tests for all affected columns

Column	TPC-H Specification (@SF=100)			PDGF			
	MIN	MAX	Distinct	MIN	MAX	Distinct	Count
S_Suppkey	1	1000000	1000000	1	1000000	1000000	1000000
P_Partkey	1	20000000	20000000	1	20000000	20000000	20000000
C_Custkey	1	15000000	15000000	1	15000000	15000000	15000000
N_Nationkey	0	24	25	0	24	25	25
R_Regionkey	0	4	5	0	4	5	5
O_Orderkey	1	6E+08	1.5E+08	1	6E+08	1.5E+08	1.5E+08

```
SELECT COUNT(*)
FROM (SELECT MOD(O_ORDERKEY,9)
MODVALS
      FROM ORDERS )
WHERE MODVALS <= 8;
```

Fig. 22. SQL to check the sparsely populated O_Orderkey

In addition to the above, for O_Orderkey we need check that the keys are only sparsely populated, i.e. only the first 8 keys of every 32 keys are used. The following SQL statement counts the number of keys that fall in residue classes small or equal than 8. If this query returns the same number of rows than the total number of rows (last column in Table 5), then only the first 8 keys of every 32 keys are populated. For a list of all columns using the Unique Value primitive see Appendix B.

Random Text Strings (min,max) is a pseudo English text generated over a fixed dictionary following the grammar defined in Clause 4.2.2.14. In order to assure that the text was generated with the grammar in Clause 4.2.2.14 one would need to write a parser for the grammar. Since the grammar of the text is not exploited in the benchmark, the authors believe that by checking i) the minimum length ii) the maximum length and iii) the uniqueness and the uniform distribution of the length, suffices to assure compliance with the specification. SQL in Figure 23 checks this.

Table 9. CoV of Random Text Strings

Column	CoV		Spec		PDGF	
	DBgen	PDGF	min/max		min/max	
L_Comment	0.00024	0.00023	10	43	10	43
O_Comment	0.00057	0.00032	19	78	19	78
S_Comment	0.00850	0.00477	25	100	25	100
P_Comment	0.00087	0.00056	5	22	5	22
PS_Comment	0.00124	0.00073	49	198	49	198
C_Comment	0.00247	0.00143	29	116	29	116
N_Comment	0	0	31	114	31	114
R_Comment	0.4	0.4	31	115	31	115

```
SELECT MIN(l)
    ,MAX(l)
    ,STDDEV(c)
    /AVG(c)
FROM(SELECT
        LENGTH(L_Comment)l
    ,COUNT(*) c
    FROM Lineitem;
```

Fig. 23. SQL to check compliance of L_Co-mment

Special Cases

O_Shippriority should be set to 0 for all orders. Compliance with the TPC-H specification can be checked with the following simple SQL query:

```
SELECT CASE WHEN c=0 THEN 'OK' END FROM (SELECT count(*) c from orders);
```

The above query shows OK for DBGen and PDGF on a SF=100 database.

L_Returnflag is set to "R" or "A" if L_Receiptdate <= Currentdate. Otherwise it is set to "N". The following SQL query counts the number of rows with L_Returnflag equal to R, A and N when L_Receiptdate is less or equal than currentdate and when L_Receiptdate is greater than currentdate. If the following SQL query returns 0 for lessAndN, largerAndR and largerAndA, then L_Returnflag conforms to TPC-H:

```
SELECT SUM(CASE WHEN L_Receiptdate<=TO_DATE('1995-06-17','YYYY-MM-DD')
               AND L_Returnflag = 'R' THEN 1 ELSE 0 END) lessAndR
    ,SUM(CASE WHEN L_Receiptdate<=TO_DATE('1995-06-17','YYYY-MM-DD')
               AND L_Returnflag = 'A' THEN 1 ELSE 0 END) lessAndA
    ,SUM(CASE WHEN L_Receiptdate<=TO_DATE('1995-06-17','YYYY-MM-DD')
               AND L_Returnflag = 'N' THEN 1 ELSE 0 END) lessAndN
    ,SUM(CASE WHEN L_Receiptdate>TO_DATE('1995-06-17','YYYY-MM-DD')
               AND L_Returnflag = 'R' THEN 1 ELSE 0 END) largerAndR
    ,SUM(CASE WHEN L_Receiptdate>TO_DATE('1995-06-17','YYYY-MM-DD')
               AND L_Returnflag = 'A' THEN 1 ELSE 0 END) largerAndA
    ,SUM(CASE WHEN L_Receiptdate>TO_DATE('1995-06-17','YYYY-MM-DD')
               AND L_Returnflag = 'N' THEN 1 ELSE 0 END) largerAndN
    ,COUNT(*) CNT
from lineitem;
```

Fig. 24. SQL compliance query for L_Returnflag

The above query shows returns 0 for lessAndN, largerAndR and largerAndA for DBGen and PDGF on a SF=100 database. DBGen and PDGF show a count of 0 for this query.

P_Retailprice is set to P_Retailprice = (90000 + ((P_Partkey/10) modulo 20001) + 100 * (P_Partkey modulo 1000))/100. The following SQL query counts the number of rows where P_Retailprice is not computed correctly:

```
SELECT SUM(CASE WHEN P_Retailprice-(90000+(MOD((P_Partkey/10),20001))
                            +100*(MOD(P_Partkey,1000)))/100
            THEN 1 ELSE 0 END) cnt
from part;
```

Fig. 25. SQL compliance query of P_Retailprice

L_Linestatus is set to "o" if l_Shipdate > currentdate, to "f" otherwise. The following SQL query counts the correct cases where L_Linestatus should be set to O and F. If the sum of largerAndO and lessOrEqualAndF equals cnt, then L_Linestatus conforms to the TPC-H specification. DBGen and PDGF show pass this query test on a SF=100 database.

```
SELECT SUM(CASE WHEN L_Shipdate >TO_DATE('1995-06-17','YYYY-MM-DD')
                AND L_Linestatus='O'THEN 1 ELSE 0 END)largerAndO
      ,SUM(CASE WHEN L_Shipdate <=TO_DATE('1995-06-17','YYYY-MM-DD')
                AND L_Linestatus='F'THEN 1 ELSE 0 END)lessOrEqualAndF
      ,COUNT(*) cnt
 From Lineitem;
```

Fig. 26. SQL compliance query for L_Linestatus

P_Name is generated by concatenating five unique randomly selected strings from a list of colors (see Clause 4.2.3 of the TPC-H specification for details). Verifying P_Name is not straight forward in SQL. One needs to extract all five colors and then check pair wise for duplicates. The following SQL query counts the number of rows with duplicate colors in P_Name. A result of 0 signifies compliance with the TPC-H specification. Both Dbgen and PDGF show 0 for this query.

```
SELECT SUM(CASE WHEN C1=C2 OR C2=C3 OR C3=C4 OR C4=C5 OR C2=C3
                OR C2=C4 OR C2=C5 OR C3=C4 OR C3=C5 OR C4=C5
            THEN 1 ELSE 0 END)
FROM (SELECT SUBSTR(P_Name,1,SA-1) C1,SUBSTR(P_Name,SA+1,SB-SA) C2
      ,SUBSTR(P_Name,SB+1,SC-SB) C3,SUBSTR(P_Name,SC+1,SD-SC) C4
      ,SUBSTR(P_Name,SD+1,LENGTH(P_Name)-SD+1) C5
      FROM (SELECT P_Name
            ,INSTR(P_Name,' ',1,1) SA ,INSTR(P_Name,' ',1,2) SB
            ,INSTR(P_Name,' ',1,3) SC ,INSTR(P_Name,' ',1,4) SD
        FROM Part));
```

Fig. 27. SQL compliance query for P_Name

O_Totalprice is computed as sum(L_Extendedprice*(1+L_Tax)*(1-L_Discount)) for all Lineitem of this order. In order to verify O_Totalprice we need to join Orders with Lineitem and calculate the sum. The following SQL query verifies this for all rows:

```
SELECT COUNT(*)
FROM(SELECT O1.O_Orderkey OK, SUM(L1.L_Extendedprice
                            *(1+L1.L_Tax)*(1-L1.L_Discount)) TP
    FROM Lineitem L1,Orders O1
    WHERE L1.L_Orderkey=O1.O_Orderkey
    GROUP BY O1.O_Orderkey),Orders O2
WHERE OK<>O2.O_Orderkey And O2.O_Totalprice<>TP;
```

N_Nationkey, N_Name, N_Regionkey is statically to a list of combinations. This list of combinations is defined in Clause 4.2.3. Both DBgen and PDGF generate a correct set of combinations.

R_Regionkey, R_Name is statically to a list of combinations. This list of combinations is defined in Clause 4.2.3. Both DBgen and PDGF generate a correct set of combinations.

PS_Suppkey defined as $(PS\_Partkey+(i*((S/4)+(int)(PS\_Partkey-1)/S))))$ modulo $S+1$, where i is the i-th supplier within $[0 .. 3]$ and $S = SF * 10,000$. The following verifies compliance of PS_Suppkey for scale factor 100. If the values of Matching and Cnt are identical PS_Suppkey is generated in compliance with the specification. Both DBgen and PDGF generate compliance data for PS_Suppkey.

```
SELECT SUM (CASE WHEN (Ps_Suppkey=MOD(Ps_Partkey+0*((1000000/4)
                        +(TRUNC((Ps_Partkey-1)/1000000))),1000000)+1)
            OR (Ps_Suppkey=MOD(Ps_Partkey+1*((1000000/4)
                        +(TRUNC((Ps_Partkey-1)/1000000))),1000000)+1)
            OR (Ps_Suppkey=MOD(Ps_Partkey+2*((1000000/4)
                        +(TRUNC((Ps_Partkey-1)/1000000))),1000000)+1)
            OR (Ps_Suppkey=MOD(Ps_Partkey+3*((1000000/4)
                        +(TRUNC((Ps_Partkey-1)/1000000))),1000000)+1)
            THEN 1 ELSE 0 END) Matching
        ,COUNT(*) Cnt FROM Partsupp;
```

Fig. 28. SQL compliance query for PS_Suppkey

5   Conclusion

In this paper, we have shown that TPC-H equivalent data can be generated with the generic data generator PDGF. First we analyzed the generation requirements of TPC-H data and showed how they can be implemented using PDGF. The complete configuration file for PDGF is given as supported material to this paper. To proof that our PDGF implementation is compliant with the current TPC-H specification (Version 2.14.2), we first developed a mathematical way to determine compliance based on the coefficient of variation, minimum, maximum values, among others. We also provided SQL statements to calculate these values. Examples of these statements are given in the paper, while a complete list is given as supporting material. Using scale factor 100, we generated a complete data set with both DBgen and PDGF.

Running the compliance queries on the scale factor 100 database showed that both tools generate data that is compliant with the specification. All minimum, maximum values and distributions in general are identical between the two tools. One of the major characteristics of TPC-H's data is that it is distributed uniformly. This is very important as the benchmark's execution rules rely on it. DBgen shows a wide range for the CoV of various colums. For instance, the CoV of the distribution of lineitem to orders is 0.000197 while the CoV of L_Partkey is 0.15503. It is up to the TPC to decide whether these CoV are specification conforming. For the sake of this paper, however, it is only important whether the data PDGF generates has the same or better CoV. Our data shows that in most cases the CoV of PDGF data is better than that of DBgen data. Only in a few cases, DBgen generates data with a lower CoV. For instance, Ps_Supplycost shows a CoV of 0.31573 with PDGF and 0.03469 with DBGen. In time for the completion of this paper we were not able to fully investigate these cases. We hope to have completed this work by the time of the workshop.

Apart from data generation itself, PDGF has many advantages over DBgen. Since it is written in the platform independent language Java, it is very portable to new, emerging platforms. Its generic nature, i.e. its separation into a data generation engine and a file defining the metadata about the data to be generated also suggests that PDGF could be the default data generator for the TPC. This will reduce development cost of new benchmarks and maintenance cost of existing benchmarks. Finally, previous studies have shown that PDGF is able to generate terabytes of data quicker than tools currently deployed by the TPC [2].

Acknowledgements. The authors would like to acknowledge Ray Glasstone for his support.

References

1. Poess, M., Floyd, C.: New TPC Benchmarks for Decision Support and Web Commerce. ACM SIGMOD Record 29(4), 64–71 (2000)
2. Rabl, T., Frank, M., Sergieh, H.M., Kosch, H.: A Data Generator for Cloud-Scale Benchmarking. In: Nambiar, R., Poess, M. (eds.) TPCTC 2010. LNCS, vol. 6417, pp. 41–56. Springer, Heidelberg (2011)
3. Rabl, T., Poess, M.: Parallel Data Generation for Performance Analysis of Large, Complex RDBMS. In: DBTest 2011 (2011)
4. Stephens, J.M., Poess, M.: MUDD: a multi-dimensional data generator. In: WOSP 2004, pp. 104–109 (2004)
5. TPC-D, Version 2.1, http://www.tpc.org/tpcd/default.asp
6. TPC-H Specification, Version 2.14.0, http://www.tpc.org/tpch/spec/tpch2.14.0.pdf

Author Index